BARRON'S

ACT® 36

AIMING FOR THE PERFECT SCORE

2nd Edition

Alexander Spare, M.A.
English Teacher
Littleton High School
Littleton, Colorado

Ann Summers Hirsch, M.A.
Math Resource Specialist
Littleton Public Schools
Littleton, Colorado

Jonathan Pazol, M.S.
Science Teacher
West Leyden High School
Northlake, Illinois

Krista L. McDaniel, M.A.
Literacy Liaison
Adams 12 Five Star School District
Thornton, Colorado

BARRON'S

About the Authors

Alexander Spare has taught high school English for 11 years in the Denver, Colorado, area. He currently is at Littleton High School, where he has taught both AP and IB English courses. In addition, Alex co-owns and operates The ACT Review Group, which offers both ACT preparation classes and private tutoring.

Ann Summers Hirsch has been involved in mathematics education for 17 years, the past 11 of which she has taught everything from basic skills to Pre-Calculus at the high school level. For seven years Ann prepped juniors and seniors for the ACT exam. Currently, she oversees math instruction at three high schools in Colorado and is responsible for helping to raise ACT scores in math.

Jonathan Pazol has taught high school science for more than 20 years at West Leyden High School in Northlake, IL. During that time, he has taught review courses for the ACT and SAT. He has worked in labs at the Weizmann Institute of Science, the Nanoscale Science and Engineering Center, the Feinberg School of Medicine, and spent six weeks engaged in seafloor mapping and geology aboard the US Coast Guard icebreaker *Healy* in the Arctic Ocean. Jonathan has also received local and state recognition for outstanding teaching.

Krista McDaniel currently works as a high school literacy liaison for a large school district in the Denver Metro Area, supporting adolescent literacy and standards implementation in Language Arts. Before that, she taught English at Littleton High School.

© Copyright 2012, 2009 by Barron's Educational Series, Inc.

All rights reserved.
No part of this publication may be reproduced or distributed
in any form or by any means without the written permission
of the copyright owner.

All inquiries should be addressed to:
Barron's Educational Series, Inc.
250 Wireless Boulevard
Hauppauge, New York 11788
www.barronseduc.com

ISBN: 978-0-7641-4705-0 (book only)
ISBN: 978-1-4380-7217-3 (book with CD-ROM)
ISSN 2160-3014 (book only)
ISSN 2162-318X (book with CD-ROM)

Printed in the United States of America

9 8 7 6 5 4 3

Contents

Introduction

Are you tired of *ordinary* ACT coaching? Does advice telling you to narrow your options, pace yourself, and plug in answer choices seem overly simplistic and not enlightening? If so, you're reading the right book.

You know there's more to achieving a 36 on the ACT than just pacing yourself and making sure you answer each question. Maybe you already know that every correct reading question is worth another point but haven't been able to get beyond missing one or two per passage. Maybe you trip over the same trigonometry questions, no matter how much you practice. Maybe you're just goal-oriented and know that a score of 30 places you in the top 5 percent of the approximately 1.5 million students who take the test each year.

If any of these scenarios sounds familiar, congratulations! You're ahead of the game already. You are the target audience of this book: students who already meet high expectations in math, English, reading, and science, and yet want to achieve the perfect score on the ACT. You know the value of a high score and its ability to earn you the higher education positions you want and deserve.

If you strive for perfection on the ACT, you've opened the right book. This book is designed to help you gain skills and strategies that go far beyond the basics. You are reading the correct preparation guide if you possess the following qualities:

1. You have a general understanding of the ACT but would like to learn some of the test's many nuances.

2. You are a solid student: one who is focused, who has worked hard all along, and who will continue to work hard.

3. You answer many of the easier questions correctly already. This book hones in on questions that the ACT writes specifically to set the great students apart from the good ones.

4. You are willing to plan and practice. The effectiveness of this book will increase exponentially if you use it methodically and practice consistently. Begin preparing several weeks, if not a few months, before your test date, and consider supplementing this book with other practice materials.

5. You are ready for a textbook that offers fresh advice and is written in a conversational voice that speaks directly to you.

WHAT CONTENT IS ON THE ACT?

You have two options when registering for the ACT. You can take the ACT or the ACT Plus Writing, which includes a thirty-minute essay. Although not all schools require the writing portion, many of the most competitive ones do. Before deciding which test to take, check with your counselor about schools that require the writing section, or find the information at *ACT.org*.

What Do the Sections of the Test Look Like?

English Section—36 points

- 45 minutes to read 5 passages and complete 75 questions

- Multiple-choice format—4 answer choices for each question

- Questions that test your knowledge of sentence structure, grammar, usage, and punctuation (about 40 questions)

- Questions that test your sense of style, strategy, revision, and organization in writing (about 35 questions)

Mathematics Section—36 points

- 60 minutes to complete 60 questions

- Multiple-choice format—5 answer choices for each question

- Questions that test your knowledge of pre-algebra and elementary algebra (about 24 questions)

- Questions that test your knowledge of intermediate algebra and coordinate geometry (about 18 questions)

- Questions that test your knowledge of plane geometry and, to a lesser extent, trigonometry (about 18 questions)

Reading Section—36 points

- 35 minutes to read 4 passages and answer 40 questions

- Multiple-choice format—4 answer choices per question

- Passages that cover four different content areas: prose fiction, humanities, social studies, and natural sciences

- Questions that test your ability to extract detail, draw conclusions, determine main points and tone, and define vocabulary in context

Science Reasoning Section—36 points

- 35 minutes to read 7 passages and answer 40 questions

- Multiple-choice format—4 answer choices per question

- Passages that cover the subject areas of biology, chemistry, earth/space science, and physics

- Questions that test your ability to analyze charts and graphs (about 15 questions), compare data from multiple experiments (about 18 questions), and scrutinize the viewpoints of two hypotheses (about 7 questions)

Writing Section (Optional)—12 points

- 30 minutes to read a short prompt, plan, and write an essay in response to the given prompt

- Designed to test your ability to argue a position on an issue, to write a focused—and organized—essay, to use logic and detail to support your argument, and to use language effectively

HOW ARE SCORES FIGURED?

Your composite score reflects the average of all four subject-area scores. The number of correct responses for each category, called a "raw score," is entered into a computer, which in turn sends it through a complex formula to give you a "scaled score." Because each testing session offers a different test, the ACT company has developed a complex algorithm so that all students, no matter which test they take, end up with comparative scores for comparative performances.

Each content category, except science and writing, has sub-categories. For example, English has two sub-categories: usage/mechanics and rhetorical skills. You also receive a scaled score for each sub-category (1–18); however, the sub-category scores and the overall score for the category have no mathematical correlation. The sub-category scores help you assess your strengths as well as areas in which you could improve. The writing section is scored separately, so if you take the ACT Plus Writing, you'll receive a composite score out of 36 points for the four content areas, plus a separate English/Writing score out of 36 points, along with a sub-score for writing out of 12 points.

How Many Questions Can I Miss and Still Earn an Exceptional Score?

To get into the 99th percentile, which is a score of 32, you can miss approximately 5 questions on each test for English, reading, and mathematics; however, you can miss only 2 science questions. In order to achieve a perfect score of 36 on the ACT, you will need to answer every question correctly on the mathematics, English, and science sections. The reading test offers you the only leeway: you can miss up to two questions on the reading test and still earn a perfect score of 36 overall. In order to reach the 99th percentile on the writing test, you need to score an 11 or 12. The rubric is based on 6 points. Your scaled score is obtained by doubling the points you get. Your writing scaled score is then meshed with your English score; you will receive a composite English/Writing score. For example, if you score a 33 on English and a 10 on writing, your composite English/Writing score will be a 32. In order to achieve a 36, you must earn a 12 on the writing test and a 36 on the English test.

How Should I Use This Book to Achieve the Perfect Score?

As you work your way through this book, focus on perfection. Read through each section and complete all practice questions. This book gives a solid review of the content you need to know along with specific strategies for answering different types of problems and questions. In order to achieve the perfect score, you need to know how to answer all questions. As you work through each section of the book, identify which questions cause you the most difficulty; then go back and review the sections of the book that apply directly to those areas.

Along the way, you will see test-taking tips—specific, easily remembered advice about the best ways to approach the test.

WHAT SHOULD I BRING ON TEST DAY?

1. **Test center administration ticket**—if you are testing on an established ACT test date.

2. **Identification.** Your administration ticket is not identification. Your administration ticket tells you which type of identification to bring, or you can go to www.actstudent.org if you need further assistance.

3. **Sharpened soft lead No. 2 pencils** with good erasers. You may *not* use mechanical pencils or pens (ink or felt tip).

4. **A watch without an alarm.** Pacing yourself is critical if you expect to achieve the perfect score. Your cell phone does not count as a watch; do not bring a phone in the room. If your watch alarm or phone sounds during testing, you will be dismissed and your answer document will not be scored.

5. **Graphing calculator.** *ACT.org* outlines specific parameters for allowable calculators.

POISE AND PREPARATION

This book guides you through the nuances of the ACT. It helps you reach a strong understanding of the content and provides plenty of practice questions to test your understanding of the concepts. But there are some basic things you can do to prepare for the ACT, as you should for any test. You may well be familiar with these guidelines, but it never hurts to have a reminder.

1. Make sure you have registered and paid for the right test.

2. Know the test location and how to get there.

3. Get plenty of sleep the night before the test.

4. Eat a healthy breakfast.

5. Don't overload on sugar, caffeine, or energy drinks.

6. Bring a healthy snack for the break to keep you going.

7. Double check that you have all your materials.

8. Relax—this is only a test.

Some of you may read this last piece of advice and think, "Relax?! Doesn't the author know that this is the most important test of my life?! If I don't do well, I'll never get into (insert your college of choice here), and my life will be ruined!"

The authors of this book do know how you are feeling and that you may be under a tremendous amount of pressure and stress to do well on the ACT. You would not be taking the time to read this book if you were not concerned about your scores. We repeat the last bit of advice: **Relax. Stay Calm. It's only a test.**

The ACT is only one factor that colleges and universities consider when making admissions decisions. Your high school courses, grades, extracurricular activities, community service, application essays, and recommendations are put together to give a more complete picture of you as an applicant. Admissions officers realize that ACT scores are a snapshot of how you did on one test on one particular day and that they do not define you as a person. Plus, you can (almost) always retake the test and submit your best scores.

Keeping the ACT in perspective is one of the best ways to ensure that you earn the scores that you are capable of getting. Too many students allow panic to set in on the day of the test. They forget the strategies they've practiced and start making simple mistakes. Do what you can to help yourself stay calm and focused. Listen to music, take deep breaths, work out, quote lines from your favorite movie, or tell jokes to your friends. Do something to help distract you from obsessing about the test.

That said, the focus that you direct to your preparation will give you the confidence you need on test day to achieve the perfect score. As a strong student, trust your abilities. *ACT 36* will reinforce the knowledge you already have without wasting time on information you don't need to know. Use this book to hone your skills and to enhance your understanding of the ACT testing format and questioning practices. Once you have refined the skills you already possess and have identified areas in which you need more work, use the book to turn your areas of concern into areas of strength. When you have practiced and prepared diligently, you can rest the night before the test and walk into the ACT room poised for greatness—ready to achieve the perfect score.

TIP

Don't study or review for the ACT the night before the test. Take some time off, watch a movie, or hang out with friends. Give your brain some down time.

INSIDE THE ACT 36 MIND

Throughout the book you will see boxed text like this. These boxes contain helpful insights about how the test questions are structured, how to avoid distracters that are meant to confuse you, and how to arrive at correct answers—all within a limited time frame. Pay attention to them and good luck!

ENGLISH

CHAPTER 1

Fundamentally Speaking

- Makeup of the test
- Four pillars worth knowing
- Finding the correct answer

Forty-five minutes is all the time you have to complete the ACT English section. Sounds rushed, doesn't it? It is fast, but it's doable provided you have mastered the fundamentals of language. By the end of these chapters, you'll have every tool you need to ace the English section. You'll also know most of the rules that govern writing in both academic and professional realms.

PREPARATION

The ACT English section measures your formal knowledge of writing. Working through this section is not a creative process, so set your creativity aside for now. To get a perfect score in this section, you'll need to trust the skill and intuition you already have as an editor *and* commit to memory a number of the rules governing English usage. Hopefully, you've had a few English teachers who held you accountable for "CUPS" (Capitalization, Usage, Punctuation, and Spelling). If you haven't, it's time for a crash course. To obtain the high English score you covet, you'll need to commit the laws of English to memory. Induction into the 36 Club requires thorough knowledge of the conventions, strategies, and tips provided in the following chapters.

TIP

Master the basics of the English language and you'll benefit long after you've forgotten about the ACT.

Believe it or not, there are even more important reasons than college admission for memorizing this information. You might have all the great ideas in the world. You might even feel like you know the nuts and bolts of English. Without instant recall of all of the fundamentals, though, you run the risk of being misunderstood. Strive to know this information so well that it becomes instinctive.

These chapters will teach you the skills you'll need to edit with confidence. They will also review the conventions of English and provide strategies that will help you both ace the test *and* use language in a way that satisfies everyone, even the strictest grammarian.

OVERVIEW OF THE ENGLISH SECTION

When you sit down to take the English section, you'll have 45 minutes to answer 75 questions. Perhaps you're already dividing those numbers in your head. Yes, the ACT allots you about 36 seconds per question. But don't think about it that way.

In order to maximize your score, you have to budget your time. Do the quick, easy questions first. Easy questions carry the same value as difficult, time-consuming ones. Never spend so much time on a challenging question that you lose the opportunity for easy points somewhere else.

Here are some basic ground rules.

1. **There will be five nonfiction passages on the test.** Each passage will have 15 questions associated with it. The passages will cover a variety of subjects, but the reading itself will be easy—about ninth-grade level.

2. **The degree of difficulty is random.** Unlike the SAT, which orders questions from easiest to hardest, the ACT attempts to throw you off by intermittently offering more difficult (or, really, more time-consuming) questions. The trick is to attempt all of the easy and medium questions before you tackle the tough ones. As is always the case on the ACT, there is no guessing penalty. Even if a question stumps you completely, guess.

3. **The ACT English test does not cover spelling or vocabulary.** Even if you recently spell-checked the word *English*, you can ace the English section. There's no easy way to fairly test spelling, so the ACT doesn't bother. Although you might be asked to fix some commonly misused words (*there, their,* and *they're,* for example), you won't have to spell anything correctly. You also won't be asked to define any words, although you will be asked to replace misused words with more acceptable or precise ones.

In short, the English section tests your sense of style and sentence structure, your ability to punctuate, your sense of organization, and your knowledge of grammar and usage. The topics break down as follows (approximately):

Sentence Structure	25%
Grammar and Usage	15%
Writing Strategy and Revision	15%
Sense of Style	15%
Organization	15%
Punctuation	15%

FOUR KEYS TO THE ENGLISH SECTION

The four keys to the English section are as follows: economy, order, pacing, and intuition. Before you review the necessary skills, commit the following test-taking method to memory.

Here are some helpful strategies for answering questions on the ACT.

1. **Economy**. The simplest sounding answer is right a lot of the time.

2. **Order**. Always tackle questions in the order that maximizes your potential to score well.

3. **Pacing**. Find the right gear. For many students, slowing down will be more important than working quickly.

4. **Intuition**. Consider order and pacing, but work confidently.

Economy

Do not forget this one! The ACT knows that students add extra verbiage to "sound smart." Think about it. Have you ever said something like "utilized" instead of "used?" Have you ever written an essay in which you admired your mom's "maternal, nurturing, caring, protective, motherly way"? That kind of "fake-fancy" writing is a trap on this test. Be economical. Whether you're answering a question about punctuation, sentence structure, style, or grammar, less is usually more. Here are two examples.

> **REMEMBER**
>
> The simplest sounding answer is often the correct answer.

Stew Michaels wanted to <u>form</u> a nonprofit organization to help people in Darfur and Eastern Chad.

48. A. NO CHANGE
    B. begin and found
    C. formulate
    D. provide the formation of

Correct answer: (A) "Form" is the most economical choice here. "Begin and found" (B) is redundant, "formulate" (C) is used incorrectly, and "provide the formation of" (D) is unnecessarily wordy.

<u>Lance, and his buddy,</u> think NASCAR is righteous.

49. F. NO CHANGE
    G. and his buddy,
    H. and his buddy
    J. , and his buddy

Correct answer: (H) The phrase "Lance and his buddy" is a compound noun, just like "he and I." The entire phrase, as one entity, warrants the plural verb *think*, so no commas are necessary. In the next chapter, you'll learn exactly when to use a comma. For the purposes of this test, it's usually best to avoid heavily punctuated answers.

Order

The English section gives you 45 minutes to answer 75 questions. Within those bounds, work in any order that suits you. Do the quick questions first. Mark and come back to the ones that are going to take a while. Remember: A ten-second question gets you the same number of points as a two-minute question!

Here's an example:

[4]

[1] The Wheaton family shuddered; they had never seen a live brown bear. [2] Miraculously, the bear approached the family and, ignoring them, began eating peanut butter. [3] It was all John could do to keep from laughing. [4] They knew they had <u>none</u> time to run for safety, so they stuck together

Line
(5)   in the tent and hoped for the best. 13

TIP

Easy questions are worth the same number of points as difficult ones.

12. **A.** NO CHANGE
    B. ample
    C. no
    D. few

13. Which of the following sequences of sentences would make paragraph 4 most logical?
    F. 1, 2, 3, 4
    G. 1, 4, 2, 3
    H. 2, 3, 1, 4
    J. 4, 1, 2, 3

If you glance at the above questions *before* reading the passage, you already know that question 13 will require more time than question 12. Why? It takes longer to read an entire paragraph than it does to read one phrase and consider word choice. As a general rule, questions with a "stem," a statement that precedes the answer choices, will take longer than questions without one. Always tackle questions in the order that maximizes your potential to score well!

Answers: 12. **(C)**   13. **(G)**

Pacing

You'll probably be able to work quickly and efficiently through 75 percent of the English section, but don't let speed make you careless. A variety of traps in this section depend on students working too quickly. Listen to wording, be aware of context when reading underlined portions, and never assume an answer is correct without considering every option. If you are the type of student who is within reach of a perfect score, you already possess countless English skills that you take for granted. You're likely to have ample time to complete this section.

Slow down and read as an editor would read—quickly but conscientiously. All too often, your intuition about how a sentence *should be* takes over, and you will gloss over the error without acknowledging it. Read exactly what is on the page, and be aware of what you read. For many students, slowing down will be more important than working quickly.

TIP

Don't rush so much that you make silly mistakes.

Intuition

If you're aiming for a perfect score on this section, you're probably highly proficient in English. Trust yourself! On some English questions, you can trust your ear for language. Does it sound wrong, especially when you whisper it to yourself? If so, it probably is. On other questions, trust your eye. Does it look wrong? Sometimes, you can trust your sense of style, organization, or development. Consider order and pacing, but work confidently.

On the other hand, remember that some questions can trap students because they haven't considered that an abundance of casual, conversational English is unconventional. By *intuition*, we mean intuitive knowledge of formal, written English. Intuitive does not mean "lazy," "casual," or "colloquial."

TIP

Remember that all the answers are right in front of you, and one of them is correct!

BREVITY, CLARITY, AND LOGIC

As a writer, it's important to practice economy, but it's equally important to employ clarity and logic. Some colloquial language—language that is informal and spoken but not considered "proper"—has developed out of a desire for economy that supersedes clarity or logic. Most native speakers of American English, for example, pronounce the word *have* in "could have" as "of" or "uh." The result sounds like "I could of," or, "I coulda." These informal versions are incorrect, of course.

Prepositions and adjective/adverb agreement are two other realms where you might have to sacrifice economy for formality. To your peers, you might say, "That bike *I rode on* yesterday handled *nice!*" when formal English dictates that you say, "That bike *on which I rode* yesterday handled *nicely!*" You might sound strange if you talked this way to your friends, but for the sake of this test, you'll need to shift gears. Just pretend you're talking to your grandmother or your English teacher and you should be fine. First, ask yourself, "Is it economical?" Then ask, "Is it clear?" and "Is it logical?"

FINDING THE CORRECT ANSWER

For a high-achieving student with good language instincts, sorting through wrong answers shouldn't be too difficult. The right answer is in front of you. You don't have to think of it; you just have to find it. Asking yourself a few basic questions will help.

Does It Sound Right?

The ACT tests your ability to distinguish among fragments, sentences, and run-ons. Consider the following example:

> *Although I love cheese.*

Read it out loud. It just sounds wrong, doesn't it? The period doesn't work, because your ear wants something more. It wants to add something like . . .

> *. . . the kind with built-in mold isn't my favorite.*

This added phrase would make the thought sound complete:

> *Although I love cheese, the kind with built-in mold isn't my favorite.*

Trust your ear to determine whether a thought is incomplete, just right, or over-extended (fragment, sentence, or run-on). Chapter 2 addresses independent and dependent clauses, which you'll need to know thoroughly in order to ace the English section, but keep in mind that your ear can help at times. Listen for errors in syntax, diction, parallelism, and redundancy as well. Even during the test, don't be afraid to double-check an answer by silently whispering a word or phrase to yourself.

Does It Look Right?

Sometimes your ears will fool you (remember *could of*?), so you'll need your eyes, too. Consider this example:

> *The senators have decided to take there tea in the Oak Room.*

Your ear won't help you here; the sentence sounds fine. But what *looks* funny? Did you notice the incorrect use of *there*? To spot homonym errors such as this one, you'll need your eyes, not your ears.

Does It Make Sense?

The ACT loves to play hide-and-seek with logical relationships. If you know the test's tricks, you can see how simple a question really is. When you sense a subject-verb agreement question, for example, focus on the essentials: subject and verb. Here's an example:

> *The mountain lake surrounded by elk and their offspring are usually filled with icebergs.*

NOTE

If you need to review words that sound the same but are spelled differently, study the list of the most common word-choice goofs in Chapter 4.

Now try cutting some dead wood:

The ~~mountain~~ lake ~~surrounded by elk and their offspring~~ are ~~usually~~ filled with icebergs.

which gives you:

The lake are filled with icebergs.

You know this sentence is incorrect, but can't you imagine rushing through the question and missing the subject-verb error? Once you understand the logic of the traps on the test, use it to your advantage. Logic will help you identify misplaced modifiers, adjective/adverb issues, and colloquialisms—all of which are covered in the English section of this book.

FIVE POINTS TO REMEMBER

1. You will face five passages—15 questions per passage. Altogether, you'll have 45 minutes to answer 75 questions about style, sentence structure, punctuation, organization, grammar, and usage.

2. The reading itself will be relatively easy, and the degree of difficulty of the questions will be random.

3. The ACT will not test your knowledge of spelling or vocabulary. Word choice questions all have to do with usage. You may be asked to clarify or correct language, but you won't be asked to spell or define words.

4. Remember the Four Keys to the English Section.

   - **Economy**. The simplest sounding answer is right most of the time, but not if it compromises precision or clarity.
   - **Order**. Always tackle questions in the order that maximizes your potential to score well.
   - **Pacing**. Find the right gear. For many students, slowing down will be more important than working quickly. Traps on the ACT depend on students getting overconfident and rushing through answers.
   - **Intuition**. Consider order and pacing, but work confidently.

5. Don't forget to ask yourself:

   - Does it sound right? This technique works best with sentence structure questions.
   - Does it look right? Sometimes your ear will fool you, especially on questions related to word choice. Be careful.
   - Does it make sense? Sometimes, you'll have to sift through extra verbiage to discover logical relationships among words.

TIP

As is always the case on the ACT, if you don't know the answer, guess.

Punctuation: Minimize the Madness

CHAPTER 2

- Punctuation basics
- Four keys to punctuation questions
- Anti-punctuation rules
- Practice questions

Were you weaned on grammar worksheets? Have you spent hours mulling over lists of appositives, conjunctive adverbs, and introductory dependent clauses only to end up more confused? You may have come to view punctuation the way hunt-and-peck typists view a computer keyboard: as a tiresome process of searching for the right spot to insert something.

LESS IS MORE

One of the most important rules of thumb in punctuation is simplicity. Punctuation marks aren't there to decorate your sentence. They're there to clarify. Extra punctuation does just the opposite. The less you punctuate, the better!

Conquer the confusion that surrounds the forbidding comma, the intimidating colon, and the ever-scary dash by learning to *minimize the madness*. By adopting a minimalist approach to punctuation, you will see these pesky marks for what they are: a useful and simple way to clarify your thinking to a reader, nothing more.

It's best to think of punctuation the way the ACT asks you to think about all writing: **Less is more.** Consider the following example:

> *The Littleton football team won <u>it's first game;</u> and hopes to enter league play with a perfect record.*

After that setup, you may have guessed, correctly, that the previous sentence needs exactly one punctuation mark: a period. But look again at the sentence. Might you have been tempted to replace the semicolon with a comma? Might you have paused before removing the apostrophe in *it's?*

Learning how to tackle punctuation questions is an exercise in avoiding the unnecessary. You must get out of the habit of adding extra punctuation when you're unsure.

TIP

Worth repeating: The less you punctuate, the better!

FOUR KEYS TO PUNCTUATION QUESTIONS

You Can Maneuver by Feel to a Certain Degree

Consider the following example:

> *Bob, and his best friend, decided they would spray paint Bob's car pink and put princess decals on the hood.*

Look at it. It looks a bit awkward, doesn't it? Read it out loud to yourself. Don't you read the first part of the sentence without pausing? You might pause after *pink*, but it's not underlined, so don't worry about it. Finally, do the commas make sense to you on a gut level? It seems nonsensical to place a comma in between a noun and a verb, the way *friend* and *decided* are separated in this sentence. Three strikes, wouldn't you say? Get rid of those commas!

It's Mostly About the Commas

TIP

Whisper the sentence to yourself. If you hear a pause, you may need punctuation.

The comma is the most heavily tested punctuation mark. Learn to use it sparingly. You may, through no fault of your own, punctuate something like this:

> *Wow, commas are important, therefore, I should, like, use them, and use them, and use, them.*

If you tend to over-punctuate, simply do what you've secretly longed to do since sixth grade. Assume that sentences can go and go and go and go and go without the help of the oppressive and bossy comma!

By knowing the anti-comma rules we address later in this chapter, you can narrow your understanding of comma placement so that it fits easily into your head on test day. Of the ten or so punctuation questions on the test, half will test comma use. Comma use is much simpler than you might think.

Forget About Quotes

You do not need to know how to use quotation marks properly to do well on this test! Furthermore, you'll never be tested on how commas or colons introduce quotation marks.

Remember the Comma's Less Popular Cousins

Knowing *a few* other rules about semicolons, colons, dashes, and apostrophes can help you when another punctuation mark is being tested or when multiple punctuation marks are used in answer choices to distract you.

ANTI-PUNCTUATION RULES

Before you proceed to the rules you do need to know, make sure you understand these five technical terms.

> ## TERMS TO KNOW
>
> 1. **Clause:** a group of words that contains a subject, an object, or both, plus a verb.
>   *Example: "I love the Beatles."*
>   In this case, *I* is the subject, *love* is the verb, and *the Beatles* is the object.
> 2. **Independent Clause:** a clause that can stand on its own as a sentence.
>   *Example: "I love the Beatles."*
> 3. **Dependent Clause:** a clause that cannot stand on its own as a sentence. A dependent clause "depends" on the rest of the sentence to make sense.
>   *Examples: "because I love the Beatles"*
>   *"After I loved the Beatles"*
>   *"loving the Beatles"*
>   *"that I loved the Beatles"*
>   *"and I loved the Beatles"*
> 4. **Possession:** showing ownership or belonging.
>   *Example:* **Bob's** *copy of "Abbey Road" remains on the shelf.*
> 5. **Conjunction**: a word that connects words, phrases, or clauses.
>   *Example: The Beatles went through a trippy phase,* **but** *I still picture them as fairly clean-cut.*

It's not necessary to know that nonessential parts of sentences are sometimes called appositives or that *however* is a conjunctive adverb. However, you should follow these simple rules:

DON'T Use a *Comma* Unless . . .

1. . . . it separates introductory words from the main part of the sentence.

Correct: <u>*After seven hours of studying*</u>*, I raised my ACT score by five points.*

Correct: <u>*Over the years*</u>*, our band has gotten better.*

Correct: <u>*Knowing my teacher had "a thing" about being late*</u>*, I made sure to be on time to class.*

Introductory Phrase = Comma

Practice Question

Upon completing the <u>building the contractor</u> sent us the bill.
   A. NO CHANGE
   B. building the contractor
   C. building, the contractor
   D. building the, contractor

Explanation: What are the main subject and action? The main subject is the contractor. What did he do? He sent us the bill. These two phrases make up the core sentence. The clause "Upon completing the building" only indicates the time period when the bill was sent. You could just say, "The contractor sent us a bill," and it would be correct. Remember, introductory phrase = comma. Answer: (C).

2. . . . it sets off words or phrases that are nonessential to the integrity of the sentence. Information can be *relevant* but still not necessary to make a grammatical sentence. Think about nonessential clauses this way: If you can remove it and the sentence still makes sense, it needs a "comma hug."

Nonessential? Give It a Hug!

, Nonessential,

Nonessential phrases can also be thought of as "by the way" phrases or "BTW" phrases. You could add "by the way" somewhere within any phrase and it would still make sense: *I am freaking out now, by the way, because the prom is coming up.* BTW phrases are nonessential because you can leave them out of the sentence. Many BTW phrases add clarifying information and should not be removed from a sentence unless they really are just extra fluff.

, BTW,

> Correct: *Joey, the homeless man at my subway stop, plays "Stairway to Heaven" on a flute.*
>
> Correct: *Steve, who loves tennis so much he wears white shorts to school in winter, has a tournament in Phoenix next week.*

Practice Question

My brother Ron, an optometrist owns his own practice.
- **A.** NO CHANGE
- **B.** Ron an optometrist owns
- **C.** Ron, an optometrist, owns
- **D.** Ron; an optometrist, owns

Explanation: You say: *My brother Ron, (who by the way is) an optometrist, owns his own practice.* If you remove it and say the sentence aloud, it sounds like a complete sentence: *My brother owns his own practice.* A nonessential or BTW phrase needs a comma hug. Answer: (C).

3. . . . it separates two independent clauses and you see one of the following words: *for, and, nor, but, or, yet, so.* If you're into boy bands, or if you like making fun of them—which pretty much takes care of everyone—you can remember that the first letters of these words spell "**FANBOYS.**"

FANBOYS

For
And
Nor
But
Or
Yet
So

Correct: *I'm thinking of going to Georgetown, <u>but</u> I enjoyed visiting U of A.*

Correct: *Steve was the best soccer player in his region, <u>so</u> they invited him to try out for the national team.*

Correct: *I'll take the #2 with a Coke, <u>and</u> I'll go ahead and "Jumbo Size" it.*

Think in terms of relationships! Sometimes when two independently minded people are together, they need a buffer between them so that they don't butt heads. The comma is the buffer between two independent clauses.

Independent, (FANBOYS) Independent

In relationships where there is an independent individual and a dependent individual, no buffer is necessary because the dependent person relies on the independent person for support.

Independent (FANBOYS) Dependent = No Comma

Practice Question

Mike was the first person on the scene of the <u>accident, and tried</u> to help the injured passenger.
- **A.** NO CHANGE
- **B.** accident and tried
- **C.** accident and, tried
- **D.** accident; and tried

Explanation: Remember FANBOYS? When you see a conjunction like *and,* always split the sentence in half. Say the first part of the sentence alone: *Mike was the first person on the scene of the accident.* Then, say the part of the sentence that comes after the conjunction (*and*) alone: *tried to help the injured passenger.* The second half of the sentence doesn't sound like a complete sentence, so no comma is necessary. Answer: (B).

Practice Question

My mother either wanted to ride her unicycle to <u>work or she</u> wanted to work out at the jujitsu gym in the evening.
- **A.** NO CHANGE
- **B.** work; or she
- **C.** work or, she
- **D.** work, or she

Explanation: Remember FANBOYS? There is an *or* in this sentence. Split the sentence in two, divided by the conjunction. In this sentence, the conjunction *either* works together with *or*; don't say the word *either* when testing the sentence. You say: *My mother wanted to ride her bike to work.* This clause is independent. You say: *she wanted to work out at the jujitsu gym in the evening.* This clause is also independent; it stands alone. Answer: (D).

4. . . . it separates words in a list or series. This is the easy one, A gift from the ACT!

> Correct: *For summer camp, they say I need <u>two pairs of pants, bug spray, sunscreen, and a llama</u>.*
>
> Correct: *How could you <u>dump me, tell Julie you love her, go to the prom with her, and then tell</u> me <u>you love me</u>!*

THE ADJECTIVE TEST

If you can say the word *and* between the adjectives that modify a noun, then you need to use a comma. If you can't, omit the comma. Another way to determine the need for a comma is to reverse the order of the adjectives. If the new combination still makes sense, then you need a comma.

The following examples **DO** need a comma.

* *The relentless, overwhelming, powerful wind caused our ice-fishing tent to fly across the lake.*

* *My friend has a relaxed, happy grin every day.*

* *Completing Ms. Worksheet's tedious, treacherous tasks exhausts me.*

The following examples **DO NOT** need a comma.

* *Ms. Worksheet lives in a <u>small brick</u> house.*

* *She often wears a <u>gray wool</u> sweater with apples on it.*

* *While basking in the <u>powerful summer sun</u>, I dream of acing the ACT.*

Practice Question

I found an <u>expensive, long, turquoise prom dress</u> on the discount rack.
> **A.** NO CHANGE
> **B.** expensive long turquoise prom dress
> **C.** expensive long, turquoise prom dress
> **D.** expensive, long, turquoise, prom, dress

Explanation: Test the adjective combinations by placing *and* between them:

- *expensive and long dress*—sounds correct
- *long and turquoise dress*—sounds correct
- *turquoise and prom dress*—sounds incorrect

Through this test, you've determined that *prom* is not one of the adjectives; therefore, it does not need a comma between itself and *turquoise*. *Prom* and *dress* make a special pair; they are a team and can't be separated, like you and your date.

Reversing the adjectives also works, as in the following examples:

- *long, expensive . . . dress*—it works

- *turquoise, long . . . dress*—may sound strange but it still works

- *prom, turquoise dress*—Whoa, this sounds funny. *Prom* must stay with *dress*. Answer: (A).

5. . . . you see a verbal phrase at the end of a sentence, especially one that contains a verb plus "ing," and the verbal phrase in question seems to refer to the entire sentence, not just the word right before it. This rule has popped up so often on the ACT test recently that the writer of this section has come to refer to it as "the 'ing' thing." Thanks to the clever student who coined this term!

The following example is straightforward.

Correct: *Barbara did well, considering she hadn't studied at all.*

That you can change the order of the two halves of the sentence without changing the meaning reinforces the idea that the verbal phrase refers to everything before it:

Considering she hadn't studied at all, Barbara did well.

The next two examples are subtler, but they help explain the rule more clearly:

Correct: *Mr. Spare offered rewards to students <u>trying</u> to improve their test scores.* (The absence of a comma indicates that the "ing" word refers only to the word right before it: "students." Therefore, no comma is necessary.

Correct: *Mr. Spare offered rewards to students, <u>trying</u> to improve their test scores.* (The comma clarifies the meaning of the sentence, indicating that the "ing" word refers to the entire sentence, namely the subject, "Mr. Spare," and not just the "students." Therefore, a comma is necessary.

Practice Question

The seven-year-old looked away from me <u>when he lied reinforcing my suspicions.</u>
    A. NO CHANGE
    B. when he, lied reinforcing my suspicions.
    C. when he lied, reinforcing my suspicions.
    D. when he lied; reinforcing my suspicions.

Explanation: It is clear that the "ing" word in this case modifies the whole clause preceding it, not just the word "lied" that precedes it. So the sentence needs a comma before "reinforcing." Answer: (C).

Note: Your intuition will come into play on these kinds of questions because a natural pause will almost always occur when the "ing" word refers to the whole sentence.

> **INSIDE THE ACT 36 MIND**
> The ACT will never test you on the serial comma. In other words, you will never be asked to determine the correctness of the last comma in a list. There's a lot of debate about the serial comma, and the ACT never addresses debatable issues.

DON'T Use a *Semicolon* Unless . . .

1. . . . it separates two independent clauses and you *do not* see one of the following words: *for, and, nor, but, or, yet, so.* Again, remember the acronym FANBOYS.

    Independent clauses without a FANBOYS word still need a buffer between them. A comma just isn't enough. The two sides of the sentence are still seen together, yet they can't touch.

Independent; Independent

Correct: *I'm thinking of going to Georgetown; D.C. is an ideal place for me to begin my political career.*

Correct: *Steve was the best soccer player in his region; his knuckle-ball free kicks were nothing short of lethal.*

Correct: *I'll take the #2 with a Coke; it's got the most trans fat, which is what I'm shooting for.*

2. . . . you see *thus, furthermore, however, moreover, therefore,* or *nevertheless* between two independent clauses. Unlike FANBOYS conjunctions, words such as *however* and *therefore* are tricky. When placed between two independent clauses, these words are considered conjunctions, but they take on a more prominent position in the sentence than FANBOYS words do. Therefore, it becomes necessary to place a semicolon in front of them and a comma behind.

Independent; *however*, Independent

Correct: *I like gigantic pickup trucks; however, they're not practical in New York City.*

Correct: *Cats aren't friendly and often spray on the couch; therefore, I have decided to become a dog person.*

Be mindful of using the word *however* as a guide for using a semicolon. Words such as *however* and *therefore* can be used without separating two independent clauses. When words like *however* interrupt a thought, they become BTW phrases and are, therefore, nonessential. If you remove a word from the above list and the sentence still makes sense, you have a nonessential, BTW phrase.

Here is a more thorough list of words that behave as *however* and *therefore* do when placed between two independent clauses:

accordingly

also

likewise

afterward

consequently

indeed

nonetheless

similarly

still

*otherwise (An exception to the rule: *Otherwise* does not need a comma when it follows a semicolon.)

*so (An exception to the rule: *So* does not need a comma when it follows a semicolon.)

Practice Question

I enjoy playing volleyball in the sand; however, I love volleyball so much that I will play on grass as well.

    A. NO CHANGE

    B. sand; however I love

    C. sand, however, I love

    D. sand however I love

Explanation: If you see conjunctions like *thus, furthermore, however, moreover, therefore,* or *nevertheless,* test for independent clauses on each side. Say, *I enjoy playing volleyball in the sand.* Independent. Then, say the second half of the sentence without *however: I love volleyball so much that I will play on grass as well.* Independent. You need a semicolon, then *however,* and then the comma. Answer: (A).

After the rigorous ACT test, I plan on going home and taking a <u>nap, I</u> may also find a large container of ice cream and gorge myself.
- **A.** NO CHANGE
- **B.** nap I,
- **C.** nap; I
- **D.** nap: I

Explanation: Look at your options carefully; the semicolon and the colon look similar. When you are in a hurry, you may accidentally choose the wrong one. The easiest way to determine the correct answer is to notice that there is not a conjunction linking the two halves of the sentence. You know that a comma is incorrect because of the "don't use a comma unless" rules we reviewed previously. Remember that two independent clauses need a stronger buffer than just a comma. Test the clauses to determine whether or not they are independent: Say the two halves of the sentence separately. Again, if they make their own sentences, they are independent. Answer: (C).

DON'T Use a *Colon* Unless . . .

1. . . . it follows an *independent* clause and introduces an example, explanation, short phrase, or list. The word, phrase, or clause that *follows* the colon need not be an independent clause.

Complete sentences (independent clauses) always precede colons! If the sentence in front of the colon is a fragment, either use a different punctuation mark or complete the fragment. A colon connects the sentence in front of it to the information that follows. The information after the colon is always referred to in front of the colon.

Correct: *There's only one city where I'd ever live: Boulder, Colorado.*

Sentence: Detail about Topic

Correct: *The teacher had only three rules in her class: be on time, sit quietly, and check your attitude at the door.*

Sentence: List

Practice Question

Martha has a serious <u>problem; she's fourteen and</u> doesn't know how to tie her shoes.
  A. NO CHANGE
  B. problem, she's fourteen and
  C. problem she's fourteen and
  D. problem: she's fourteen and

Explanation: Rule out B and C because of the fact that there isn't a FANBOYS word and because these two independent clauses need a buffer between them. Determining whether the answer should be A or D is tricky. The key word in the first half of the sentence is *problem.* The second half of the sentence indicates the nature of Martha's problem, which means that a colon and not a semicolon should follow. The second half of the sentence refers to the first half of the sentence. Remember that a colon is more of a connector than a buffer. Answer: (D).

Practice Question

Charles took several items to <u>the beach; a football</u>, a towel, an iPod, his cell phone, and an apple.
  A. NO CHANGE
  B. the beach: a football
  C. the beach a football
  D. the beach—a football

Explanation: This example isn't that tricky. "Several items" is the most important phrase to notice in this sentence. The phrase should tell you that a list could be forthcoming. When you introduce a list, you need a colon. Remember that the section of the sentence prior to the colon must be a complete sentence. Answer: (B).

DON'T Use a *Dash* . . .

1. . . . pretty much ever, because it's not tested frequently.
2. . . . unless there's a major break or interruption in thought, in which case you need one on either side of the break. This last statement is key, because if the ACT tests you on a dash, it will usually want you to use two, one on each side of the statement.

The ACT rarely tests the use of a dash because, all too often, a "comma hug" will adequately punctuate a nonessential clause (see comma rule #2). Nonessential clauses that require dashes express a clear break in thought. An author might want a major break for emphasis, or she might need to place an entire sentence within the body of another sentence, in which case no other punctuation will suffice.

Correct: *Skiing at Vail is expensive—<u>it cost me ninety-seven bucks last time I went</u>— but the back bowls are worth every penny.*

—Complete Sentence/Nonessential Clause—

Dashes can also be used when placing a list within a sentence.

Correct: *Three of my most difficult classes—history, physics, and English— are all first thing in the morning.*

Correct: *My friends—Jill, Kim, and Sophie—all teach gymnastics with me during summer vacation.*

Practice Question

Because of the unbelievable heat today—it is 110 degrees—I need to find some shade.
  A. NO CHANGE
  B. today, it is 110 degrees, I
  C. today; it is 110 degrees, I
  D. today: it is 110 degrees, I

Explanation: When you read this sentence aloud, you can hear the emphasis on the phrase "it is 110 degrees." Yikes! Besides adding emotion to the sentence, the phrase is an independent clause that needs extra support from two dashes. Answer: (A).

Practice Question

I used to play with Barbie dolls, only when I felt lonely and I would make my brother play with me.
  A. NO CHANGE
  B. only when I felt lonely; and
  C. only when I, felt lonely, and
  D. —only when I felt lonely—and

Explanation: Keep in mind that the ACT wants you to demonstrate that you understand the best answer. Responses A, B, and C don't work. The phrase "only when I felt lonely" is a BTW phrase that definitely needs some extra support. The answer options don't include a comma hug, so the only logical response is D.

Practice Question

There are three primary issues on the ballot this season; health care, education, and tax reform, so I sure hope changes are coming soon.

   A. NO CHANGE
   B. season, health care, education, and tax reform, so I
   C. season—health care, education, and tax reform—so I
   D. season, health care, education, and tax reform; so I

Explanation: Your knowledge of punctuation may be tested here. In this instance, a nonessential clause already has commas within it and needs to be offset by a dash on each end. Answer: (C).

DON'T Use an *Apostrophe* Unless . . .

1. . . . the word shows possession.

'**s = singular possession**

Correct: *Danny's hat says "Duke" on it.*

s' = plural + possession

Correct: *Both of my parents' siblings live in Rochester.*

Key thought: Make sure the noun actually possesses something. You may rush to place an apostrophe just because the word is plural and "feels" like it needs one. Don't forget that "feel" is only your first line of defense. Slowing down helps distinguish between plurality and possession. (Review the introductory remarks about "pacing.")

   Incorrect: *The Daltons' and the Larsons' traveled to Charleston during the month of June.*

The Daltons and the Larsons don't possess anything in the previous example; they don't own the "traveling," and they certainly don't possess Charleston. Remove all apostrophes.

   Correct: *The Daltons' boat and the Larsons' car washed away in the flood.*

This example shows possession, so apostrophes are necessary.
   Note: When two nouns possess the same item or idea, the second noun is given the punctuation, not the first:

   Correct: *Joe and Anne's basement was also destroyed by the flood.*

Practice Question

I didn't like Mr. <u>Morrisons'</u> advice about talking to girls, so I decided to talk to my hamster, Lyle, instead.

    A. NO CHANGE
    B. Morrisons
    C. Morrisons,
    D. Morrison's

Explanation: Placing a comma between *Morrisons* and *advice* (choice C) doesn't fit with any of the comma rules, so you know that this question tests your knowledge of the apostrophe. First, make sure Mr. Morrison actually possesses something by looking at the word that immediately follows the noun. Ask yourself: *Can Mr. Morrison "possess" advice?* Your parents give you advice all the time, and they have to possess it to give it. Because Mr. Morrison possesses advice, an apostrophe is needed. Next, ask: *Is the noun singular or plural?* Because "Mr." indicates only one person, we know that the apostrophe comes before the *s*. The correct spelling is *Morrison's*. Answer: (D).

Practice Question

We drove to the lake <u>in Angie's and Paige's</u> convertible, dressed as the latest all-girl band.

    A. NO CHANGE
    B. in: Angie and Paige's
    C. in Angie and Paige's
    D. in Angie and Paiges

Explanation: Be careful! Except for that sneaky colon in answer B, it looks correct. The ACT will at times make sure you are being precise and throw in other punctuation, either to distract you or in the hope that you'll overlook it. The first noun in the phrase "Angie and Paige" does not receive an apostrophe. Only the noun immediately before the object that is being possessed receives that honor. Answer: (C).

2. . . . the word is a contraction.

    The only ones you're likely to see are

    it's (it + is)
    there's (there + is)
    they're (they + are)
    who's (who + is)

Correct: *It's a fact that elephants are bigger than mice.*
Correct: *My cousin, who's a genius on the violin, will attend Juilliard.*

Unsure if the apostrophe correctly indicates a contraction? Pull the word apart to make sure it makes sense. Make sure you "hear" it correctly.

Example*: They're going to dig a deep hole in my backyard.*
You say*: They are going to dig a deep hole in my backyard.*
Example: *I am going to take a ride on they're boat.*
You say: *I am going to take a ride on they are boat.*

When you say "they are boat" aloud, it doesn't make sense; therefore, you know that you're (*you are*) dealing with a pronoun and not a contraction. Commonly confused words (i.e., *there, their* and *they're*) are addressed in Chapter 4.

Practice Question

<u>Whose</u> going to the luau with us tonight?
    A. NO CHANGE
    B. Who's
    C. Whose,
    D. Who has

Explanation: When the ACT tests your contraction knowledge, it may try to check your knowledge of other words that sound the same as the contraction. Try separating the contraction *who's* (choice B) to *who is.* "Who is going" makes sense and sounds correct. Separating the word does not produce *who has,* so D is incorrect. The word in the sentence does not contain a contraction and is therefore not correct; the question has incorporated the wrong *whose.* Rule out A and C. Answer: (B)

INSIDE THE ACT 36 MIND

Because it's so easy to do, the ACT will often try to convince you that a question tests punctuation when really it assesses some other skill. Look at the answer options. If the answer has punctuation in some responses and not others or moves punctuation around, punctuation may be a distracter. Knowing the anti-punctuation rules thoroughly is the best way to avoid this trap.

SIX TIPS TO MINIMIZE PUNCTUATION MADNESS

1. Stop! Look! Listen! Does the sentence look correct? Does it sound correct? Use your eyes, ears, and instincts to help you identify punctuation problems.
2. Know your anti-punctuation rules, especially with regard to commas. Simplify your life with the "don't use unless" mentality.
3. Know your FANBOYS words: *for, and, nor, but, or, yet,* and *so,* and know how to punctuate them.
4. Don't worry about quotations.
5. Know how to identify independent and dependent clauses.
6. Know how to identify BTW, or "by the way," phrases, and don't forget about those comma hugs.

CHAPTER 3

Sound Sentences

- Subject-verb agreement
- Plural nouns
- Tense agreement
- Pronoun usage
- Syntax and style

Here's an obvious statement: A noun must agree in number with its verb.

The <u>boy</u> <u>takes</u> the test seriously.
The <u>girls</u> <u>take</u> the test seriously.

You will often instinctively know if a sentence sounds, looks, or feels awkward. Questions on the ACT will test your instincts and may try to confuse you.

BACK TO THE BASICS: SUBJECT-VERB AGREEMENT

Your first defense is to "hear" agreement in your head. Say the sentence aloud in your mind. Read everything exactly as it is printed on the test. But pace yourself! Be careful! Your instincts about subject-verb agreement are so strong that your mind will often correct sentences unconsciously. Because it would sound funny to say, *The <u>boys takes</u> the test seriously*, your mind immediately corrects the mistake without any effort on your part.

Reading out loud is one simple way to make sure you hear the simplest mistakes. In this chapter, we offer a few more ways to ensure that you don't make silly mistakes. By pacing yourself and learning this test, you can at least guarantee that you won't miss questions for reasons that make you say "duh."

TIP

Train your brain to read sentences on the ACT exactly as they are written. That's the key in choosing the correct answer.

Sentence Simplification

One of the easiest ways to identify issues with subject-verb agreement is to simplify the sentence.

Incorrect: *Claudia and Kevin, who want to join the speech and debate club together, first decides to start dating after Claudia's sister's boyfriend brings Kevin over to play Guitar Hero.*

1. Ask yourself: Who or what is the subject of the sentence? Answer: Claudia and Kevin

2. Then ask: What is he or she doing? Answer: deciding

3. Remove all BTWs and other words or phrases that are not critical to the subject or the action. In the punctuation chapter, we addressed BTWs or "by the way" phrases, which require a comma hug.

Claudia and Kevin, ~~who want to join the speech and debate club together,~~ first decides ~~to start dating after Claudia's sister's boyfriend brings Kevin over to play Guitar Hero.~~

After simplifying the sentence above, it is obvious that the subject and verb disagree.

Claudia and Kevin decides.

The *and* between *Claudia* and *Kevin* makes them a plural subject. Change *decides* to *decide* to make the sentence correct.

Problems arise when the introductory or BTW phrases contain words that come immediately before the verb. Often these words—which the ACT inserts intentionally to try to confuse you—appear to be the main subject of the sentence when they're not, especially if you're just scanning the underlined areas for an answer.

Consider This Sample Question

George, encouraged by his <u>friends, are</u> finally going to get that "Mom" tattoo.
   A. NO CHANGE
   B. friends, is
   C. friends are
   D. friends: are

When approaching this question, first decide what the question is asking. The BTW phrase in the sentence is punctuated properly, so rule out C and D, which indicate a change in punctuation. A and B are now the only possible answers. Looking at the sentence again, you realize that your task is simple: decide between *is* and *are*. "Friends are finally" *going* sounds correct until you simplify the sentence. Find the main subject and verb so that you don't make a hasty error. *George, encouraged by his friends, are finally going to get that "Mom" tattoo.* "*George are going*" is the simplified version of the sentence. This sentence sounds awkward, and therefore B is the correct answer.

Practice Questions: Subject-Verb Agreement

Simplify each of the following sentences. Circle the subject-verb agreement error and then correct it in the blank at the end of the sentence.

1. Beth and her boyfriend Jeff is going to the movie this weekend. _____

2. James or Phylicia are traveling to the extreme bike races with me this weekend.

   _____

3. Neither Camille nor Theresa are chasing after the hottest guy in school. _____

4. Neither he nor I are waiting for someone to ask us to the dance; we are going to ask someone ourselves. _____

5. Either the principal or the committee members is going to determine the Homecoming parade route. _____

Answers

1. When the word *and* joins two subjects, it immediately brings them together in harmony, making them a nice couple. The subject is plural and requires a plural verb. Change **is** to **are**. Simplified: *Beth and Jeff are going*.

2. When the word *or* joins singular subjects, the subjects remain singular. James and Phylicia are not doing anything together. Change **are** to **is**. Simplified: *James or Phylicia is traveling*.

3. This sentence is tricky; sometimes either example sounds correct. Camille and Theresa are associated with each other, but they aren't lumped into the same category. Think of *or* and *nor* and *neither/nor* and *either/or* as barriers that relate subjects without joining them. Change **are** to **is**. Simplified: *Neither Camille nor Theresa is chasing*.

4. When *I* is a subject in a *neither/nor* or *either/or* combination, it is placed second in the subject combination and followed by a singular verb. Change **are** to **am**. Simplified: *Neither he nor I am waiting*.

5. When **or, nor, either/or,** and **neither/nor** are used with a combination of a singular and a plural noun, the verb agrees with the noun closest to it. In this sentence, the verb must agree with the word *members*. Change **is** to **are**. Simplified: *Either the principal or the committee members are going*.

Looks Plural, Acts Singular: "Each Is One Body"

The first set of pronouns that look plural yet act singular can be remembered by thinking about the phrase "Each is one body." This phrase will help you remember that the pronoun *each*, as well as pronouns that end in -*one* and -*body*, are singular and require a singular verb such as *is*. The pronouns *either* and *neither*, when not used in combination with *or* or *nor*, also fall into the singular category.

The "Singles" Club

Pronouns	Amount	Plural sounding (but still singular)	Collective nouns
each everyone every one everybody anyone anybody someone no one either neither	dollars years decades	civics news mathematics measles	group team committee class family

There are three more categories of words that form the "Singles Club," but pronouns and collective nouns are most likely to appear on the test.

Practice Question

Each of the <u>boys dance</u> well enough to be in a music video.
>   **F.** NO CHANGE
>   **G.** boys' dance
>   **H.** boys, dance
>   **J.** boys dances

TIP

Use the phrase "each is one body" to remember that the word *each* and pronouns that end in *-one* and *-body* are singular.

Explanation: Read the sentence to hear how it sounds. Because you are working so quickly through the test, your initial sound check may not instantly call attention to a problem. When said aloud, *boys dance* sounds fine. When you look at the answer options, you realize that the boys don't own anything; therefore, no apostrophe is necessary and answer G is not correct. When you consider answer H, you realize that it doesn't fit any of the comma rules that we reviewed in the punctuation chapter. Your only other choices are F or J. The phrase *of the boys* points to the pronoun *each* as the subject of the sentence. Remove *of the boys* and say it correctly, remembering that the pronoun *each* belongs to the Singles Club. ***Each dances well enough to be on a music video.*** Answer: (J).

Amount Words: Special Circumstances

Words indicating amount, like the word ***none***, when used as the subject of a sentence, do not hang out in the Singles Club. They are married to one word—the word *of*. The noun at the end of an "of" phrase dictates the verb status.

- **None** <u>of my friends</u> want to see the new Tom Cruise movie with me. (friends want)

- A **fraction** <u>of my friends</u> work retail in the mall during the summer. (friends work)

- Seventy **percent** <u>of the student body</u> works during the summer. (student body works)

Simplifying these sentence may, at times, be problematic, so pay careful attention to amount words such as *percent, fraction, part, majority, some, all, none,* and *remainder.*

KEEP IT CONSISTENT: TENSE AGREEMENT

Consistency, consistency, consistency! When a passage starts in one tense, it needs to stay in one tense, usually for the entire paragraph. Consider the following examples:

Incorrect: *Joe <u>ran</u> the race and <u>wins</u>.*

Correct: *Joe <u>ran</u> the race and <u>won</u>.*

Incorrect: *Caitlin <u>tries</u> to teach her mom how to text but didn't expect her to get it.*

Correct: *Caitlin <u>tried</u> to teach her mom how to text but didn't expect her to get it.*

Incorrect: *Mirth <u>has dressed</u> up like a ballerina every year since the third grade, and every year her friends <u>laughed at her</u>.*

Correct: *Mirth <u>has dressed</u> up like a ballerina every year since the third grade, and every year her friends <u>have laughed</u> at her.*

An exception: If it is obvious that the tense has changed, then a shift in tenses is allowed.

Bruce <u>asked</u> Georgia to go to the independent movie today and <u>will ask</u> Chuck to go to the action thriller with him tomorrow.

The independent movie happens today, so the tense remains in the present. The action thriller happens tomorrow, necessitating the future tense.

Practice Question

As soon as the last bell rang, Mr. Brooks's class <u>rushes</u> the door.
- **A.** NO CHANGE
- **B.** will rush
- **C.** has been rushing
- **D.** rushed

Explanation: Because the underlined word, *rushes,* is a verb, check for possible verb issues—in this case, tense issues. Find other verbs that need to match, and remember that the clue to the correct answer will probably *not* be in the underlined portion. The verb *rang* and the verb *rushes* should match. Because *rang* is in the past tense, *rushes* should be **rushed.** Answer: (D).

Pronoun Usage: Singular or Plural?

The rule that applies to subject-verb agreement applies to pronoun agreement: pronouns must agree in number.

> ### INSIDE THE ACT 36 MIND
>
> The pronouns *each*, *any*, and *body* dominate agreement questions on the ACT. In short, the ACT tries to trick you into using colloquial forms that sound good to your ear. Refer to the Singles Club chart on page 30 for a list! These pronouns are singular and agree with other singular pronouns, even though, when speaking we often use plural ones.

Circle the correct pronoun for the following sentences.

1. Everyone took (his/their) water guns to the Spring Fling, which is held on the ball fields at the end of the school year.

2. If anybody wants to go to the water park this weekend, (she/they) should give (her/their) number to Abby so she can get (her/them) a discounted rate.

Everyone and *anybody* are singular!

Answers

1. his
2. she, her, her

When you are speaking casually, you often use the plural form of the above pronouns, because in your mind you know that you are talking about a group of people. The ACT test assesses how well you know formal English. **Memorize your "Each is one body" pronouns!**

Other Issues You Might Encounter

The following sample questions and explanations review other areas of pronoun agreement that could appear on the ACT test.

Sample Question: Agreement "in Person"

When the juniors come to class, we know that not all of <u>you will have you're</u> homework done.

    F. NO CHANGE
    G. you will have your
    H. them will have their
    J. you, will have your

Explanation: Do you remember these: first person (*I*), second person (*you*), and third person (*he, she, they, it*)? The above question tests person without using the "Each is one body" trap. When considering the answer options, look first at the options that rephrase the underlined portion. Only one answer response deals with punctuation, and because placing a comma after *you* interrupts the flow of the sentence, ignore answer J. Answer G doesn't make sense because *you're* really means *you are*, and when you say *you will have you are* out loud, it sounds absurd. Be aware of consistent "person." This sentence should stay in the third person. Replace the underlined portion with *them will have their* and read the sentence again. Answer: (H).

Sample Question: Unclear Reference

When Jeremy and Justin went to the rodeo in Kansas, they met the rodeo clowns and <u>they</u> showed them how to rope.

    A. NO CHANGE
    B. they,
    C. , they
    D. Jeremy

Explanation: Read through the sentence. Tune into the ambiguity surrounding who taught whom to rope. *They* in the underlined portion could really refer to either *the rodeo clowns* or *Jeremy and Justin*. Don't even bother looking at the punctuation answers; replace *they* with *Jeremy* (answer D) and see if it sounds correct. It does—Jeremy taught them (the clowns) how to rope. Answer: (D).

One More Pronoun Issue

Reflexive pronouns like *myself, herself, themselves* and *ourselves* may challenge you because they are often used incorrectly in everyday speech. Reflexive pronouns reflect back on the subject of the sentence; they are not used as the subject of the sentence. Some people like to use reflexive pronouns to sound more proper, when in reality they are often incorrect.

Incorrect: *Tammy and <u>myself</u> spent the day at the go-cart track.*

Correct: *Tammy and <u>I</u> spent the day at the go-cart track.*

Reflexive pronouns match the subject:

Correct: *Freida and Freddy sent <u>themselves</u> postcards while on their trip to Dubai.*

Correct: *Flo sent <u>herself</u> flowers after she broke up with Forrest.*

Correct: *We sent candy to <u>ourselves</u> before we even knew we won the contest.*

SYNTAX AND STYLE
Sentences, Fragments, and Run-Ons: Part or Whole?

Get back to the basics. Knowing whether or not a sentence is truly a sentence is essential on the ACT English section. Figure out whether the sentence has a subject and a predicate, which includes at least a verb and often a verb and an object. If it doesn't, it is a fragment. If the sentence sounds long and includes too many independent clauses joined by improper punctuation, it is a run-on. Your knowledge of punctuation is key to identifying a grammatical sentence, so review the chapter on punctuation.

<u>Our school joined with a neighboring school and developed</u> a girls' lacrosse
₁
team. After two years as a team, they made it to the state playoffs <u>and the</u>
₂
<u>team worked hard and placed second in the state this year.</u> <u>Being incredibly</u>
₂ ₃
<u>proud. The</u> athletic director threw the team a party the weekend after they
Line ₃
(5) played. Next year, the team is looking to win the state championship and
maintain a standard of excellence for years <u>to come, each</u> school will likely
₄
develop separate teams in the future.

1. **A.** NO CHANGE
   B. Our school, joined with a neighboring school and developed
   C. Our school joined with a neighboring school, and developed
   D. Our school joined with a neighboring school; developing

2. **F.** NO CHANGE
   G. ; the team worked hard and placed second in the state this year.
   H. . And the team worked hard, and placed second in the state this year.
   J. : and the team worked hard and placed second in the state this year.

3. **A.** NO CHANGE
   B. Being incredibly proud—the
   C. Being incredibly proud, the
   D. Being incredibly proud the

4. **F.** NO CHANGE
   G. to come: each
   H. to come. Each
   J. to come and each

Answers and Explanations:

> **NOTE**
>
> The answers and explanations for these questions will review many of the anti-punctuation rules from Chapter 2. We cannot emphasize enough how much knowing the anti-punctuation rules will help you with these kinds of questions!

1. **(A)** The sentence has a subject and a verb. Because *and* connects the independent clause, *our school joined with a neighboring school,* with the dependent clause, *developed a girls' lacrosse team,* no comma is necessary.

   Independent (FANBOYS) Dependent = No Comma

2. **(G)** The word *and,* one of the FANBOYS words, connects two independent clauses. Remember that independent clauses tend to butt heads too much; the *and* just isn't enough to keep them comfortable.

   Independent, (FANBOYS) Independent

   TIP

   Do not join two independent clauses together with a comma. That's a comma splice—a big no-no!

   Because inserting a comma isn't one of the options, a semicolon without a FANBOYS word works just as well.

   Independent; Independent

3. **(C)** *Being incredibly proud* can't stand alone as a sentence; it exists to describe something else. In this instance, it describes *the athletic director* in the subsequent independent clause. *Being incredibly proud* needs to be connected to the independent clause with a comma and set in front of *the athletic director* so it can describe him specifically.

   Nonessential Introduction = Comma

4. **(H)** The error in this sentence is called a comma splice: two independent clauses "spliced" together using a comma. Avoid comma splices at all times. When separating two independent clauses, or groups of words that can work independently as sentences, you have two options besides using a FANBOYS word. Use either a semicolon or an old standby that you may have forgotten about because of its simplicity: a period plus a capital letter.

Modifier Agreement

Incorrect: *The tennis player asked the swimmer to help change her tire in a short skirt.*

Who has the short skirt, the tennis player or the swimmer? Did the tennis player ask the swimmer to wear a short skirt when changing her tire? This sentence could indicate some strange form of sexual harassment, or it could just mean that the clause describing the tennis player is in the wrong location.

Correct: *The tennis player in a short skirt asked the swimmer to help change her tire.*

The phrase that describes the noun or verb must be located immediately next to the noun or verb that it is describing; otherwise, confusion ensues.

Incorrect: *The group of freshmen boys admired the cluster of senior girls with grins on their faces.*

Who is grinning, the freshmen boys or the senior girls? In this instance, it is likely that the boys have larger grins than the girls do.

Correct: *With grins on their faces, the group of freshmen boys admired the cluster of senior girls.*

Sample Question

The flowering trees and the yellow bushes that bloom in early spring smell like rotten meat and sour milk in the front of the school and next to the school sign cause many students to park in the back of the building in order to save their noses a little torture.

    F. NO CHANGE
    G. Many students park in the back of the building in order to save their noses a little torture because of the flowering trees that smell like rotten meat and the yellow bushes that smell like sour milk, bloom in early spring in front of the school and next to the school sign.
    H. The flowering trees smell like rotten meat and the yellow bushes smell like sour milk, bloom in early spring in front of the school and next to the school sign cause many students to park in the back of the building in order to save their noses a little torture.
    J. Blooming in early spring, the flowering trees in front of the school, which smell like rotten meat, and the yellow bushes next to the school sign, which smell like sour milk, cause many students to park in the back of the building in order to save their noses a little torture.

TIP

Rereading a sentence to figure out what it is saying is a clear tipoff that something's wrong.

Explanation: First of all, what a sentence! Ask yourself, "Does it sound correct?" No. It sounds strange and choppy. A long underlined portion of text almost always sounds strange, though, so hearing the sentence will only take you so far. Fortunately, you have another clue: Each option shows a rewrite of the sentence with a different arrangement of phrases, so find the one that makes the most sense. Do the trees smell like rotten meat or sour milk? Are the trees and bushes in front of the school or next to the school sign?

This type of question will take you longer to answer than some, so consider leaving it until you've done the less time-consuming ones. The sentence that reads most smoothly and that has all of its modifiers in the correct place is answer J. Answer: (J).

TIP

Remember the modifier rule: The modifying phrase should be located next to the noun or verb that it modifies.

Parallel Structure: Achieving the Perfect Balance

Incorrect: *Miss Sharp sang, danced, and was cooing as she entered the room for our first-period class.*

Incorrect use of parallel structure is common in writing. No doubt your teachers have made comments on your papers about this issue. If you want to ace the ACT, know how to identify unparallel phrases and fix them.

The word *parallel* refers to two or more items in a sentence that have similar "roles." In the above example, note the list of actions. All three have similar roles: they describe an action of the apparently eccentric Miss Sharp. Words in a list, because they have parallel roles, must be *parallel* grammatically—that is, they must match in structure. Lists offer great potential for faulty parallelism, so naturally the ACT loves to use them. Fixing parallel structure requires that you use a skill you learned from Sesame Street years ago. Do you remember the song, "One of these things is not like the other?" When the ACT gives you a list, find the mismatched item and make it match the others.

Correct: *Miss Sharp sang, danced, and cooed as she entered the room for our first-period class.*

Practice Sentences

In the following sentences, underline the problem with parallel structure and then correct it in the space above the sentence.

1. Gerome likes to hike, to bike, and running.
2. Mr. Spare's AP students were asked to write their essays accurately, thoughtfully, and in a detailed manner.
3. The IB student received a D for the semester because he turned in assignments late, waited until the night before to complete the project, and was sleeping during the semester final.
4. Matt's parents told him to clean the kitchen, clean his room, and give the cat a haircut.

5. In honor of the first day of school, Jessi wore her new jeans, borrowed a shirt from her friend, and her sister's shoes.
6. Vishnu's semester exam was rigorous, painful, and 150 questions.

Answers and Explanations

1. *Gerome likes to hike, to bike, and <u>to run</u>.* You can also say *Gerome likes to hike, bike, and run.* Each verb needs to begin and end in the same way. Change *running* into *to run*.

2. *Mr. Spare's AP students were asked to write their essays accurately, thoughtfully, and <u>thoroughly</u>.* The phrase "in a detailed manner" doesn't match the other two words, which are adverbs (words that end in –*ly*). If a list contains mostly adverbs, then every phrase or word in the list should also contain adverbs. Change "in a detailed manner" to *thoroughly*.

3. *The IB student received a D for the semester because he turned in assignments late, waited until the night before to complete the project, and then <u>slept</u> during the semester final.* *Sleeping* ends in *-ing* while *turned* and *waited* both end in *-ed*. Mismatched endings are a big clue when checking parallel structure. Think back to your Sesame Street childhood: "One of these things is not like the other." Find the mismatched item and fix it.

4. *Matt's parents told him to clean the kitchen, clean his room, and <u>groom the cat.</u>* This sentence may sound OK in its original form, but if you pay careful attention, each of the phrases begins with a verb and ends with a noun, and each phrase is three words long. The phrase "give the cat a haircut" seems awkward. "Groom the cat" matches nicely: verb + *the* + noun.

5. *In honor of the first day of school, Jessi wore her new jeans, <u>her friend's shirt</u>, and her sister's shoes.* Two of the phrases begin with *her* + whatever it was that Jessi wore. All of the phrases should match.

6. *Vishnu's semester exam was rigorous, painful, and <u>lengthy</u>.* Again, words in a list need to match. Each word in the list should be an adjective. Change *150 questions* to *lengthy*.

EIGHT CONCEPTS FOR KEEPING SENTENCES SOUND

Let's review what you'll need to know inside and out in order to ace all questions on sentence structure:

1. Listen to the "sound" of the sentence. If a sentence doesn't sound right, there is probably something wrong with it.
2. Read as an editor would read. Intuition is your first line of defense, except when you change the words instinctually because your brain "hears" a sentence or phrase correctly. Read the words as they appear on the page.
3. Know how to simplify a sentence to determine the subject and the verb. Be wary of distracting BTWs, or "by the way," phrases. They can keep you from

identifying the main subject and verb. Simplify the sentence to make sure that a simple subject-verb agreement issue doesn't elude you.

4. Remember the Singles Club: "each is one body." The ACT loves to test your knowledge of the pronoun *each* and pronouns that end with *-one* and *-body*. These pronouns are singular.

5. "Amount" pronouns like *none, fraction,* and *percent* when married to the word *of* do not determine the subject-verb agreement. In these exceptional cases, the noun at the end of the "of" phrase dictates whether or not the verb is singular or plural.

6. Punctuation! Know how to identify independent and dependent clauses, and know the anti-punctuation rules from Chapter 2.

7. Identify misplaced modifiers. It must be clear which noun a pronoun modifies and which phrase modifies which noun or verb.

8. To identify nonparallel structure, ask, "Which of these things is not like the other?" The use of a list is the biggest clue that you are being tested on this skill.

World of Words

- Word choice
- Colloquialisms and slang
- Misused verbs and other words

- Adjectives and adverbs
- Incorrect conjunctions

People misuse words all the time. Consider these examples, made by teachers themselves:

- "It's getting cold, so I think I'll go to my room and achieve some pants." (high school history teacher)

- "This idea is true in and out of itself." (MIT linguistics professor)

- "For every useful Web site in cyberspace, there's 100 useless ones." (the author of this section)

Did you spot all three errors? Surprisingly, spell check caught only one. *Achieve* should be *retrieve*, *in and out of* should be *in and of*, and *there's* should be *there are*.

SPOTTING WORD-CHOICE MISTAKES

See if you can identify these other common word choice mistakes.

1. Bob and myself are thinking about founding an Internet company.
   Incorrect word: _____

2. Sadie is the biggest of my two golden retrievers.
   Incorrect word: _____

3. My car is old, but it looks like its engine might of been replaced.
   Incorrect word: _____

4. Stan is the person that left his keys at the front desk.
   Incorrect word: _____

5. I was worried over the idea that I had acne.
   Incorrect word: _____

You should have found the following *incorrect* uses: 1. *myself,* 2. *biggest,* 3. *of,* 4. *that,* 5. *over.* If you missed a couple, don't feel bad; word use errors are rampant in English. If you're shooting for the perfect score, solidify your knowledge of the most subtle errors in usage and diction.

It's easy for a high-achieving student to dismiss word choice when studying for the ACT. If you're aiming for the thirties in English, you already know to replace items on the test that sound too casual, and you know that slang *is out.* But you might not be as aware of a group of colloquialisms and word use errors so common that they often feel, look, or sound correct. Remember Sadie the golden retriever from example two above? Put her next to an elephant, and she's the *smaller* of the two. Put her next to two or more elephants, and she's the *smallest* animal in the group. Even so, people use *smallest* all the time when referring to a pair, though formal English dictates the use of *smaller.*

Here's another example, which was covered in detail in Chapter 3: *Everyone get out their notebook.* Instinctively, you know *everyone* refers to a group of people, so you might be tempted to use the plural pronoun *their.* Besides, it's what you're used to saying in casual conversation, isn't it? You'd never arrive at a study group session and say, "Everyone get out *his or her* notebook and we'll study the invertebrates." Formal English dictates that you use a singular pronoun with words that end in *-one* such as *someone, anyone, everyone,* and *no one.* (See page 29, "Looks Plural, Acts Singular.") If you want an exceptional English score, be aware of rules such as this one.

TIP

Don't use the plural pronoun *their* to refer to the singular noun "everyone."

HOW TO THINK ABOUT WORD-CHOICE QUESTIONS

First and foremost, remember that the English section tests your knowledge of formal, written English. This means you can't always trust your instincts when choosing the right word, and you can't assume you'll catch every mistake without effort. Read the words precisely as they are on the page, not the way your mind unconsciously interprets them.

TIP

The ACT wants you to simplify word choice more often than it wants you to formalize language. Be economical and clear, not fancy!

Conversely, having strong word choice skills is not just a matter of running through the passage correcting slang. Often you'll find formal, clunky language in need of clarification. Consider one of the examples above: *Bob and myself are thinking of founding an Internet company.* Chances are you've heard this incorrect use of *myself* a thousand times. For some reason, people think they sound more intelligent when they overuse reflexive pronouns, which are pronouns that "reflect" back on the subject, as in "I did it by myself." Spoken English breaks rules constantly. There's no obvious reason why incorrect uses develop, and often they complicate things. *Bob and I* is easier to say than *Bob and myself,* and, it's correct!

To reign over the World of Words, you'll need to be able to do the following:

1. Identify incorrect colloquial, idiomatic, and slang expressions and replace them with more formal language.

2. Know a small list of misused homonyms—*except* versus *accept,* for example.

3. Understand when to use an adjective and when to use an adverb.

4. Develop good instincts when it comes to keeping verb tense consistent and pronoun use proper (covered in Chapter 3).

5. Know the difference between comparatives and superlatives.

6. Identify and clarify wordy, imprecise, or redundant language.

COLLOQUIALISMS AND SLANG

Have you ever called anyone *laid back*? Have you ever read a *make-believe* story or seen a *sappy* movie? All three of these phrases qualify as colloquial, but you'd likely read past all three without thinking of them as too casual.

INSIDE THE ACT 36 MIND

Identifying colloquialisms and determining their appropriateness requires you to sense tone in a passage. The ACT chooses either formal, academic passages or informal, friendly passages. If the passage is formal, avoid all colloquial expressions. If the passage has an informal feel, colloquial language might be appropriate.

Here's an example of the difference:

1. Formal: As stated, the student's belligerent behavior resulted in serious harm to the desk, to wit: a broken and mangled left desk leg, lacerations to the desktop, and four conglomerations of chewing gum beneath the afore-mentioned desktop. Witnesses, including but not limited to one student and one classroom teacher, corroborated that the student had in fact caused the damage. In short, the desk was destroyed.

2. Informal: I went into class and, feeling angry, began to mess with my desk. After I'd worked the leg back and forth until it popped off, I broke it into a few pieces. Then having dismantled the leg completely, I wrote angry phrases on the desktop and stuck some gum underneath. Bobby turned to me and said, "Man, that desk is all jacked up." I felt much better until I realized Mr. Loupe was standing right behind me.

> **REMEMBER**
>
> Knowing the difference between clear, precise writing and overly "fancy" writing will serve you well on the ACT.

Here are the major hints that passage two is informal:

1. first-person *I*

2. colloquial verbs such as *mess*

3. contractions

4. dialog

Be sure you can recognize the difference between informal and formal writing on the English section so that you can spot incorrect usage accordingly. Remember three rules:

1. The ACT prefers clear writing to formal writing.

2. Informality does not excuse imprecision.

3. If the tone is formal, colloquialisms are never correct.

MISUSED VERBS: SUBSTITUTE ANOTHER WORD

If you see an underlined verb but don't notice a tense issue, you have a word choice question. What follows is a helpful strategy in such a situation:

1. Pretend to "white out" the underlined word.

2. Read the sentence again, substituting a word that makes sense.

3. Check the answer choices for a word that matches the word you substituted.

Consider the following example:

Around a child's first birthday, his awareness of his surroundings suddenly <u>heightens</u>.
  A. NO CHANGE
  B. improves
  C. raises
  D. rises

If you "white out" the underlined portion, you get the following:

Around a child's first birthday, his awareness of his surroundings suddenly _____.

Reading back over the sentence and attempting to fill in the blank, you probably realize that the sentence calls for a verb that means "gets better":

Around a child's first birthday, his awareness of his surroundings suddenly <u>gets better</u>.

Consider the answer choices. *Heightens* (A) can mean either "intensifies" or "increases in height." *Raise* and *rise* (C and D) have similar meanings; they also mean "intensify," "increase," or "move upward." *Improves* (B) is the only word that fits the definition "gets better" and is therefore correct. Answer (B).

The substitution method is an invaluable tool for word choice questions. If you sense even slight imprecision, you probably need to make a change.

PREPOSITIONAL IDIOMS

Idioms are words that make sense only through common use. Some idioms are easy to identify because they have become common figurative expressions: *nailing Jell-O to a wall* or *a couple sandwiches short of a picnic.* Other idioms are embedded in our language so deeply that we use them without considering their illogical nature. When was the last time you thought about hands when you said *on the other hand* . . . ? Idioms sound correct to us only because most of us have used them all our lives.

The ACT tests you on the most subtle of idioms: those that employ prepositions. Consider the following phrases, all of which use the word *look*:

Do you . . .

. . . look *up* a word or look *in* a word?

. . . look *out* for traffic or look *on* for traffic?

. . . look *over* a document or look *inside* a document?

. . . look *to* grandma for advice or look *at* grandma for advice?

. . . look *into* an issue or look *inside* an issue?

TIP

Read carefully so that you don't miss an incorrect preposition in an idiom.

You're able to identify the correct ones, but you don't know why. You just *know*, for the same reason you know that a new trend is *in*, Bob is a little *off*, and something's wrong *with* that guy. Be careful: your unconscious use of prepositional idioms can work against you. The ACT tries on occasion to add an incorrect idiom surreptitiously. When you encounter a prepositional idiom question, slow down. As we've mentioned before, think like an editor to ace this section.

Sample Questions

When I met Joan, she was so <u>onto</u> dance that she wore a tutu to school. Now, she
₁

thinks <u>off</u> dancing as little more than something to do on a Saturday night.
₂

1. A. NO CHANGE
   B. in
   C. into
   D. in for

2. F. NO CHANGE
   G. in
   H. on
   J. of

Answers

1. **(C)**   2. **(J)**

You don't need explanations for these. In fact, there are no logical explanations for why these uses are correct; they just *are*.

"Lucky 13" Misused Words

Luckily for you, the ACT plays favorites when it comes to commonly misused words. This section gives you the ACT's favorites and explains them. If you want to explore misused words further, there is a short list at the end of the section. Web sites offer even more. Because of the remote chance that you'll see a misused word that isn't on this lucky list of 13, you might want to develop a personal misused word list using the Internet.

No matter what you do, memorize this "Lucky 13" list:

TIP

Memorize these commonly missed words—and create your own list.

1. *accept / except*

Accept is the verb.

Except means "apart from" and indicates a contrast. It often appears in its noun form, *exception*. *Accept* is a verb that usually means "recognize" or "take on."

Examples:

- "I recently *accepted* a Fulbright Scholarship to study in Munich."
- "*Except* for Harleys, I hate motorcycles."

Remember: There is no such word as *acception*!

2. *effect / affect*

As far as the ACT is concerned, *effect* is never a verb.

Affect is a verb that means "to influence." Although *effect* can be a verb, assume for the purposes of the ACT that it will always be a noun synonymous with *result*.

Examples:

- The results of the homecoming vote *affected* the freshman class enormously.
- I don't really trust that Rogaine will have the desired *effect*, so I'm going for the comb-over.

Remember: *Effect* can be a verb meaning "to bring about," as in, "Through a petition, he was able to *effect* change." File this exception away; its appearance on the test is highly unlikely.

3. *fewer / less*

Fewer refers to a number, to something you can actually count. *Less* refers to an amount of something.

Thinking about cooking helps with this distinction. You have *fewer* cherries but *less* flour. You have *fewer* tomatoes but *less* tomato sauce. Counting cherries and tomatoes is possible, while counting flour and tomato sauce is a little tricky. As another guideline, *fewer* modifies plural words, while *less* modifies singular words.

Examples:

- I liked the presidential candidate a little *less* after he said he would solve global warming and joblessness by hiring people to build windmills.
- *Fewer* people voted in 2000 than did in 2008.

4. **then / than**

Then refers to time; *than* indicates a comparison.

Then indicates one of two things: either something is coming next or something has occurred in the past. *Than* always appears when comparing two ideas or items.

Examples:

- I did crunches, and *then* I blasted my pecs.
- It was *then* that I discovered my talent for losing things.
- It's better to have loved and lost *than* never to have loved at all.
- Horses are generally bigger and more aggressive *than* ponies, but ponies are cuter.

Remember: If you pronounce these two words and accentuate the vowels, *than* sounds like "and" (comparison) and *then* sounds like "when" (time).

5. **to / too / two**

To is a preposition, *too* means "also," and *two* is the spelled-out version of *2*.

You probably know these distinctions already; they are on the list to remind you not to rush and become trapped by an easy concept.

Examples:

- Charlie failed the first *two* chemistry tests of the semester, at which point he decided to major in English.
- Going *to* the beach is Lance's favorite pastime.
- Kelly likes the beach, *too*.

Remember: You are probably such a good reader that you'll fix these issues unconsciously. It's possible to be trapped by mistakes that appear too easy to study.

6. **it's / its**

It's means "it is." *Its* is possessive.

This is an easy mistake to make because your eye is trained to read apostrophes as possessive. *Its* is an exception.

Examples:

- After battling *its* rival, the lion licked *its* wounds.
- *It's* unrealistic to think things will turn out well every time you do something, but assume you'll succeed.

Remember: A few other pronouns forego the apostrophe when they're possessive. Thinking about *his, hers, theirs,* and *ours* may also help you remember the rule about *its*.

7. **farther / further**

   Farther indicates physical distance, while *further* indicates level or degree.

   This error is rampant, which makes it an ideal ACT trap.

   Examples:

   - Littleton, Colorado, is *farther* from Beijing than it is from Tokyo.
   - When it comes to manipulating perspective, Picasso goes *further* than Cézanne.

   Remember: *Farther* contains the word *far*, which will help you identify its relationship with *distance*. Further contains the word *fur*—wearing fur increases your body heat by many *degrees*.

8. **could / would / should / might have** versus **could of / would of / should of / might of**

   Of is never correct following one of these words.

   Many people say "might of" instead of "might have." Because the two phrases sound so similar, do not trust your ear on this one. Read carefully.

   Examples:

   - Incorrect: I *might of* taken the EMT class, but I didn't have enough time in the evenings.
   - Correct: I *might have* taken the EMT class, but I didn't have enough time in the evenings.

   Remember: Like the rule of "to, too, and two," this one is easy to gloss over. The "might of" trap is a great example of how trusting your ear can deceive you on a word choice question.

9. **their / they're / there**

   Their indicates possession. *They're* is a contraction of *they are*. *There* refers to location, as in "over there."

   Examples:

   - *Their* SUV now costs $180 to fill up.
   - *They're* considering buying a Prius.
   - The Prius dealership is over *there* by Starbuck's, where they buy *their* $4 lattes.

   Remember: *There's* and *theirs* are slight variations on this goof. *Theirs* is possessive. *There's* is short for "there is." Also, don't forget *your* and *you're*. *Your* is possessive while *you're* means "you are."

10. *that / which*

That is restrictive and *which* is used as part of a nonrestrictive or "by the way" phrase (BTW). *Restrictive* clauses "restrict" the meaning or identity of a word. A nonrestrictive clause tells you something about the subject but doesn't limit its meaning. Clauses using *which* are "by the way" and need a comma hug!

- The waterfall *that* empties into Phelps Lake starts above the tree line.
- The waterfall, *which* empties into Phelps Lake, starts above the tree line.

In the first sentence, the restrictive clause *empties into Phelps Lake* defines the waterfall, so *that* is the appropriate choice. In the second sentence, the meaning has changed. *Empties into Phelps Lake*, no longer "restricts" the waterfall; it adds information but doesn't define. In other words, it becomes a BTW or nonrestrictive phrase and *which* is the appropriate choice.

Remember: Punctuation will be the key to determining whether or not a phrase is restrictive. See the section on BTW phrases in the punctuation chapter.

11. *that / which* **versus** *who*

Forget about restrictive and nonrestrictive clauses here. When the subject is human, *that* or *which* is never correct; substitute *who* for either *that* or *which*.

- Incorrect: The security guard *that* works at Target is actually Marilyn Monroe's cousin.
- Correct: The security guard *who* works at Target is actually Marilyn Monroe's cousin.
- Incorrect: The pet store owner, *which* loves Milky Ways, was waiting on a shipment of toucans.
- Correct: The pet store owner, *who* loves Milky Ways, was waiting on a shipment of toucans.

12. *who / whom*

In order to understand the difference between these two pronouns, you need to know the difference between a subject and an object of a sentence. Here's the quick version: subjects do the action, objects are the recipient of the action. Substitute *who* for a subject and *whom* for an object.

- Incorrect: *Whom* is the favorite to win Wimbledon?
- Correct: *Who* is the favorite to win Wimbledon?

Who and *whom* often appear in interrogative sentences, which works to your advantage. Answer the question, and you'll often learn whether you're dealing with a subject or an object. The answer to the above example might be, "Roger Federer is the favorite to win Wimbledon." "Roger Federer" is the subject of the sentence, so he's also the subject of the interrogative or "question" version

If you're confused about when to use *who* and *whom*, remember that who refers to a subject and whom refers to an object.

of the sentence. Whether it's a question or an answer, it still has the same subject.

- Incorrect: *Who* do you want to win Wimbledon?
- Correct: *Whom* do you want to win Wimbledon?

This example is a little counterintuitive, because in everyday speech we misuse this rule. Turn the phrase around, though: "I want Raphael Nadal to win Wimbledon." If you want Nadal to win, he is the object of the sentence. Substitute the pronoun *whom*.

An even quicker way to test *who* and *whom* is to again make the question into a statement and then substitute either *he* or *him*. *Him* has the same ending as *whom*, and both words refer to objects. *He* and *who* refer to subjects.

- Question: Who is the favorite to win Wimbledon? Answer: He is. Use *who*.
- Question: Whom do you want to win Wimbledon? Answer: I want him. Use *whom*.

Remember: If *who* or *whom* is used in a declarative statement, the same rule applies. Substituting *he* or *him* becomes easier in this case, because you don't have to turn the phrase into a question.

- The painter *who* did the mural downtown is up for a major award.

You'd say, ". . . he did the mural downtown . . . ," so *who* is correct.

- The painter, *whom* we contacted to do the mural downtown, is up for a major award.

You'd say, ". . . we contacted him . . . ," so *whom* is correct.

13. *I / me*

Linking verbs don't act on objects. Instead, they connect two words, a noun with another noun, as in, "Larry is an avid reader." When deciding whether to use *I* or *me* with a linking verb (*am, is, are, was, were, be, been*), restructure the sentence to determine the correct use of the pronoun.

Example: "This is he." (Someone answering a phone)

- You ask: Who answered the phone? Answer: He answered the phone. You wouldn't say, "Him answered the phone." *He* is the correct pronoun. Note: Forget about how you *actually* answer the phone and think *formal English*.

Example: The guy who dressed up like Shrek and scared the kids was *he*!

- You ask: Who dressed up like Shrek? Answer: He dressed up like Shrek. You wouldn't, say, "Him dressed up like Shrek." *He* is the correct pronoun.

Example: My brother is as unhappy as *I*. (implied verb)

- You might be tempted to say, "*My* brother is as unhappy as me." In the example sentence, an implied *am* could be added to the end of the sentence but isn't: *My brother is as unhappy as I (am). I* is the correct pronoun even if *am* is implied. Two words that often precede an implied clause are *as* and *than.*

Another example: Tim is happier than he.

- Again a verb is implied. You wouldn't say "Tim is happier than him is." You would say: "Tim is happier than he is." *He* is the correct pronoun.
- Another way to test this sentence is to reverse the order. You would say *He is happier than Tim,* not *Him is happier than Tim.*

Remember: When the comparison words *as* and *than* are used, the pronouns become reversible. The same pronoun form that works at the beginning of the sentence works at the end. It might help to think of the verb "to be" as an "eqauls" sign. You can often "flip" sentences like these the way you "flip" an equation.

Other Word Choice Goofs That Didn't Make the Lucky 13 List

Although it's not as likely, the following items may appear on the test. The ACT will avoid some of them, because they involve spelling, but understanding the distinction between these word pairs is always helpful.

your/you're (mentioned briefly above)	die/dye	imply/infer
lie/lay	feat/feet	counselor/councilor
many/much	idle/idol	discreet/discrete
can/may	incite/insight	capital/capitol
set/sit	passed/past	climatic/climactic
there's/there are	peace/piece	principle/principal
between/among	plain/plane	illusion/allusion
beside/besides	right/rite/write	compliment/complement
board/bored	stationary/stationery	precede/proceed
brake/break	way/weigh	hanged/hung
clothes/close	which/witch	elicit/illicit
	wood/would	

Here are some commonly misused phrases you might see. You'll be a step closer to achieving the perfect score if you memorize them.

supposed to (*not* suppose to)

used to (*not* use to)

toward (*not* towards)

no one (*not* noone)

anyway (*not* anyways)

couldn't care less (*not* could care less)

intents and purposes (*not* intensive purposes)

going to (*not* gonna)

supposedly (*not* supposably)

ADJECTIVES AND ADVERBS

You know the following distinction already: adjectives modify nouns; adverbs modify verbs, adjectives, and other adverbs. You can usually spot an adverb because it contains the suffix *-ly*.

The ACT may try to tempt you into "formalizing" the sentence with an adverb. Don't be fooled.

Sample Question

As <u>gently</u> as my dog is, she would still protect my family in an emergency.
  - **A.** NO CHANGE
  - **B.** gentle and tender
  - **C.** gently and tenderly
  - **D.** gentle

Answer: (D).

A linking verb "links" a noun with an adjective. It defines them as equal, or at least as a pair. Linking verbs are often versions of "to be": *am, is, are, was, were, be, being,* and *been.* The following sentences are short to help you see the common use of noun + linking verb + adjective.

- She is gentle.

- They are perfect.

- We seem happy.

The third word in each sentence modifies the pronoun (the first word) in the sentence. When an active verb is added, the adjectives change to adverbs.

- She is smiling gently.

- They are playing perfectly.

- We seem to be singing happily.

Identify and fix the adverb problems in the following sentences.

  1. The man's vision returned gradually, until finally he could see clear enough to make out the horizon.

  2. Even though late-night television commercials often tell you it's easy, in reality it's difficult to get rich quick.

Answers:
  1. *Clear* should be changed to *clearly. Clearly* describes how the man could see. *See* is a verb, so only an adverb can modify it.
  2. *Quick* should be changed to *quickly. Get* is a verb that needs an adverb to modify it. Incidentally, even though you might be tempted to change *easy* to *easily,* don't be fooled. *It's,* a contraction of "it is," contains the linking verb "to be." The adjective *easy* is the correct choice.

Remember: *Good* is an adjective and *well* is an adverb, unless you're talking about someone's physical or emotional state.

- Tiger Woods is so *good* at golf. (*Good* modifies Tiger.)

- Tiger Woods played *well* in his last tournament. (*Well* modifies how Tiger plays.)

- Tiger Woods is not *well,* so he won't play in the Open Championship. (*Well* refers to Tiger's physical state.)

COMPARATIVES AND SUPERLATIVES

Use comparatives (*bigger, faster, hotter, funnier*) when comparing *two things.* Use comparatives with *than,* as in, "Elephants are bigger than monkeys."
   Use superlatives (*biggest, fastest, hottest, funniest*) when comparing *more than two things.*

Incorrect: Of the two 100-meter runners on the track team, Tim has the *fastest* time.

Correct: Of the two 100-meter runners on the track team, Tim has the *faster* time.

Incorrect: Ryan is the *stronger* of the three discus throwers.

Correct: Ryan is the *strongest* of the three discus throwers.

INCORRECT CONJUNCTIONS: CONTINUATION OR CONTRAST?

The ACT may try to trick you by hiding an incorrect conjunction within the body of a sentence. If you exhaust the strategies from Chapter 3 and your sentence still doesn't seem sound, look at transitional words or phrases. Possible transitions include the FANBOYS words plus the following: *because, when, that, who, whose, which, if, before, after, since, unless, therefore,* and *although.* If the second clause is a *continuation* of an idea, you'll need a word such as *and, since,* or *because.* If the second clause *contrasts* the original statement, expect *but, yet,* or *although.*

INSIDE THE ACT 36 MIND

The ACT loves to mix up transition words to catch people who are scanning the underlines for mistakes. In these kinds of questions, the sentence may look fine grammatically. Logically, though, it won't make sense.

Sample Questions

I had to get to work by 7:00, but the buses weren't running until 8:00. My grandmother told me that I could borrow her Buick, <u>and</u> I couldn't get it started. At
₁

6:45, I thought to call my co-worker Randy, <u>and luckily</u> he hadn't left his house
₂

yet and could come get me.

   1. A. NO CHANGE
      B. even though
      C. but
      D. but it wouldn't start and

   2. F. NO CHANGE
      G. which
      H. but
      J. and unfortunately

Answers

  1. **(C)**   2. **(F)**

IMPRECISE AND REDUNDANT PHRASING

Chapter 1 explained that the ACT favors concise, economical writing. Whenever you can omit words and achieve the same meaning, do so. Count on a few questions that test your ability to "cut the dead wood."

Redundant: I value *each and every* student's opinion.

Concise: I value *every* student's opinion.

Redundant: My mom has a maternal, nurturing, caring, protective, motherly way about her.

Concise: My mom cares, nurtures, and protects.

Redundant: After building a campfire, which quickly became hot and smoldering, we settled in and relaxed for the evening.

Concise: After building a smoldering campfire, we rested for the evening.

Assume you're facing a question about imprecision or redundancy when . . .

. . . you don't see anything grammatically wrong in or around the underlined section.

. . . you sense that there are too many words, phrases, or clauses in the underlined section.

. . . you see answer choices that reword the same idea.

. . . you see the word OMIT in the answer choices.

TIP

If you can remove words from a sentence without changing its meaning, do so.

Sample Questions

1. Because I had seen the band twelve times, I knew I was witnessing <u>a fantastic show</u>.
  A. NO CHANGE
  B. a show of tremendous magnitude.
  C. a show that was truly fantastic.
  D. a fantastic, great show.

2. When I saw the player do a 360-degree dunk, I <u>became aware</u> that I was on the wrong practice court.
  F. NO CHANGE
  G. realized
  H. gained consciousness of the fact that
  J. saw the truth

3. When my parents returned <u>and arrived</u> from their trip to the Bahamas, I greeted them at the airport.
  A. NO CHANGE
  B. and touched down
  C. and landed
  D. OMIT

Answers

1. **(A)**   2. **(G)**   3. **(D)**

EIGHT WAYS TO CHOOSE THE RIGHT WORDS

1. For the most part, the ACT tests your knowledge of formal, written English. Except in rare cases, and *especially* if you sense formality, avoid colloquialisms and slang.

2. Know the "Lucky 13" list by heart, and review the list of other common mistakes.

3. Slow down and think like an editor, especially when you see a preposition.

4. Substitute your own word when you sense an inaccuracy.

5. Keep it simple when it comes to adjectives and adverbs, and know the rules.

6. Use a comparative with two and a superlative with more than two.

7. Think, "Continuation or contrast?" when a transitional phrase is in question.

8. Remove redundant or imprecise language. Be economical without being unclear.

CHAPTER 5

Thinking Like a Writer

- Writing strategy and style questions
- Relevance questions
- Transitions
- Key concepts

When you revise a piece of writing, you consider numerous factors besides grammar and mechanics. You delete irrelevant information to make ideas concise, and you add additional information to make ideas clear. You adopt language that is more accurate, and you reorganize sections to make ideas flow more logically. The English section includes questions that test your ability to communicate effectively, clearly, and accurately—essentially, your ability to "think like a writer." These questions are more time-consuming and are therefore more difficult for some students. If you have a high score already, though, these questions are an opportunity to set yourself apart. Strategy and style questions account for 25 to 35 percent of the test, or about 20 to 25 questions.

Writing strategy and style questions may feel like reading questions. You'll often need to read an entire paragraph—even an entire passage—before you can answer them. The ACT will alert you to one of these questions by numbering either sentences or paragraphs. If you see bracketed numbers, pay attention to the main idea, purpose, tone, and style of the passage. Attempt all the other questions first, before attempting these. If you struggle with one of these questions, remember the golden rule of "Order" from Chapter 1. Never spend so much time on one of these questions that you miss an opportunity to answer a quick, easy one.

TIP

If you see numbered sentences or paragraphs, expect a style question.

IMPORTANT STRATEGIES

Look for question stems in the right-hand column

Other questions simply pose four possible answer choices; strategy and style questions contain specific prompts that precede the answer choices. Question stems that test your ability to think like a writer may sound similar to the following:

- To end this passage, the author wants to find a sentence that links the conclusions clearly to the introduction. Which of the following is the best choice?

- Which of the following sentences most effectively and clearly conveys the author's intended message?

- Given that all are true, which sentence best introduces the passage and clarifies the author's purpose?

- The author is considering deleting the preceding sentence from the paragraph. Should the author make this decision?

TIP

The question stem may give you a clue that you're dealing with a strategy and style question.

  F. Yes, because . . .

  G. Yes, because . . .

  H. No, because . . .

  J. No, because . . .

- In which order should the sentences in this paragraph appear?

  A. NO CHANGE

  B. 1, 3, 4, 2

  C. 2, 1, 4, 3

  D. 3, 2, 1, 4

- If the writer were to make this deletion, the essay would primarily lose:

  F. important information . . .

  G. logical flow . . .

  H. articulation of the main purpose . . .

  J. the appropriate tone . . .

Look for bracketed numbers within or between paragraphs

Bracketed numbers within or between paragraphs indicate organization or strategy questions. If you see them, know that you will be asked to rearrange, add, or delete information. Passages with bracketed numbers will look like the one that follows:

> [1] Eighty degrees with brilliant sunshine provided the perfect backdrop for our trip. [2] The water cooled and refreshed us and was still high enough so that we rarely became stuck on sandbars. [3] A great blue heron stood on
> *Line* the bank of the river. [4] We watched it for awhile until this grand, yet shy
> *(5)* bird flew away as we approached; it then landed behind us once we floated past its feeding area.

Consider the "big picture"

Determine the main idea, purpose, tone, and style of the passage.

- **Main idea**: What is the topic? What is the author trying to say about the topic? Answering these two questions helps you with strategy and style questions.

- **Purpose**: Determining the author's purpose helps you decide whether or not information is relevant and logical. Does the author want to entertain, inform, explain, or persuade?

- **Tone**: You may be asked to consider whether or not the tone of a specific passage matches the author's purpose. To determine tone, seek to understand the author's attitude toward the topic. Is it distant? Sarcastic? Ironic?

- **Style**: While reading the passage, take note of the author's style. Is it conversational? Formal? Direct? Academic? Sensing the style of the passage will help you assess specific stylistic issues.

QUESTION CATEGORIES

Writing strategy and style questions fit into one of the following categories. Please note: Practice questions and explanations follow the section on categories.

Relevance

Relevance questions test your ability to determine which sentences or phrases are relevant to the essay and which ones can be omitted. The purpose and tone of the passage guide you when answering relevance questions. Answer the relevance question after you have read the entire passage, as you may not completely understand the author's purpose until you have read the concluding sentence. Relevance questions also test your ability to determine whether a sentence adheres to or deviates from the focus of a paragraph.

Meaning

A question stem may ask you to assess the effect of changing, adding, or omitting a section based on the purpose or tone of the writing. If so, you will be asked to identify the effect of the change on a single sentence or the passage as a whole. These questions appear infrequently; you may only see one or two per test.

Clarity and Precision

Which phrase or sentence most clearly or precisely expresses an idea? This question type is covered in more depth in Chapter 3. There may be no question stem for questions that ask you to choose the most precise sentence or phrase or to match the tone of a sentence or phrase with the tone of the rest of the passage. In the case of a clarity or precision question, a section of the passage will be underlined and the answer options will offer alternative ways to say the same thing. You must choose the best response.

Organization and Relationships

If a passage has bracketed numbers prior to each paragraph, a question will appear that either asks you to place a sentence correctly within one of the paragraphs or to identify which order is best for the paragraphs within the essay. The ACT may also bracket a specific sentence, or it may ask you to reorder a group of sentences. Remember these guidelines about paragraph organization:

- The topic sentence gives a general overview of the content in the paragraph. Unless it's the topic sentence of an essay's introductory paragraph, it should flow seamlessly from the previous paragraph.

- The body of the paragraph gives details and examples that either support a claim or define a concept or idea. An example illustrates and reinforces an idea while a detail is a specific element of an idea.

- The concluding sentence of a paragraph should allow your mind to transition easily to the next paragraph and may evaluate or reflect on details or examples.

INSIDE THE ACT 36 MIND

Understanding basic paragraph structure is essential when approaching questions about organization. As a rule, the ACT chooses only paragraphs that are organized in a traditional way.

Passages will be organized traditionally as well. Again, remember the basics:

- An opening paragraph hooks the reader and introduces the topic of the essay. An introduction also introduces the central purpose of the essay, whether it be argumentation, description, narration, or explanation, and it will often contain a thesis or central claim.

- Body paragraphs offer details or examples to support the introductory paragraph and may build from ideas stated in previous body paragraphs. The ACT will often ask you to determine the proper placement of or order of details.

- A concluding paragraph should refer again to the central idea of the essay and reflect on it in a way that may depart somewhat from the way the idea was originally stated. Above all, a conclusion should feel like it "wraps up" the essay.

A Word About Transitions

Organizational questions also test your knowledge of transitions, both between sentences and between paragraphs. Transitions should enhance clarity and support the logical sequence of ideas. Pay careful attention to the following transitional phrases:

- **Transitions that signify cause/effect relationships**: *therefore, as a result, because, consequently, so, thus*

- **Transitions that signify contrast**: *however, although, but, despite, on the other hand, though, while, yet*

- **Transitions that lead to examples or convey emphasis, similarity, and continuation:** *for example, for instance, in addition, in fact, likewise, moreover, similarly*

When the ACT asks you to identify the most appropriate transition, think about the relationships of the ideas involved. Does a contrast exist between clauses, sentences, or paragraphs? If not, the word *however* is inappropriate. As practice, try writing sentences that include each of the above transitional phrases. You will notice that the transitional word or phrase always dictates the rest of the sentence.

PRACTICE THINKING LIKE A WRITER

Answer the questions associated with the following sample passages and then assess your understanding of writing strategy and style questions with the explanations that follow.

Sample Passage 1

[1]

[1] This past summer my mother and I spent an afternoon tubing down the Niobrara River with my cousin Sarah and my Aunt Karla. [2] My mother called the tubing outfitter the week before to make arrangements. [3] We prepared for the trip by purchasing river-worthy snacks: licorice, soda, water, trail mix, and chips. [4] We then asked my brother to meet us at the end to pick us up and deliver us back to our car. [1] [5] When we reached the launch area, we placed our cooler of snacks and drinks in the tube that holds the cooler and then attached the tubes together.

1. Adding ", which unbeknownst to us would be the most entertaining part of the trip" to the end of sentence 4 adds which of the following to the essay?
   A. whimsy
   B. sadness
   C. seriousness
   D. anticipation

[6] <u>Each large tube has a smaller tube in the</u>
  ₂
<u>center and is covered with a canvas tarp that</u>
  ₂
<u>kept us from sitting in the water.</u>
  ₂

[2]

[1] Eighty degrees with brilliant sunshine provided the perfect backdrop for our trip. [2] The water cooled and refreshed us and was still high enough so that we rarely became stuck on sandbars. [3] A great blue heron stood on the bank of the river. [4] We watched it awhile, until this grand yet shy bird flew away as we approached; it then landed behind us once we floated past its feeding area. [5] <u>My aunt's 60th</u>
  ₃
<u>birthday was the following weekend, and we</u>
  ₃
<u>chose to make this trip down the river our</u>
  ₃
<u>celebration with her.</u>
  ₃

[3]

[1] The trip was supposed to take four hours; however, it took five hours because we stopped at Smith Falls to enjoy the scenery and the spray from the waterfall. [2] The trip also took longer because we kept getting stuck in the slow-moving current, and we were too relaxed to get off our tubes to push the tubes into the stronger current. [3] <u>Family acquaintances</u>
  ₄
<u>own an elk ranch near where we got off the</u>
  ₄
<u>river. As we relaxed in the sun, we reminisced</u>
  ₄
about previous tubing trips, family stories, and other travels we had experienced recently.

2. The author is considering a different ending for this paragraph. Which of the following options matches the purpose of this paragraph?
   F. NO CHANGE
   G. OMIT the current sentence and leave sentence 5 as the final sentence of the paragraph.
   H. OMIT the sentence and replace it with the following sentence: "We jumped on the tubes, pushed off the edge of the river, and settled into a relaxing afternoon trip."
   J. Move sentence 6 so that it precedes sentence 5.

3. The author feels that this sentence does not fit with this paragraph and would like to place it in the first paragraph. Which of the following options is most appropriate?
   A. after the first sentence of paragraph 1
   B. after the second sentence of paragraph 1
   C. after the third sentence of paragraph 1
   D. after the fourth sentence of paragraph 1

4. While revising this essay, the author senses that something is wrong with the placement or use of this sentence. Which of the following options is best?
   F. NO CHANGE
   G. Move this sentence so that it precedes the first sentence in this paragraph
   H. OMIT this sentence; it doesn't match the other details in the paragraph that describe the trip down the river.
   J. OMIT the sentence and replace it with the following sentence: "We ran out of bug spray trying to keep the biting flies off of us."

[4]

[1] As we reached the end of our trip, we heard a motor revving loudly, as if a vehicle was stuck in the mud. My mother and I hoped that it wasn't my brother; otherwise, we wouldn't have a ride home. My brother was waiting for quite a while because it took us longer to get down the river than anticipated. He was parked in the middle of the road taking a nap. A group of young campers tried to go around his vehicle and didn't see the large washout created by the river next to the road. Their small pickup truck dove headlights first into the washout and became stuck. When we reached the unloading area, my brother was trying, unsuccessfully, to help them out of the large ditch. 5 We were unable to help them out of their predicament, but we drove to the site of a nearby outfitter and sent someone back to help them get their

truck out of the ditch. 6

5. The author would like to add a detail that best describes the humor of the situation without criticizing the driver's actions. Which of the following options most effectively meets this purpose?
   A. The sight of that small truck in the middle of that large ditch was quite humorous because of the massive size of the ditch and how ridiculous it was that the driver hadn't seen it.
   B. The truck was buried in the ditch.
   C. The image of that truck in the ditch was hysterical. I don't know how the driver hadn't seen the big hole in the ground.
   D. The truck sat precariously in the ditch as the driver climbed out of his window, looking like a shy turtle poking his head out of his shell.

6. The author is considering adding a sentence to this paragraph. Which of the following options wraps up the paragraph as well as the essay as a whole?
   F. NO CHANGE
   G. The memories of our tubing trip will probably blend in with the many other relaxing floats down the river and be forgotten, but the ending added a comedic twist that we will remember forever.
   H. The young campers eventually became unstuck and were able to continue with their relaxing weekend.
   J. We enjoyed our trip and hope to have another trip down the river next year.

Sample Passage 2

[1]

[7][1] Fort Niobrara National Wildlife Refuge is nestled along the river and hosts longhorn cattle and prairie bison along with white-tail and mule deer. [2] Smith Falls, the tallest waterfall in Nebraska, is located on the Niobrara River, and Smith Falls State Park provides camping opportunities throughout the spring, summer, and fall. [3] Also, bird lovers may have the opportunity to view over 200 species of birds that live in the river valley. [4] A man-made boardwalk runs from the river valley to the base of the falls, providing easy

access for visitors.[8]

[2]

Local tubing and canoeing outfitters are plentiful throughout the area. If you want to be more active, you can rent a canoe, kayak, or raft. If you want a leisurely day without a paddle in sight, tubing is the activity for you. During the middle of the summer, sandbars appear in the river where you can stop and

7. The author has been asked to write a section of a tourism brochure about the Niobrara River area near Valentine, Nebraska. Which of the following sentences creates the best introduction for the essay as a whole and the specific details included in this paragraph?
   A. NO CHANGE
   B. Valentine is the nearest town and provides many hotels and even some bed and breakfasts if you are seeking accommodations other than a tent.
   C. The Niobrara River valley near Valentine, Nebraska, offers a relaxing environment for water lovers and wildlife watchers.
   D. Besides floating down the river, the Niobrara River offers other opportunities for summer fun.

8. Which of the following sequences of sentences will make paragraph one most logical?
   F. NO CHANGE
   G. 1, 3, 2, 4
   H. 1, 4, 2, 3
   J. 1, 2, 4, 3

9. The author would like to revise this sentence so that it better reflects the content of the rest of the paragraph. Which of the following options best introduces the content of the paragraph?
   A. NO CHANGE
   B. Local tubing and canoeing outfitters can provide the proper equipment and accommodations for enjoying the river.
   C. Local tubing and canoeing outfitters can provide assistance getting on and off the river.
   D. Local tubing and canoeing outfitters can provide tubes and canoes for your river trip.

build a sand castle, swim in the water, or view the natural waterfalls. Many outfitters have camping areas along the river and help you get on and off the river or shuttle you to and from your vehicle. If you want to float down the river on the weekend, make plans early; outfitters may be completely booked as early as April for spring and summer weekends

<u>Bring lots of cash; the cost of going down the</u>
₁₀
<u>river is priccy and you may want to have some</u>
₁₀
<u>money left over to purchase souvenirs.</u>
₁₀

Choosing to visit the area during the middle of the week may make your trip planning easier, and the river is often less crowded at that time as well.

[3]

<u>When you are not letting loose on the river,</u>
₁₁
local area activities provide even more family-friendly fun. Go on a horseback ride or drive out to Merrit Reservoir State Recreation Area for a fun afternoon at the lake. Merrit is located about thirty minutes from Valentine and offers camping, fishing, boating, and other water recreation activities. The Valentine National Wildlife Refuge, located forty minutes south of Valentine, protects thousands of acres of sand dunes, prairie, wet meadows, and natural lakes. <u>The Niobrara River Valley</u> and the area
₁₂
surrounding Valentine are filled with western history and open spaces that take you back to a slower and more peaceful time.

10. The author is considering removing this sentence from the essay. Is this the best decision to make and why?
   F. Yes, costs shouldn't be included when writing a travel brochure.
   G. Yes, the tone of this sentence gives a negative impression of the outfitters and may deter tourists from visiting the area.
   H. No, the sentence gives important information about the cost of the vacation.
   J. No, the sentence adds a more relaxed tone to the essay, which is inviting to readers.

11. **A.** NO CHANGE
   B. When you are not relaxing on the river,
   C. When you are not chillin' on the river,
   D. While relaxing on the river,

12. Which of the following transitional phrases most effectively links the essay's introduction to the information in the last sentence?
   F. NO CHANGE
   G. Along with natural water and wildlife wonders, the Niobrara River Valley
   H. Besides a variety of water sports, the Niobrara River Valley
   J. Considering all of the wonderful activities and sights, the Niobrara River Valley

Answers and Explanations: Sample Passage 1

1. **(D)** Category: Meaning

   By adding information that prepares the reader for the truck story at the end of the essay, the phrase adds more anticipation to the essay. Readers want to know why the end of the trip was the most interesting. Options A and B aren't reasonable choices; eliminate them immediately. If anything, the phrase adds more of a relaxed feel to the essay; therefore, option C, *seriousness*, doesn't make sense.

2. **(H)** Category: Relevance

   The last sentence of the first paragraph discusses the structure of the tubes. Because the purpose of this essay is to tell the story of the tubing trip, the information about the tubes is not important to the action; therefore, the sentence should be omitted. Option F (NO CHANGE) is incorrect. When considering option G, remember the purpose of the paragraph, which is to describe who was on the trip, how they prepared for the trip, and how they eventually ended up on the water. Sentence 5 doesn't show the individuals getting on the river, so it isn't an effective concluding sentence. Option H provides a conclusion for the introductory paragraph and moves the action of the narration forward. Narrative texts usually include information in chronological order. Without this sentence, it appears that the tubers remained on the bank of the river. Option J fails for the same reason option F fails. Regardless of where you put sentence 6, it doesn't provide information that fits the paragraph.

3. **(A)** Category: Relevance

   Option A is the best response. The sentence in question establishes the purpose of the trip and should be placed in the introductory paragraph. Because Aunt Karla is mentioned in the first sentence, referring to her 60th birthday party in the next sentence makes the most sense. Inserting the sentence anywhere else disrupts the flow of the paragraph.

4. **(H)** Category: Relevance

   The sentence in question has no relevance to the essay. The purpose of the second paragraph is to describe the sights of the trip. The fact that the narrator has an acquaintance with an elk ranch nearby is not an event that happened on the trip; therefore, it should be omitted, making options F and G incorrect. Only options H and J suggest omitting the sentence. Option J replaces the sentence with a sentence about bug spray. The rest of the paragraph contains descriptions of the beauty of the river, and a negative detail about the bug spray ruins the relaxed mood established throughout the rest of the paragraph. Option H is a stronger option than J.

5. **(D)** Categories: Relevance, Tone

   Option A describes the driver's actions as ridiculous and, therefore, criticizes the driver. The factual nature of option B does not reveal the humor of the situation. Option C is also too critical of the driver. The image of the driver climbing out the window like a turtle poking his head out of his shell gives the sentence a humorous tone without being too critical of the driver.

6. **(G)** Category: Organization
As it is written, the essay lacks a conclusion, ending instead with a detail that has little to do with the trip down the river. Option F does not work. Option G makes the truck story relevant to the rest of the essay, and reveals the emotional impact of the event on the narrator: The tubing trip is correctly described as relaxing, and the truck in the ditch makes it memorable as well. Option H shifts the focus too much on the truck stuck in the ditch, when the story is also about the trip down the river. Option J helps to wrap up the story, but it doesn't connect the truck incident to the rest of the essay.

Answers and Explanations: Sample Passage 2

7. **(C)** Category: Organization
The first sentence jumps immediately into detailed information about the wildlife refuge, leaving the reader confused about the purpose of the essay. Option A will not work. Option B expresses a specific detail about Valentine without offering a general introduction to the Niobrara River Valley. Option C is the correct response because the sentence introduces the area the essay discusses and suggests who might enjoy the Niobrara River Valley: water lovers and wildlife enthusiasts. Option D is incorrect because of the transitional phrase "besides floating down the river." The word *besides* indicates a contrast between two ideas, which necessitates a preceding sentence.

8. **(G)** Category: Organization
Sentence 3 feels out of place and needs to be linked to the other sentence that refers to the wildlife in the area (sentence 1). Another indicator that sentence three is linked to the other sentence about wildlife is the word *also*. Sentences 2 and 4 are connected because sentence 4 continues to give more detailed information about the waterfall and the boardwalk that leads to it. Sentence 3 disrupts the flow between these two sentences. The correct order is 1, 3, 2, 4 (option G).

9. **(B)** Category: Organization
Option A does not work because the original sentence only states that the outfitters are plentiful, which does not address the main content of the paragraph—the services provided by the outfitters. Option B is the best response because it shows that the outfitters provide accommodations and equipment. Option C is too general, and option D is too specific.

10. **(G)** Category: Relevance

Tourist brochures highlight the positive aspects of a community and never reveal the negative. Costs *are* relevant to a vaction, making Option F incorrect. The sentence in question does not put the outfitters in a positive light. Although tourist brochures do reveal the costs involved in planning a trip, they never label them as "pricey," as this sentence does. Option G is the correct response.

11. **(B)** Categories: Clarity and Precision

Even though a tourism brochure is a casual piece of writing, *letting loose* is too casual, which makes option A incorrect. Option B replaces *letting loose* with *relaxing*. The word *relaxing* appeals to a larger audience, which is important when developing a tourism brochure. Option C offers the word *chillin'* which is just as problematic as *letting loose*. The phrase "while relaxing on the river" (option D) changes the meaning of the paragraph. The intent of the paragraph is to give alternative activities for families when they are <u>not</u> on the river.

12. **(G)** Category: Organization

The last sentence feels out of place because it brings in new details about the area: western history and open spaces. It needs to be more connected to the rest of the essay, so F is not an option. Option G reviews the main contents of the essay by referring to the "variety of water and wildlife wonders." Because the essay discusses more than just the water sports in the area, option H doesn't include enough information. Option J employs the transitional word *considering*, which indicates a cause and effect relationship. The rest of the sentence does not reveal a cause and effect relationship, so option J is incorrect.

SIX CRITICAL CONCEPTS TO HELP YOU THINK LIKE A WRITER

1. Watch for question stems. They often ask you to consider revisions.

2. If paragraphs or sentences are numbered, an organization question is coming. Maintain a holistic sense of the passage as you answer detail questions, and refer to the numbers once you get to the organization question.

3. Answer all other questions first before tackling questions that ask you to consider entire paragraphs or an entire passage.

4. While you read, be cognizant of topic, main idea, purpose, tone, and style. When you attempt a strategy/style question, keep these concepts in mind.

5. Strategy and style questions test your understanding of the relevance and meaning of sentences, phrases, passages, and transitions. Consider the clarity and precision of language and the relationships between ideas.

6. Remember, there are no short cuts that help with style and strategy questions. Sometimes you'll have to slow down and work at them, but they will separate higher scores from lower ones!

CHAPTER 6

English Practice Test

Sample Passage 1

Directions: The following passage has underlined words that may or may not contain errors or inappropriate expressions or that asks general questions about the passage. Compare each with the four alternatives in the right-hand column. If you think the original version is best, select A or F: NO CHANGE. If you think another alternative is best, circle the corresponding answer choice. Compare how you did with the answer explanations that follow.

Home Cooking

[1] Down the street from my mom's old house in Albuquerque, Padilla's Restaurant sits
quietly in a strip mall. [2] A gas station and a

grocery store occupying spots on either side of
it, with all three structures built just out of
sight of a main intersection. [3] As a kid I
played tennis just a block away, and as I got

older, if she asked, I would stop at the grocery

store on the way home to pick something up
for her. [4] Getting out, I'd feel proud of myself
for being old enough to drive there. [5] One
time, backing out in a hurry, I impaled my
mother's tail light on the store's mailbox, right
across the street from Padilla's. [6] Many don't
notice the restaurant because of its

location on Girard Street in an area that boasts

1. **A.** NO CHANGE
   B. Albuquerque Padilla's
   C. Albuquerque: Padilla's
   D. Albuquerque, Padillas

2. **F.** NO CHANGE
   G. occupied
   H. occupy
   J. occupies

3. **A.** NO CHANGE
   B. if my mother asked,
   C. if my mother, asked
   D. —if she asked—

4. **F.** NO CHANGE
   G. restaurant, because of
   H. restaurant in spite of
   J. restaurant due to the fact that

little through traffic. [5]

If you stand just outside the front door of Padilla's, the sights, noises, and stenches practically pull you inside. The pungent spiciness of red and green chile and the warm sweetness of heated corn tortillas pull your nose

---

inside. Once your through the door, the sounds of dishes banging in the back and waitresses placing orders rise above the sounds

---

of satisfied diners. If you scan the place, and you'll see two rooms: one tiny and another larger. The second room seems like an add-on, as though the restaurant owners bought an adjacent business and knocked a wall down in order to seat more red chile fanatics.

Fast service and the city's best New Mexican food characterize a Padilla's dinner. Water, chips, and homemade salsa usually beat you to the table. Hard-working waitresses, people who know turning tables earns them money, greet you as you push your chair in and ask if you'd "like a few more minutes."

5. For the sake of logic and coherence, sentence 6 should be placed
   A. where it is now.
   B. before sentence 1.
   C. after sentence 1.
   D. after sentence 3.

6. In keeping with the tone of the essay, the author would be wise to change this phrase to which of the following?
   F. NO CHANGE
   G. thuds, and whiffs
   H. resonances, and odors
   J. sounds, and aromas

7. A. NO CHANGE
   B. Once you make it through the entrance;
   C. Once you walk through the door's entrance,
   D. Through the door,

8. F. NO CHANGE
   G. If you were to try to scan the place,
   H. Scan the place
   J. You scanned and inspected the place,

9. A. NO CHANGE
   B. cities
   C. citys'
   D. citys

10. F. NO CHANGE
    G. people who know
    H. ; people who knew
    J. ; who know

When I was a kid, we often wasted no time. Why not order right away if you already know

which item on the memorized menu you want?

For my mother and stepfather, it was always the same order: chicken enchiladas, half red, half green (or "Christmas," as some call it) with extra onions and lettuce. I liked red chile enchiladas, sometimes with an over-easy egg. My sister was a little less predictable, sometimes·

going with the tamales and sometimes

selecting a burrito with green salsa.

I still remember the cozy feeling in my stomach after a Padilla's meal. After wiping our plates clean with warm tortillas, we'd exit past clusters of families clinking forks and cooling their palates from red plastic cups. We'd then climb in our car and head home, arriving in

about three minutes.

[1] I live in Denver now, and I wish the restaurant could pick itself up for one night and move into my new neighborhood. [2] The chile here's just not the same. [3] We craved it, just couldn't get our "fix" often enough. [4] Of course, a week later we'd come back to Padilla's all over again. [5] In fact, I'd say that the *only* thing that disappoints me about Padilla's is that it's not portable. [15]

11. The author is considering deleting the underlined sentence. If the writer did this, the paragraph would primarily lose:
   A. information comparing the author's experience at Padilla's with the experiences of the rest of his family.
   B. details describing Padilla's food.
   C. information informing the reader that the author frequents Padilla's.
   D. details about the fast service at the restaurant.

12. F. NO CHANGE
   G. ordering
   H. deciding
   J. coming to the decision of

13. A. NO CHANGE
   B. she would select
   C. selected
   D. she selects

14. F. NO CHANGE
   G. at which we arrived in about three minutes.
   H. where we arrived at in about three minutes.
   J. and arrive in about three minutes.

15. Which configuration represents the most effective sequence of sentences in this paragraph?
   A. NO CHANGE
   B. 4, 5, 3, 1, 2
   C. 2, 4, 5, 3, 1
   D. 4, 3, 5, 1, 2

Answers and Explanations

1. **(A)** The introductory dependent clause in the sentence, "Down the street from my mom's old house in Albuquerque," calls for a comma (see comma rule 1. Answer B is incorrect because it lacks punctuation between the introductory dependent clause and the clause that succeeds it. Answer C is incorrect because colons only come after an independent clause and before an example, explanation, short phrase, or list (see colon rule 1). Answer D is incorrect because the name "Padilla's" implies possession and therefore needs an apostrophe (see apostrophe rule 1).

2. **(H)** Answer F is incorrect because *occupy* is the main verb in the sentence. *Occupying* cannot stand on its own; it requires a helping verb such as *is* (*is occupying*), or else the result is a fragment. Answer G is incorrect because of inconsistent verb tense. Because the rest of the paragraph is in present tense, the verb *occupy* must remain in present tense as well. Answer J is incorrect because the subject, "A gas station and a grocery store," is plural and necessitates the plural verb *occupy*, not the singular verb *occupies*.

3. **(B)** Answer A is incorrect because no antecedent precedes the underlined phrase to identify the *she* in the underlined portion. Answer C is incorrect because the comma between *mother* and *asked* is unnecessary—you should never place a comma between the subject of a clause and the verb within the same clause. Answer D is incorrect for the same reason that answer A is incorrect: Without a reference provided by an antecedent, it's incorrect to use a pronoun.

4. **(F)** Answer G is incorrect because the second part of the sentence, "because of its location on Girard Street in an area that boasts little through traffic," is a dependent clause. Unless both "sides" of the sentence are independent, they do not need a comma between them (see comma rule 3). Answer H is incorrect because the phrase "in spite of" implies that the second half of the sentence should contrast with the first. In fact, the second half of the sentence flows logically from the first: It makes sense that people wouldn't notice a restaurant on a street with little through traffic. Answer J is incorrect because it is wordy. It is more economical to say "because" than it is to say "due to the fact that."

5. **(C)** Sentence 6 offers primary detail about the location of Padilla's and therefore works best after the first sentence. Answer A is incorrect because the information contained in sentence 6 does not logically follow the secondary information about the car accident. Answer B is incorrect because the sentence does not provide a proper introduction to the passage and therefore should not be the first sentence of the passage. Answer D is incorrect because sentences 3 and 4 connect logically; breaking their flow by placing a sentence in between them creates an awkward arrangement of ideas.

6. **(J)** This question tests your sense of how words convey tone. Your best strategy is to gain a sense of the tone of the passage as a whole and then determine whether the connotations of the underlined words fit the tone of the passage. Answer F is incorrect because the word *stenches* has a negative connotation and therefore doesn't fit the positive tone of the review. Answer G is incorrect because the word *whiffs* is too colloquial and rarely used as a noun. Answer H is incorrect for two reasons: the word *resonances* is out of place within the context of the passage, and the word *odor* carries a slightly negative connotation that is rarely associated positively with food.

7. **(D)** Answer A is incorrect because the use of *your* is incorrect. *Your* in the underlined portion actually means "you are" and therefore needs to be spelled *you're*. Answer B is incorrect because the underlined portion is an introductory dependent clause, making the semicolon incorrect (see comma rule 1). Answer C is incorrect because the phrase "door's entrance" is redundant. The word *door* implies an entrance, so *entrance* in this context is unnecessary.

8. **(H)** The answer to this question hinges on the word *and*, which allows you to rule out answers G and J immediately. The word *if* at the beginning of these answers makes the introductory clause dependent, which means the second half of the sentence must be independent. *And*, a subordinating conjunction, can't follow an "if" statement. Answer J is incorrect for three reasons. First, verb tense is inconsistent. Second, the phrase "scanned and inspected" is redundant. Third, the entire phrase, if placed next to the non-underlined portion of the sentence, renders the whole thought ungrammatical.

9. **(A)** *City's* shows possession and needs an apostrophe (see apostrophe rule 1). Answer B is incorrect because *cities* is the plural form of the word, not the possessive form. Answer C is incorrect because *citys'* is an incorrect spelling of the plural-possessive form of the word. Answer D is incorrect because it is an incorrect spelling of the plural form of the word.

10. **(F)** The phrase "people who know turning tables earns them money" is a "BTW" phrase that needs a comma hug (see comma rule 2). Answer G is incorrect because it is missing the first comma needed to offset the BTW phrase. Answer H is incorrect because verb tense is inconsistent. Answer J is incorrect because a semicolon is not appropriate (see semicolon rule 1).

11. **(C)** Answer A is incorrect because the underlined phrase does not compare the diner's experience with the experiences of the rest of his family. Answer B is incorrect because the phrase does not describe details about the food. Answer D is incorrect because the phrase describes the family's tendency to order quickly, not the fast service of the restaurant.

12. **(G)** Answer F is incorrect because the phrase "going with" is too colloquial and not specific enough. Answer H is incorrect because the word *deciding* is only grammatical if a preposition follows it, as in "decided on." Answer J is incorrect because it is redundant. "Ordering" is more economical and specific than "coming to the decision of."

13. **(A)** This question is slightly tricky, because your answer to 12 dictates your answer to 13. Because of the rules of parallel structure, the verb form you choose must match the preceding verb, *ordering*. Answers B, C, and D all break the rule of parallel structure, so all are incorrect. (See Chapter 3 for more information.)

14. **(F)** Answer G is incorrect because the phrase "at which" is awkward in general but even more awkward when placed right next to the word *home*, which it describes. Answer H is incorrect because the phrase "where we arrived at" misuses the preposition *at*. Answer J is incorrect because the resulting sentence, "Then we'd climb in our car and head home and arrive in about three minutes," is wordy and ungrammatical.

15. **(D)** This question depends on your understanding of how sentences are organized within a paragraph. Obtaining the correct answer hinges on knowing that sentence 4 makes the best transition between the second-to-last paragraph and the last one. In any other combination, sentence 3 feels out of place. Furthermore, sentences 3 and 4 are a continuation of the previous paragraph, while sentences 1, 2, and 4 move on to talk about the author's relocation to Denver and his longing for the restaurant. Answer A is incorrect because sentences 2, 3, and 4 make the paragraph seem disjointed and illogical. Answer B is incorrect because sentence 5 sounds illogical when placed before sentence 3. Answer C is incorrect because sentence 2 sounds illogical when placed in front of sentence 4.

Sample Passage 2

Directions: The following passage has underlined words that may or may not contain errors or inappropriate expressions or that asks general questions about the passage. Compare each with the four alternatives in the right-hand column. If you think the original version is best, select A or F: NO CHANGE. If you think another alternative is best, circle the corresponding answer choice. Compare how you did with the answer explanations that follow.

Unfathomable

[1]

On an August morning in 2008, a Serbian-American swimmer named Milorad Cavic glides toward the wall. The entire world believes he'll

win the biggest race of his life. Suddenly, a tsunami of chlorinated water rushes forward in the next lane. Two hands the size of Frisbees propel another swimmer's body toward the finish. In a moment impossible to see with the naked eye, the swimmer next to Cavic surges forward and arrives just before him.

This desperate attack, which seconds earlier

seemed in vain, has proven to be the difference. The swimmer in the lane next to Cavic has won.

[2]

The swimmer in the next lane is, of course,

Michael Phelps. His margin of victory is one one-hundredth of a second.

1. A. NO CHANGE
   B. believed he'd
   C. believed he was going to
   D. believe he'll

2. F. NO CHANGE
   G. his.
   H. his arrival.
   J. he does.

3. A. NO CHANGE
   B. lunge
   C. jump
   D. pounce

4. F. NO CHANGE
   G. in the next lane were,
   H. on the next lane is,
   J. in the next lane is

[3]

[1] The story of Michael Phelps at the Beijing Olympics includes countless mind-boggling specifics; eight gold medals, seven
₅
world records, two miraculous finishes, and a

never-ending stream of priceless images:
₆
however, none of these details captures the
₆

essence of Phelps the athlete best than his
₇
astonishing win against Cavic in the 100-meter butterfly.

[2] This moment, seen only by underwater cameras,
₈
embodied Phelps's performance at the 2008 games. [3] Why? [4] Because it drove home the idea that no matter where he was in the pool— or in the eyes of the world for the other 200 weeks between Olympic meets—he inevitably came from nowhere, defeats his opponents and
₉
dominating our collective consciousness.

5. **A.** NO CHANGE
   B. specifics—eight gold medals
   C. specifics, eight gold medals
   D. specifics: eight gold medals

6. **F.** NO CHANGE
   G. images; moreover, none
   H. images; therefore, none
   J. images. None

7. **A.** NO CHANGE
   B. as good
   C. as well
   D. better

8. **F.** NO CHANGE
   G. only seen to underwater cameras,
   H. and seen by underwater cameras only,
   J. seen only by underwater cameras

9. **A.** NO CHANGE
   B. defeated his opponents
   C. defeating his opponents
   D. defeating his opponents—

[4]

[1] Phelps is a rare athlete who *always*
10
believes he can win, regardless of the odds or
10
how many people doubt him. [2] Like Tiger
10

Woods, the only similarly dominant athlete in
11
recent memory, Phelps gets better as the stakes get
higher. [3] Normally an affable diplomat of his
sport, Phelps morphs instantly when necessary
into a fierce, relentless competitor.

[5]

[1] All week, Deborah Phelps's face had
shown television viewers the roots of Michael's
success. [2] Sure, his six-foot-seven-inch arm
span contributing too his achievements, but
12
family played at least as big a role. [3] When
Phelps finished his stunning run by helping his
team win the 400 meter medley relay, he took
one more swim, around an ocean of
13

10. The author is considering omitting the
underlined phrase and rewriting the
sentence. If she did so, the sentence would
primarily lose:
   F. An important detail explaining why
   Phelps is the only truly rare athlete.
   The author should not remove the
   phrase.
   G. An important transition between
   paragraphs 1 and 2 that also explains
   why Phelps is a rare athlete. The
   author should not remove the phrase.
   H. Only a minor point about how Phelps
   responds to doubt. The author should
   remove the phrase.
   J. Nothing. The author should remove
   the phrase.

11. A. NO CHANGE
    B. similar dominant
    C. similar, dominant,
    D. similarly different

12. F. NO CHANGE
    G. contributed to
    H. contributed too
    J. contributed

13. A. NO CHANGE
    B. across an ocean
    C. across a desert
    D. over a mountain

photographers to hug his mother and sisters. 14
[4] When Phelps kissed his mom on the cheek,
it was clear that he credited her with making
his dreams possible. [5] As spectators, we can
only guess what they said to each other. [6]
What would you say to the person who taught
you that no matter where you were in the pool,
and regardless of the odds, you had the ability
to out-touch your opponent? 15

14. In paragraph 5, sentence 3 would work
best if the author placed it:
    F. where it is now.
    G. before sentence 1.
    H. after sentence 4.
    J. after sentence 5.

15. In order to explain that Michael Phelps has
a sense of his place in history, the author is
considering adding the following sentence
to the essay:

After his final race, Phelps seemed humbled by
the complimentary words of Mark Spitz, whose
"unbreakable" records Phelps broke in Beijing.

If added, this sentence would most logically be
placed:

    A. after sentence 1 in paragraph 3.
    B. after sentence 3 in paragraph 4.
    C. before sentence 1 in paragraph 5.
    D. The author would be better off
       omitting the sentence altogether.

Answers and Explanations

1. **(A)** This question tests subject-verb agreement and verb tense consistency. Answer B is incorrect because the past tense "believed he'd" is inconsistent with the rest of the paragraph. Answer C is also incorrect because it's written in past tense, which is inconsistent with the rest of the paragraph. Answer D is incorrect because the phrase "The entire world," as one collective group, requires the singular verb *believes*. (See Chapter 3.)

2. **(J)** This question tests your knowledge of pronoun use. Answer F, although it represents a form commonly used in spoken English, is technically incorrect. The subjective case of this pronoun is necessary because the verb *arrives* is implied at the end of the sentence—it would be incorrect to say "him arrives." (See Chapter 4.) Answer G is incorrect because the possessive *his* creates the nonsensical phrase "just before his." Answer H is incorrect because it creates a redundancy by placing *arrives* and *arrival* in the same phrase.

3. **(B)** This question tests your sense of style, especially relating to the connotations and specific definitions of words. The correct answer is hinted at in the preceding sentence when the author uses the word *surges*—obtaining the correct answer means finding its closest synonym. Answer A is incorrect because the word *attacks* doesn't describe the situation—a desperate move forward—accurately. Answer C is incorrect because the action described is not a *jump* but a move forward in the water. Answer D is incorrect because the word *pounce* implies a move to quickly cover something, as a cat does to a mouse.

4. **(F)** Answer G is incorrect because the plural verb *were* does not agree with the two nouns it links: *swimmer* and *Michael Phelps*. Answer H is incorrect because of a preposition error: Conventional English dictates that the phrase "in the next lane" makes sense while "on the next lane" does not. Answer J is incorrect because it lacks the comma necessary to separate the "BTW" phrase "of course" (see comma rule 2).

5. **(D)** This question tests your knowledge of punctuation. Colon rule 1 dictates that you should use a colon when it follows an independent clause and introduces an example, explanation, short phrase, or list.

6. **(J)** This question tests both your ability to punctuate properly and your sense of style with regard to ideas within a sentence. Answer F is incorrect because the word *however*, succeeded by an independent clause, necessitates a semicolon, not a colon (see semicolon rule 1). Answer G is incorrect because the word *moreover* implies a continuation of the thinking from the first part of the sentence, when in fact the second part of the sentence contrasts with the first part. Answer H is incorrect for the same reason: *therefore* implies continuation when in fact the beginning of the sentence contrasts with the end.

7. **(D)** Answer A is incorrect because the result is the incorrect phrase "best than." Answer B is incorrect because it uses the adjective *good* to modify the verb *captures*. Answer C is incorrect because its result is the awkward phrase "as well than." Conventional English dictates that we use the phrase "as well as" in this case.

8. **(F)** Answer G is incorrect because of the improper preposition *to*. Answer H is incorrect because it creates the incorrect phrasing "this moment, *and* seen by underwater cameras only, embodied. . ." Answer J is incorrect because it lacks the necessary comma to set apart this BTW phrase (see comma rule 2).

9. **(C)** This question tests your sense of style as it relates to parallel structure. Answer A is incorrect because the verb form *defeats* fails to match the form of *dominating*, another verb within the same phrase. Answer B is incorrect for the same reason. Answer D is incorrect because it misuses a dash (see dash rule 2).

10. **(G)** This question tests writing strategy. Answer F is incorrect because it is too extreme. Although Michael Phelps is a rare athlete, he is not "the only truly rare athlete." In fact, the paragraph goes on to describe another rare athlete, Tiger Woods. Answer H is incorrect because the point of the sentence is not minor at all; in fact, it defines the topic of the entire paragraph. Answer J is incorrect because, without the first sentence, the paragraph feels incomplete; its subject is not stated overtly enough.

11. **(A)** This question tests your knowledge of both adverb use and punctuation. Answer B is incorrect because it contains an adjective, *similar*, modifying another adjective, *dominant*. Answer C is incorrect because no comma is necessary between the word *dominant* and the word *athlete*. Answer D is incorrect because the phase "similarly different" is paradoxical and therefore illogical in this case.

12. **(G)** Answer F is incorrect because the verb *contributing* makes the first clause of the sentence dependent, which renders the entire sentence ungrammatical. Answer H is incorrect because it employs the incorrect form of *too* (see Chapter 4). Answer J is incorrect because the phrase "contributed his achievements"—as someone with an ear for conventional English knows—lacks the necessary preposition *to*.

13. **(B)** This question tests both your ear for prepositions and your understanding of figurative language. Answer A is incorrect because the *ocean* of photographers implies a mass of people that Phelps must go *through*, not *around*. Answer C is incorrect because *desert* does not complete the metaphor. It would not make sense, especially in an essay about swimming, to depict Phelps "swimming across

a desert." Answer D is incorrect for similar reasons. A mass of people is not a figurative *mountain* Phelps must climb; it's a figurative *ocean* he must cross.

14. **(G)** This question tests your sense of paragraph organization. In reading through the paragraph, you may have sensed some disorganization, which should have told you that answer A probably isn't the right choice. In fact, it's incorrect because sentence 1 refers to *Deborah Phelps* without introducing her. Although some readers might infer that the author is talking about Phelps's mother, her relationship with him is more obvious when sentence 1 follows sentence 3. Answer H is incorrect because the information in sentence 3—from a chronological standpoint—comes before the information in sentence 4, not after it. Answer J is incorrect for the same reason: In the passage, Phelps must make his final "swim" across the crowd before we can guess what he says to his mother.

15. **(D)** This time-consuming question tests your sense of the passage as a whole. Answering it correctly involves a process of elimination. Answer A is incorrect because a sentence about the historical context of Phelps's achievements doesn't fit within a paragraph that describes a single Olympic moment in detail. Answer B is incorrect because, although the sentence makes more sense in paragraph 4, it disrupts the paragraph in two ways. First, it adds another piece of information not asserted by the topic sentence. Second, it attaches a final sentence to the paragraph without evaluating the significance of the sentence. In order to make this sentence fit, the author would have to develop paragraph 4 further. Answer C is incorrect because a sentence about historical context does not fit within a paragraph that describes Phelps's relationship with his family.

Sample Passage 3

Directions: The following passage has underlined words that may or may not contain errors or inappropriate expressions or that asks general questions about the passage. Compare each with the four alternatives in the right-hand column. If you think the original version is best, select A or F: NO CHANGE. If you think another alternative is best, circle the corresponding answer choice. Compare how you did with the answer explanations that follow.

Wii Love It!

[1]

A video game system is like a new family member that everyone must adjust to.
₁

1. **A.** NO CHANGE
   B. member: to which everyone has to adjust
   C. member, to which everyone must adjust.
   D. member: everyone has to adjust to it.

I know: I bought one a few weeks ago. It
₂
arrived with much fanfare, a little like a

2. **F.** NO CHANGE
   G. I know I
   H. I know, I
   J. I know; I

newborn child. My three boys had gawked
₃
lighthearted at their cousin's system, just like
₃   ₄

3. **A.** NO CHANGE
   B. have gawked lightheartedly
   C. had gawked, lightheartedly,
   D. had gawked lightheartedly

children who are expecting a new brother or
₄
sister might want or need to spend a little extra
₄
time around a friend's baby brother or sister.
₄

4. **F.** NO CHANGE
   G. children, expecting a new brother or sister, may likewise want to spend time around a friend's baby brother or sister.
   H. as children expecting a new brother or sister might show curiosity toward someone else's baby.
   J. much as around a new baby, children might want to spend a little extra time who are expecting one, or need to.

We had never owned their own game system,
₅
unless you count the hand-me-down Nintendo 64 we inherited when my oldest son was three.

[2]

None of us predicted the effects our new game system would have on the family. It was
₆
fun, but it also made everyone in the family,
₆
except my wife, temporarily insane, after the
₇
initial, tedious setup, we began playing.

Sam, the oldest of my three sons,
₈

took an immediate liking and got lots of
₉
enjoyment out of the sports games right away.
₉
Henry enjoyed the system somewhat but mostly

got frustrated—its hard to ski jump in perfect
₁₀
balance when you're four. Willie, my two-year-old, didn't really understand the games, but he

did learned quickly that unplugging the little
₁₁
box made Sam and Henry fume in anger.

5. **A.** NO CHANGE
   B. We had never owned our own
   C. Having never owned our own
   D. We have never owned her own

6. **F.** NO CHANGE
   G. It was fun
   H. It was fun;
   J. It was fun—

7. **A.** NO CHANGE
   B. insane. After
   C. insane; after
   D. insane. After,

8. **F.** NO CHANGE
   G. , the older of my three sons,
   H. the oldest of my three sons
   J. , the oldest of my three sons;

9. **A.** NO CHANGE
   B. liked
   C. immediately liked
   D. got lots of enjoyment out of

10. **F.** NO CHANGE
    G. it's
    H. it was
    J. it isn't

11. **A.** NO CHANGE
    B. learned fast
    C. learn more quickly
    D. learn quickly

[3]

Despite an occasional conflict, everything
                                        12
went good until Lego Star Wars arrived. One
     12
night, after my kids went to bed, I decided I
should "figure out" the new game for them.
I played for five hours. When I finally came to
bed—at 3:00 A.M.—my wife, Christina, looked
sleepily at the clock and said, "*What* are you
doing?" At that moment, I wished I had an
answer besides, "I'm a thirty-five-year-old

moron who likes to played video games until
                              13
dawn. *Yawn.*" But that's all I could come up
with. My wife rolled over, certain she had
married the wrong man.

[4]

The next several days saw great conflict
between Sam and Henry because Sam, under-
standably, was able to figure out Star Wars more
quickly then his brother was.
              14
Countless times after work I heard the same
complaint:

[5]

"Dad, I'm trying to get over this bridge, but
Henry is in the other corner bumping his head
against the wall so I can't move. Can you help
me?"

[6]

Things have settled down a little now that a
few weeks have passed. Sam and Henry now
have a system for playing Star Wars together,
which includes Henry "dropping out" periodi-
cally so Sam can conquer a particularly challenging section.

12. Which choice is the most effective first
    sentence of paragraph 3?
    F. NO CHANGE
    G. Despite an occasional conflict,
       everything went fairly well until Lego
       Star Wars arrived.
    H. Besides the occasional conflict, nothing
       went well until Lego Star Wars arrived
    J. Lego Star Wars arrived, before which
       everything went well besides the
       occasional conflict.

13. A. NO CHANGE
    B. that likes to play
    C. who likes to play
    D. whom likes to play

14. F. NO CHANGE
    G. then his brother was able.
    H. than his brother was.
    J. than his brother had the ability to do.

[7]

Now, while I am making their dinner, I often hear Sam squawking, "Drop out, Henry! Drop out!" I cringe a little. Inside, I hope desperately that our acquisition of a video game system doesn't set Sam, Henry, or William on a path that culminates in their high school guidance counselor using the same phrase. 15

15. In which order should the last four paragraphs be arranged?
   A. NO CHANGE
   B. 5, 4, 6, 7
   C. 6, 5, 4, 7
   D. 4, 6, 5, 7

Answers and Explanations

1. **(D)** This question tests your knowledge of prepositions, your understanding of punctuation, and your ability to distinguish between *whom* and *which*. Answer A is incorrect because, in formal English, sentences may not end with a preposition. Answer B is incorrect because a colon may not precede a prepositional phrase—no punctuation mark other than a comma should be considered in this instance (See Chapter 2). Answer C is incorrect because of the phrase "to which." Because the author personifies the game system, he must use the word *whom*, which refers to a noun that is human. Answer C also features an unnecessary comma after "member."

2. **(J)** This question tests punctuation. Both "I know" and "I bought one a few weeks ago" are independent clauses, so a semicolon must separate them. Answer F is incorrect because colons are used only when they follow an independent clause and introduce an example, explanation, short phrase, or list. Answer G is incorrect because, without punctuation, the sentence becomes a run-on. Answer H is incorrect because a comma in this situation produces a comma splice.

3. **(D)** This question tests your ability to use adjectives and adverbs as well as your ability to spot inconsistencies in verb tense. Answer A is incorrect because the adjective *lighthearted* cannot modify the verb *gawked*. Answer B is incorrect because the present-tense verb *have* is inconsistent with the rest of the narrative, which is set in the past. Although the author editorializes in the present, he tells the story in the past. This underlined portion is clearly a part of the narrative. Answer C is incorrect because the adverb *lightheartedly*, rather than being a nonessential or "BTW" phrase, simply modifies the verb *gawked* and therefore doesn't require a "comma hug" (see comma rule 2).

4. **(H)** This question tests your ability to use language economically. Answer F is incorrect because the phrase "want or need" is wordy and because the repeated phrase "brother or sister" loads the sentence with too much verbiage. Answer G is incorrect because the phrase "brother or sister" is repeated in the sentence, making it feel overloaded and clunky. Answer J is incorrect because phrases and clauses are mixed together in a way that destroys the flow of the sentence and renders it unclear.

5. **(B)** This question tests both your understanding of sentence structure and your ability to maintain consistent verb tense. Answer A is incorrect because the pronoun *we* does not agree in person with the pronoun *their*. Answer C is incorrect because it produces a fragment—the first clause must be independent, because the rest of the sentence is not. Answer D is incorrect because the verb *have* does not agree in tense with the rest of the sentence.

6. (F) This question tests your knowledge of punctuation. Two independent clauses with a FANBOYS word between them necessitate a comma (see comma rule 3). Answer G is incorrect because, without punctuation, the sentence is a run-on. Answer H is incorrect because a semicolon is unnecessary here: The subordinating conjunction *but* serves the same purpose (see comma rule 3 and semicolon rule 1). Answer J is incorrect because, as we mention in Chapter 2, dashes are reserved for major breaks in thought (see dash rule 2).

7. (B) This question tests your knowledge of sentence structure. Answer A is incorrect because it creates a comma splice: two independent clauses attached with just a comma. Answer C is incorrect because the clause "after the initial, tedious setup, we got to playing" is not related to the previous clause closely enough to warrant a semicolon. Answer D is incorrect because no comma is necessary between *after* and *the*.

8. (F) This question tests your knowledge of comparatives and superlatives, as well as your knowledge of punctuation. Answer G is incorrect because the comparative word *older* can only be used when comparing two things. Answer H is incorrect because the nonessential or BTW phrase "the oldest of my three sons" requires a comma hug (see comma rule 2). Answer J is incorrect because a semicolon is not necessary following a nonessential, or BTW, phrase (see comma rule 2).

9. (B) This question tests your sense of economy in language. Answer A is incorrect because it's redundant; "took an immediate liking" and "got lots of enjoyment" state essentially the same idea. Answer C is also redundant; *immediately* and *right away* (a phrase following the underlined portion) have exactly the same meaning. Answer D is incorrect because it's more economical to say "liked" than it is to say "got lots of enjoyment out of."

10. (G) This question tests your sense of the ideas in the sentence, your knowledge of punctuation, and your ability to maintain verb-tense consistency. Answer F is incorrect because it employs the possessive spelling of *its* when the contraction *it's* is necessary. Answer H is incorrect because the editorial comment "it's hard to ski jump in perfect balance when you're four" needs to be in present tense. Answer J is incorrect because it isn't logical. It is hard for most young children to maintain perfect balance, so the phrase "it isn't hard" makes little sense.

11. (D) This question tests your knowledge of adverbs and adjectives, comparatives, and verb-tense consistency. Answer A is wrong because the word "learned" is incorrect when placed next to the word "did." The result is the incoherent phrase "did learned." Answer B is incorrect for the same reason, and because—in formal English writing—the adjective "fast" cannot modify the verb "learned." Answer C is incorrect because the word "more" necessitates a comparison; without anything to compare, it is unnecessary.

12. **(G)** This question tests your sense of style and your knowledge of adjectives and adverbs. Answer F is incorrect because, although common in colloquial English, the adjective *good* cannot modify the verb *went*. Answer H is incorrect because the phrase "besides the occasional conflict" makes little sense in the same sentence as "nothing went well." The word *besides* implies a contrast, when in reality the phrases "occasional conflict" and "nothing went well" are closely related. Answer J is incorrect because it breaks up the transition between paragraphs 2 and 3, disrupting the flow of the essay and making the beginning of paragraph 3 sound disjointed.

13. **(C)** This question tests your ability to identify when to use the words *who*, *whom*, and *that*. Answer A is incorrect because the word *likes* must be succeeded by the infinitive *to play*, making *to played* ungrammatical. Answer B is incorrect because the word *that* must be replaced by *who* when the sentence refers to a human being. Answer D is incorrect because *who* is the subject of the clause. *Whom* is only correct in cases when it is the object (see Chapter 4).

14. **(H)** This question tests your ability to distinguish between *then* and *than*, as well as your sense of economy in language. Answer F is incorrect because *then* refers to time and cannot be used when comparing two things. Answer G is also incorrect, both because it employs the wrong *then* and because it contains the unnecessary word "able." Answer J is incorrect because the phrase "had the ability to do" is wordy and redundant in the context of the rest of the sentence.

15. **(A)** This question tests your understanding of the essay's organization. Answer B is incorrect because paragraph 4 sets up the quotation in paragraph 5 and therefore must precede it. Answer C is incorrect for the same reason, and also because paragraph 6 sets up the central idea in paragraph 7 and therefore must precede it. Answer D is incorrect because paragraphs 4 and 5 must go together and cease to make sense when separated by paragraph 6.

MATH

CHAPTER 7

Overview of the Math Section

- Overview of the math test
- Word problems
- Helpful strategies
- Important reminders

You can earn a perfect score on the mathematics section of the ACT. Between your skills and knowledge, the tips in this book, and the time you put into preparing, you have everything you need. The math portion of the ACT is an assessment of content knowledge through Algebra 2 (or the equivalent). That means a typical junior is on track for completing the necessary coursework to ace the math. So why doesn't everyone earn a perfect score? Well, the challenge is completing 60 questions in 60 minutes. Be efficient and manage your time.

Questions are based on everything from elementary algebra to trigonometry. The different types of questions are mixed throughout the test. The elementary algebra questions appear more frequently in the beginning of the test and are sprinkled throughout the latter part of the test. The opposite is true of the intermediate algebra, coordinate and plane geometry, and trigonometry questions. This means you can expect to move through the test more quickly in the beginning and to slow your pace toward the the end.

What makes the math section of the ACT challenging is not the content but rather the time limit. You have 60 minutes to correctly answer 60 questions (and most are word problems), so you will not have enough time to carefully solve each question. Employ strategies for finding the correct solution without fully working out each problem. By understanding the makeup of the test, you will be better able to plan your attack and get closer to reaching the perfect score. It can be done!

WORD PROBLEMS

The test is composed mostly of word problems. That's right, those tricky problems both teachers and students have avoided for the last ten years of your life. But now your job is to seek out word problems. You must solve word problems at every opportunity so they become natural for you. The more word problems you read and solve, the faster you will be at identifying what the problem is asking and determining the most efficient way of solving it. Whether your math teacher assigns word problems or not, solve them whenever you can.

TIP

The ability to decipher and solve word problems is the key to acing the math section.

MULTIPLE-CHOICE QUESTIONS

Multiple-choice questions may sound like a slam dunk, but there is a catch. Among the answer choices are wrong answers that are the results of common mistakes. Test writers include decoys among choices (wrong answers that look right) by working problems incorrectly. It is important to answer the problems quickly, but remember to balance your pace with accuracy. Be sure to go as quickly as you can while avoiding careless mistakes.

Types of Problems

TIP

Almost half of the math consists of elementary algebra.

Now that you're aware of the makeup of the exam, let's look at the good news. First of all, you are allowed to use a graphing calculator on the exam. (There are restrictions on the type of graphing calculator, which we will discuss later.) Forty percent of the test is made up of elementary algebra problems. That's right: 24 of the 60 questions will be based on pre-algebra and algebra coursework. Eighteen problems are Algebra 2 and coordinate geometry. Eighteen problems are planar geometry and trigonometry. The test will begin with mostly elementary algebra problems and then move into the types of problems that are likely to involve multiple steps. There will be some elementary algebra problems sprinkled throughout the remainder of the exam.

Makeup of the Test Questions	
24	Pre-algebra and elementary algebra
18	Algebra 2 and coordinate geometry
18	Planar geometry and trigonometry
60	Total questions

USING THIS BOOK TO PREPARE

The purpose of the mathematics section of this book is to familiarize you with the exam and prepare you to obtain a perfect score on the math section of the ACT. Six chapters make up the math portion of the book. The first chapter is an overview of the math section test. The next three chapters focus on each of the three content areas of the test. The fourth chapter includes mini-lessons on conic sections, trigonometry, and graphing calculator use, and the fifth chapter is a practice test.

TIP

The graphing calculator can be a great time saver—but only if you know how to use it.

The content chapters will be where you spend most of your time and energy. In each of the content chapters you will find an explanation for the more common topics assessed in that content area. Each topic comes with example problems and solution explanations. Throughout these chapters, you'll see content/formula boxes as well as tip boxes. Use the boxes later as a quick review of what you learned. Each content chapter will end with 12 practice questions. For this mini-test, you will need to time your performance. For elementary algebra problems, you will want to average 30 seconds per question. For the more difficult material covered in the other two chapters, you will want to average 80 seconds per question. Be sure to use the strategies provided in this section to help you solve the questions accurately and quickly.

The last two chapters include mini-lessons and a practice test. Even if you are familiar with the topics, you will want to read through the mini-lessons because they focus on the specific ways the topics are addressed on the ACT. In trigonometry, for example, the focus is on right triangle and circular trigonometry. Knowing this will help you focus your studies and preparation. Your graphing calculator can be a great tool, but only to the extent that you are familiar with using it. The use of the graphing calculator is highlighted in the Intermediate Algebra chapter as well as the mini-lesson chapter. Following the mini-lessons is a 60-question practice test. The practice test is important because it mixes all of the topics covered in the math section of this book. When taking the practice test, be sure to simulate a testing environment as best you can (time, quiet, no reference materials).

ACHIEVING A PERFECT MATH SCORE

As mentioned earlier, your skills and knowledge of mathematics will not be enough to ensure a perfect score on the ACT. You will need to take an active role, which means using the book in the most effective way as well as working outside of the book to train yourself for the exam.

Engage with the Material in This Book

Feel free to write in the margins and highlight the text. (If you are borrowing the book, use removable highlighter tape and sticky notes). When taking notes in the text, use language that will help you remember what you learned. Your notes can act as a review when you come back to the book. Highlight and code items that you want to re-read later. Mark areas that require further study. You can also write questions in the text that you want to ask your math teacher.

TIP

When studying, focus most of your attention on your weak spots.

Work Through the Content Chapters

The three content chapters are a review of the mathematics you already know. Read each chapter in the order it is presented, and work through each example before reading the solution explanation. Be sure to mark both your strong and weak areas. You will want to quickly review your strong areas and pay more attention to weak areas. Each content chapter includes practice problems specific to the material in the chapter. Treat these problems as a practice test and don't forget to give yourself time constraints.

Both Time and Accuracy Are Important

Whether you are doing the problems in one focus area or using the sample test at the end of this section, time yourself. A great strategy is to set a timer for slightly less than the allotted time (this will help you with your pacing). When the time has elapsed, change pencil or pen colors and continue to work through the problems. This will show you how much additional time you use. Once you have attempted every problem, use the answer key to check your answers. Over the course of your preparation, your goal should be to improve both your time and your accuracy. The key to a perfect score is simple: get all the questions correct within the allotted time.

Mini-Lessons Are Important, Too

The fourth chapter of this section includes mini-lessons for conic sections (circles, ellipses, hyperbolas), circular trigonometry, and graphing calculator. For some students, these lessons may not be necessary, and for others they will be beneficial. Depending on your coursework to date, read through the lessons to review the topics and make your own judgment. If you need additional instruction on these topics, talk with your math teacher about resources available at your school.

Focus on ACT Preparation in Your Math Class

Use your math class as practice before the big day. This book will be key in helping you understand what is on the test and identifying your strengths and weaknesses. But you can do a lot to improve your ACT math score simply by changing what you do in your regular math class. Focus on these four areas to improve your performance: word problems, your personal weak spots, the ballpark approach, and the graphing calculator.

Word problems make up a good portion of the ACT. Take the initiative to solve all available word problems in your math textbook as you learn a new unit of study. While these problems may not cover the same content as problems on the ACT, they will help you to hone your word problem-solving skills. When working with word problems, pay special attention to determining the important information in the problem and identifying a strategy to solve the problem. Treat each problem as a practice ACT question.

Weak areas can be strengthened with the help of your math teacher. Once you have worked through this book, take a list of your weak areas along with specific questions to your teacher. Request additional help AND additional practice problems in the areas that frustrate you. Your teacher has access to more resources than you do. Do not underestimate your teacher's dedication to your success.

The ballpark approach will help you throughout the ACT math test. When solving any problem in your math class, begin by guessing a range that the answer will fall in. Using this technique with the problems in your math class will give you lots of practice. Write your guess down, solve the problem, and then evaluate your guess. Reflect on ways that you can guess more accurately in the future. You'll be surprised how useful this technique can be when you are attempting to solve 60 questions in 60 minutes.

The graphing calculator's usefulness depends on how well you know how to use it. Increase your comfort with the graphing calculator by using it as often as possible.

TIP

Don't use time constraints when learning new material.

For starters, use it to help you determine a ballpark answer before solving problems by hand. Make sure to review your calculator's statistics, probability, and counting functions. Enlist the help of your classmates who seem the most savvy with their calculators.

MATH STRATEGIES

As you begin your quest for a perfect ACT score, let's look at seven key strategies for approaching math questions.

SEVEN KEY MATH STRATEGIES

- Buy Time
- Solve It (Whenever You Can)
- Draw/Label Pictures
- Ballpark and Eliminate
- Plug in the Answer Choices
- Use Your Graphing Calculator
- Make an Educated Guess*

*Since this book is focused on helping you obtain a PERFECT score, guessing is included only as a last resort.

TIP

Set a timer for 80 seconds and sit in silence. It is longer than you think.

Buying time is the first—and most important—strategy. One minute per problem will not be sufficient for solving the more difficult problems. You can buy time for those problems by solving the easiest problems in 30 seconds or less. These problems include topics from Pre-Algebra through parts of Algebra 1. They will not be marked in any special way, so it will be up to you to identify them as being easy and solve them quickly. The next chapter will help you with both identifying these problems and solving them efficiently. Unfortunately, even 80 seconds will not be enough time to completely solve some of the more difficult problems, so you'll need to pair this strategy with some others.

Beyond the elementary algebra problems, there will be several problems you can solve quickly (and only you can identify these). Use this book to help you determine which types of problems, in addition to the elementary problems, you are able to solve quickly. Make a list of the types that are easy for you. Review this list prior to the test. When you see a problem that is typically easy for you—**SOLVE IT!** Don't over-think this strategy. If you find it easy to solve in the allotted time (30 seconds or 80 seconds), go for it.

When a picture is provided, use the information in the word problem to **label the picture**. If there is no picture and you find yourself trying to visualize the situation in your mind's eye, **draw the picture** on paper. It is easier to work with an actual drawing that is labeled than it is to keep the information straight in your mind. This will reduce the chance of mistakes *and* the time it takes you to solve the problem (our two key areas for ensuring success).

Once you've determined that a problem won't be *easy* to solve, you will want to begin with a **ballpark-and-eliminate** strategy—ballpark the answers and eliminate the choices that aren't in the ballpark. Begin practicing this strategy with problems you are facing in math class today. Use your knowledge and experience to identify a general range of results, whether the answer is numerical or graphical, and then attempt to solve the problem. On the ACT, you may still end up testing out the solutions that your ballpark answer does not eliminate, but using this technique will reduce the number of solutions you need to test.

Plug in answer choices when the answers are numerical. This can be quicker than solving the problem because it simply requires substitution rather than actual algebra. When using this strategy, start with the middle choice because the answers are listed in numerical order. Once you have tried one number, determine if you should go to a higher or lower answer choice for your next attempt.

Your graphing calculator can be a lifesaver. Say you recognize a problem as a combination or permutation but don't remember the formula. Your graphing calculator will solve it for you. What if you are given a list of data and asked for some measure of central tendency? Your graphing calculator can calculate that for you, too. If you are given a graph and asked to find the equation, you can enter each answer choice into your calculator and examine the resulting graph. Work on becoming even more proficient with your graphing calculator and plan on using it on the ACT. Practice with it as you work through this book and you'll know when to turn to it during the exam. Remember, your calculator is only a time-saver if you're quick with it.

The last resort is to make an **educated guess**. This will not guarantee you a perfect score, but it is certainly better than leaving any problem blank. First, complete all the problems that you can answer correctly and quickly, skipping the ones you find difficult. When you have a few minutes left in the testing time, go back to the problems you skipped. Remember, the key to guessing is to make an *educated* guess. Use your ballpark answer or your graphing calculator to eliminate incorrect choices. Narrow your choices as much as you can before guessing.

So, there you have it! You now have an idea of what will be in the math section of the ACT, tips for using this book, and strategies for taking the test. Perhaps you have already written notes in these margins and highlighted the key points. Refer back to this chapter when working through the next five and again after you have worked through the entire math section of this book.

Elementary Algebra

CHAPTER 8

- Probability and statistics
- Percents and formulas
- Factors and multiples
- Expressions and equations
- Exponents and polynomials

E lementary algebra is just that—elementary! It calls upon the skills you learned in middle school through part of first-year algebra, including probability, percents, proportion, expressions, equations, and polynomials. Graphing problems are in another section. When you come across an elementary algebra problem, don't over-think it! The key here is to trust that the problem is, in fact, easy and straightforward.

Your pre-algebra and basic algebra skills should be strong enough that you can work out these problems in 30 seconds or less. Spending time looking for patterns or clues to select an answer without solving the problem may be a waste of time. The most difficult problems in this category are factoring problems, which we'll get to at the end of this chapter.

This section of the test is your chance to buy time. Elementary algebra will make up 24 of the 60 questions in the math section of the ACT. Know your basics and you have a great opportunity to earn yourself more time to think on the remaining 36 questions. Review each of the topics in this chapter and time yourself on the practice problems. Remember, limit yourself to 30 seconds or less on each problem. If an area is taking more time, find some practice problems on that topic and work to pick up your speed.

TIP

The most efficient way to answer elementary algebra questions is to solve them directly.

INTRODUCTORY PROBABILITY AND STATISTICS

The good news is that the probability and statistics material tested on the ACT is what you learned in middle school. You will use fractions and percents along with your knowledge of probability to solve simple problems.

Simple Probability

You won't have to memorize any formulas for these questions. Instead, you will use your understanding of the general concept to solve straightforward problems. To review, you will recall that the probability of something happening is represented as the fraction of the number of favorable outcomes divided by the number of possible outcomes. For instance, when you roll a six-sided die, the probability of rolling a 2 is 1/6 because there is one 2 (favorable outcome) out of six possibilities.

> ### PROBABILITY FORMULA
>
> $$\text{Probability of an Event} = \frac{\#\,of\,Favorable\,Outcomes}{\#\,of\,Possible\,Outcomes}$$

Try the following problem and then read the solution/explanation to review the concept.

Practice Question

1. A bag contains 4 red balls, 5 green balls, and 3 blue balls. If a ball is selected at random from the bag, what is the probability that the ball selected will be green?

   A. $\dfrac{1}{5}$

   B. $\dfrac{1}{12}$

   C. $\dfrac{5}{60}$

   D. $\dfrac{5}{12}$

   E. $\dfrac{5}{7}$

Solution/Explanation

1. **(D)** The answer is simply $\dfrac{5}{12}$ because there are 5 green balls and a total of 12 balls (or possible outcomes). Probability is always the number of choices considered successes divided by the number of choices that exist.

Simple Statistics

When you first started learning about statistics, you examined data sets and found the measures of central tendency and the range of the data. Those are the only parts of statistics that you will be called upon to know for the ACT. In other words, you will use *mean, median, mode,* and *range.*

- *Mode* is the number that occurs most often in a data set (there may be more than one mode).

- *Range* is the difference between the smallest data value and the largest.

Most likely, the statistics problems you encounter will involve mean or median. Examples and explanations of these two concepts follow.

Mean

The mean is determined by adding all of the data in a data set and dividing by the number of data. The problems on the ACT will not always be as straightforward as that, but they will be simple. The following example demonstrates how the mean might be used to solve a problem. Give it a try and check the solution/explanation to see if you solved it the same way.

> **REMEMBER**
>
> *Mean* is the total value of a data set divided by the number of data in the set (the average).

Practice Question

Julia went to Cancun during summer vacation. She recorded the number of pesos she spent on the first five days of her trip in the table below. How many pesos did she spend on the sixth day to make the mean expenditure per day (for six days) 220?

July	1	2	3	4	5	6
Pesos spent	250	100	150	100	400	?

F. 120
G. 200
H. 220
J. 320
K. 1000

Solution/Explanation

(J) The answer to this problem is 320. In order for the mean of six pieces of data to be 220, the sum of the data must be equal to 6(220) or 1320. If you subtract the sum of the pesos spent over the first five days (1000) from 1320, you have 320 left, which must have been spent on day 6.

Median

The median of a set of data is the value of the piece of data that is in the middle when all data are listed in increasing or decreasing order. This is considered one of the measures of central tendency, along with mode and mean. In order to find it, you must first list the numbers (data) in numerical order and then locate the middle value by counting the total number of data (how many there are). When there is an odd number of data in your set, you will simply select the value in the middle

> **REMEMBER**
>
> *Median* is the middle number (or average of two middle numbers) when data are written in numerical order.

of the list (once rewritten in numerical order). When there is an even number, you will find the two values in the middle and then find the average of those two numbers. Here are two examples that demonstrate both cases.

Practice Questions

1. What is the median of the following 9 numbers?

   61, 14, 72, 25, 36, 48, 57, 17, 81
   A. 14
   B. 81
   C. 48
   D. 5
   E. 42

2. Find the median of the following set of data.

   42, 13, 76, 61, 5, 21, 13, 37
   F. 33
   G. 21
   H. 33.5
   J. 29
   K. 13

Solutions/Explanations

1. **(C)** The first step in solving this problem is to list the numbers in numerical order from least to greatest. The set would then be listed as 14, 17, 25, 36, 48, 57, 61, 72, 81. There are nine total numbers, and if you move in evenly from either side, you will end up at the fifth term, which is 48. The median of this data set is 48.

2. **(J)** Again, you will first reorder the data in numerical order from least to greatest. The set will then be written as 5, 13, 13, 21, 37, 42, 61, 76. If you move in evenly from each side, you will end up with two values, 37 and 21, in the middle. Neither of these is the median. The median is 29, which is the average of 37 and 21.

PRE-ALGEBRA TOPICS

The quickest, easiest way to solve problems in this section is to use the context rather than trying to remember formulas or procedures. You may not have practiced these skills out of context in a few years, but you still know how to do the math. You use percents when you are shopping at the mall. You use formulas and solve for variables in formulas all the time in your science classes. Finding patterns and using tables is second nature to you. So, again, do not over-think this. These problems should be as easy as they appear, and each of them should take you under 30 seconds to solve. Read about each topic, try the examples, and review the solution/explanations.

Percents

If a percent problem is completely straightforward, use your calculator and move on. However, it is likely that percent problems will not be completely straightforward and will require a working knowledge of the meaning of percents. Remember that *percent* means "per one hundred" and you can always convert the number to a fraction. For instance, 47% is the same as $\frac{47}{100}$ or 0.47 (47 hundredths). When you are finding a percent of a number you multiply. If you are not comfortable with percents, use the context and your common sense to help you. For example, if you know what 10% of a number is, you can find 1% or 5% by using a tenth or half of 10%. Take a look at the following example along with the solution/ explanation.

> **REMEMBER**
>
> *Percent* means "per one hundred."
> Example:
> $37\% = \frac{37}{100}$
> $= 0.37$

You may be given information involving percent in a table and asked to solve problems based on the values given. This is a simple case of reading a table and applying your knowledge of percent. A common example of this type of problem would be a loan chart in which varying payment schedules are listed depending on the amount borrowed and the percent of interest charged.

Practice Question

At a given lunch period, 75% of the students buying lunch selected pizza. 60% of the students who did not select pizza selected chicken nuggets. What percent of the students selected something other than pizza or chicken nuggets?
A. 0%
B. 10%
C. 15%
D. 25%
E. 40%

Solution/Explanation

(B) For this problem it is easiest to suppose that there are 100 total students. If 75% chose pizza, then 75 students chose pizza and 25%, or 25 students, did not select pizza. If 60% of the students who did not select pizza (25) selected chicken nuggets, then 40% of the 25 did not select either. 40% of 25 is equivalent to $\frac{4}{10}$ of 25, which is 10 or 10%. In this case you are finding percents of percents. Whenever possible, make the problem more concrete for yourself.

TIP

When working with percents, you may want to draw a circle or a fraction bar.

Formulas

You will see two types of formula problems on the ACT. You will be evaluating formulas, and you will solve a formula for a given variable.

Evaluating formulas is simple—you don't even have to know the formula that you are asked to evaluate. In the past, you have probably worked with geometric formulas and distance formulas. For example, you may have been given the area and width of a rectangle and asked to find the length, using the geometric formula $A = \ell w$. Using the distance formula, $d = rt$, you might be given the time and distance and asked to find the rate at which a car is traveling. No matter the formula, you will be expected to use the problem to find the values of all but one variable, substitute those values in, and solve the equation for the remaining variable.

The second type of formula problem is one in which you are simply given a formula and asked to solve for a particular variable. If you have taken chemistry or physics, you have done this before. If you have not, don't let this kind of problem intimidate you. Solving a formula for a given variable is actually easier than evaluating a formula. Again, it is not necessary to be familiar with the formula you are asked to manipulate. Simply use the same algebraic properties that you would use when solving equations for a variable. Keep things balanced and you should be fine! Here are three examples for you to work through to become more comfortable with these types of problems.

Practice Questions

1. The circumference of a circle is given by the formula $C = \pi d$ where d is the diameter of the circle. The formula for the area of a circle is $A = \pi r^2$. If the area of the circle is 9π, what is the circumference of the circle?
   A. 9π
   B. 9
   C. 6π
   D. 6
   E. 3π

2. The Pythagorean theorem is $a^2 + b^2 = c^2$. Solve for a.
   F. $a = c - b$
   G. $a = c^2 - b^2$
   H. $a = \dfrac{c^2 - b^2}{2}$
   J. $a = \sqrt{c - b}$
   K. $a = \sqrt{c^2 - b^2}$

3. The perimeter of an ellipse is found using the formula $p = \dfrac{\pi}{2}\sqrt{2(h^2 + w^2)}$. Solve this formula for w.

A. $\sqrt{\dfrac{2p^2}{\pi^2} - h^2} = w$

B. $\sqrt{\dfrac{2}{\pi^2}(p^2 - h^2)} = w$

C. $w = \dfrac{\pi}{2}\sqrt{2(h^2 + p^2)}$

D. $w = \dfrac{\pi}{2}\sqrt{2(p^2 - h^2)}$

E. $\dfrac{2p^2}{\pi^2} - h^2 = w$

Solutions/Explanations

1. **(C)** This problem is simple even though it requires more than one step. First you use the area of 9π to recognize that r^2 is equal to 9. Therefore, r is the square root of 9, which is 3. The diameter is twice the radius of 3, so the diameter is 6 and the circumference is 6π.

2. **(K)** This is a straightforward and very common problem. The solution $a = \sqrt{c^2 - b^2}$ is found by first subtracting b^2 from both sides and then taking the square root of both sides.

3. **(A)** Yes, this formula and the solutions can appear intimidating. There are exponents and radicals, and you may not even know what an ellipse is. In order to solve this problem, you will need to use multiple steps and equation-solving skills. You will square both sides, multiply by a reciprocal, subtract a value, and take the square root of both sides. Really, the process is not difficult, but you must be careful about the exponents and parentheses. Follow the process below.

First, square both sides of the equation to eliminate the radical.

$(p)^2 = \left(\dfrac{\pi}{2}\sqrt{2(h^2 + w^2)}\right)^2$ which results in $p^2 = \dfrac{\pi^2}{4} \cdot 2(h^2 + w^2)$

Simplifying this will give you $p^2 = \dfrac{\pi^2}{2} \cdot (h^2 + w^2)$. In order to isolate the parentheses you will need to multiply both sides by $\dfrac{2}{\pi^2}$.

$\left(\dfrac{2}{\pi^2}\right)p^2 = \left(\dfrac{2}{\pi^2}\right)\left(\dfrac{\pi^2}{2}(h^2 + w^2)\right)$, which results in $\dfrac{2p^2}{\pi^2} = (h^2 + w^2)$.

The next step is to subtract h^2 from both sides.

$\dfrac{2p^2}{\pi^2} - h^2 = (h^2 + w^2) - h^2$, which results in $\dfrac{2p^2}{\pi^2} - h^2 = w^2$.

TIP

When solving equations, keep things balanced. In other words, anything that you do to one side, you must do to the other side.

Now, taking the square root of each side will isolate w and therefore solve for w.

$$\sqrt{\frac{2p^2}{\pi^2} - h^2} = \sqrt{w^2}, \text{ resulting in } \sqrt{\frac{2p^2}{\pi^2} - h^2} = w$$

Factors and Multiples

On the ACT you will be asked to solve problems involving factors and multiples without those terms being used specifically. You should be able to move from a number to its factors or its multiples with ease. Check your skill with the following example.

Practice Question

> **REMEMBER**
>
> *Factors* and *multiples* are opposite terms. For example, 9 is a factor of 72, and 72 is a multiple of 9.

One light flashes green every 15 seconds and a second light flashes red every 6 seconds. If they flash together and you begin counting seconds, after how many seconds will they next flash together?

F. 75
G. 60
H. 30
J. 18
K. 15

Solution/Explanation

(H) The solution is 30 seconds. This problem involves your knowledge of multiples, yet it does not specifically ask you to find multiples. In this case, selecting the larger number and finding its multiples while checking to see if the smaller number is a factor of each multiple is the quickest way to solve the problem. 6 is not a factor of 15, but it is a factor of 30.

> **TIP**
>
> When finding a common multiple, list the multiples of each number and find the first one they have in common.

EXPRESSIONS AND EQUATIONS

Absolute Value

The absolute value of a number is the distance the number is from zero on the number line. You may know this simply as the positive of the number. Similarly, the absolute value of an expression is the distance of the value of that expression from zero. When you are asked to work with the absolute value of an expression, treat the contents of the absolute value as a group, find the value of the contents, and then take the absolute value of that value. For instance, $|3 - 7| = |-4|$. -4 is four units from zero on the number line, which means that $|-4| = 4$. You may be given a problem like $|x - 7| = 5$ and asked to find x. In this case, you need to work backwards and understand that the contents of the absolute value symbol may be positive or negative 5 because both are 5 units away from zero. Therefore, you would need to solve for either value and report all possible solutions to the equation. In this case, you would find that $x - 7 = 5$ results in $x = 12$ and $x - 7 = -5$ results in $x = 2$. So, there are two solutions to this problem $x = 12$ or 2.

Practice Question

1. Solve $|x - 13| = 5$ for x.
   A. 18
   B. 8 or 18
   C. −18
   D. −2
   E. 8

Solution/Explanation

1. **(B)** If $|x - 13| = 5$, then $x - 13 = 5$ or $x - 13 = -5$. If $x - 13 = 5$, then $x = 18$. If $x - 13 = -5$, then $x = 8$. So the solution is $x = \{8, 18\}$.

Absolute Value Inequalities

Absolute values indicate a distance from zero. If an absolute value is less than or greater than a number, it indicates that the distance of the contents of the absolute value is less than or greater than that number. If the distance is greater than a number, then the solutions are one *or* the other, because you cannot be in both regions at the same time. If the solution is less than a number, the solutions must both be in play at the same time so you would use *and* to describe the two solutions.

Practice Question

Solve $|x - 13| > 5$ for x.
   F. 18
   G. 8 or 18
   H. $x < 8$ or $x > 18$
   J. $8 < x < 18$
   K. 8

TIP

The solution of an absolute value inequality will be between two numbers if it is < a number (indicated by **and**) and will be less than one number **or** greater than the other if the absolute value is > a number.

Solution/Explanation

(H) If $|x - 13| > 5$, then $x - 13 > 5$ or $x - 13 < -5$. If $x - 13 > 5$, then $x > 18$. If $x - 13 < -5$, then $x < 8$. So the solution is $x < 8$ **or** $x > 18$ (it cannot be both so you must use **or**).

Proportion

Proportions are simply a special kind of equation. They can help you solve problems when you have a relationship that is established and you are missing one piece of information out of four. For instance, if you know that in order to mix a fruit drink you need to use 1 cup powder for 3 cups of water, and you have 5 cups of powder available, you can determine that you need 15 cups of water. 1 is to 3 as 5 is to . . . ?

You can use a proportion to set up the equation $\frac{1}{3} = \frac{5}{x}$. You can solve this problem by multiplying both sides by $3x$ to eliminate the fractions. You would then have $x = 15$. Proportion problems will not always be this simple and may involve expressions, but the premise is the same. There will be an established relationship, you will set up a proportion, you will multiply by the denominators to eliminate fractions, and then you will solve the equation.

Practice Question

1. Gordon recently learned that his shadow is proportional to his height. He also learned that the shadows of other objects are proportional to their height. At three o'clock, his shadow measured 4 feet and the shadow of the tree in his front yard measured 18 feet. If Gordon is 6 feet tall, how tall is the tree?
    A. 108 feet
    B. 72 feet
    C. 27 feet
    D. 24 feet
    E. 9 feet

Solution/Explanation

1. **(C)** This proportion can be set up two ways. One way is $\frac{4}{18} = \frac{6}{x}$ and the other is $\frac{4}{6} = \frac{18}{x}$ or $\frac{2}{3} = \frac{18}{x}$. Either way, you may notice that the ratio of 4 to 6 is equivalent to 2 to 3. Then, using the same ratio for 18 to x, 9 goes into 18 twice and 9 times 3 is 27. You could also multiply by the denominators to find that $4x = 108$ and that $108/4 = 27$. Using the second proportion would result in the same equation.

Solving Multi-Step Linear Equations

Because you've probably had a lot of practice solving equations, it will be best to solve linear equations rather than checking the answer options. Checking the answers requires that you perform the operations multiple times (as many as it takes for you to find the correct answer). This will take more time than solving the equation once for the variable in question.

Linear equation problems will call on you to distribute, combine like terms, and use multiplication, division, addition, and subtraction to isolate the variable. When faced with a multi-step linear equation, hit autopilot and get to work without wasting time considering whether to solve or not. Solving will be the most efficient method!

Practice Question

Solve $2(4x + 7) - 3(2x - 4) = 20$ for x.

F. $\dfrac{9}{7}$

G. -3

H. 9

J. 13

K. 23

Solution/Explanation

(G) Distribute 2 and -3 through their respective parentheses to result in $8x + 14 - 6x + 12 = 20$. Then, combine like terms to result in $2x + 26 = 20$. Subtract 26 from both sides of the equation so that $2x = -6$ and divide by two on both sides to find that $x = -3$.

TIP

If an equation has fractions in it, multiply through by the least common denominator to eliminate all fractions.

Writing Linear Equations

The ACT will ask you to demonstrate your skill at writing linear equations. The most typical scenario is one in which you are given a situation and asked to depict the situation with variables in an equation. Try your hand at the following example. You may find that the context makes it easier for you to move to an equation.

Practice Problem

Josie would like to have wireless Internet in her apartment. Her phone company charges a $60 installation fee and $13.95 per month. Write an equation that will help Josie determine her cost (c) to have wireless for any given number of months (m).

A. $60 + 13.95\ m = c$

B. $13.95 + 60\ m = c$

C. $60 = 13.95\ m$

D. $c = 60 - 13.95\ m$

E. $c = 60\ m - 13.95$

Solution/Explanation

(A) The initial cost is $60, and that will be charged no matter how many months Josie has wireless Internet in her apartment. The monthly cost of $13.95 needs to be multiplied by the number of months that Josie has service. So, the total cost equals 13.95 m + 60.

Linear Equations: Special Cases

TIP

Use *x* as your variable and define all other variables in terms of *x*.

There will be problems that ask you to represent one value in terms of another in order to reduce the equation to two variables. For instance, there are times when you will be asked to work with consecutive integers or consecutive odd integers or consecutive even integers. In these cases, you name the first integer x and write the second integer in terms of the first: $x + 1$ in the case of consecutive integers and $x + 2$ in the case of consecutive even or odd integers.

Another special case of linear equations is a problem in which you are given a table of values and asked to write a rule for the given pattern. If there is a common difference, then you may simply use your knowledge of slope intercept to determine the value of the pattern for the zero term, and use the common difference as the slope. If there is no common difference, the equation is not linear and you may want to plug values into each of the possible solutions. Be careful here because it is possible that more than one choice will work for some of the values in the table, but only one will work for all the values.

TIP

If you come across a pattern that does not have a common difference, guess and check with the solutions to determine the correct answer.

EXPONENTS/POLYNOMIALS
Multiplying Monomials

In order to multiply monomials, you must use the product property of exponents. Remember that when you multiply monomials you can combine common bases by adding their exponents. This works because $x^3 \cdot x^5 = (xxx) \cdot (xxxxx) = xxxxxxxx = x^8$. This same problem could be solved simply by adding the exponents $x^3 \cdot x^5 = x^{3+5} = x^8$. Of course, the monomials you are asked to multiply will be more complicated than these, but the premise remains the same. Give it a try here and see just how simple multiplying monomials is.

Practice Question

The product of $(3m^5n^7)(-4mn^3)$ is equivalent to:

F. $-12m^5n^{10}$
G. $-12m^4n^4$
H. $-12m^{12}n^4$
J. $-12m^5n^{21}$
K. $-12m^6n^{10}$

Solution/Explanation

(K) 3×-4 is -12, $m^5 m = m^6$, and $n^7 n^3 = n^{10}$. So, the product of $(3m^5n^7)$ $(-4mn^3)$ is equivalent to $-12m^6n^{10}$.

TIP

When multiplying common bases, remember the product property: $x^a \times x^b = x^{a+b}$. For example, $x^3 \times x^5 = x^{3+5} = x^8$.

Adding Polynomials

Adding polynomials is as easy as combining like terms. Be careful that the terms are in fact alike and that you keep track of the signs of the coefficients. Feel free to write in the ACT problem book and cross off the terms that you have added so that you do not forget any. Also, writing the solutions in decreasing order will help you keep track of your work and make it easier to match your solution to the solution choices given. You may not have to work through the entire problem if you keep track of your answer's similarity to the choices given.

Practice Question

What polynomial must be added to $7x^2 + 14x - 8$ to result in a sum of $5x^2 + 18x + 1$?
A. $-2x^2 - 4x + 7$
B. $2x^2 - 4x + 9$
C. $-2x^2 + 4x + 9$
D. $-2x^2 + 4x + 7$
E. $2x^2 + 4x + 9$

Solution/Explanation

(C) In order to get from $7x^2$ to $5x^2$, you would need to add $-2x^2$, to get from $14x$ to $18x$, you would need to add $4x$, and to get from -8 to 1 you would need to add 9. Therefore, the polynomial you would need to add to $7x^2 + 14x - 8$ to result in a sum of $5x^2 + 18x + 1$ would be $-2x^2 + 4x + 9$.

TIP

When adding polynomials, pay close attention to the signs of the coefficients.

Distributing

Distributing is a skill that you use all the time. It is simply multiplying a monomial across a polynomial. In the case of multiplying two binomials, you take one monomial at a time and multiply it across the second binomial. This is often called FOIL (first, outer, inner, last). Also, multiplying two polynomials together requires taking each monomial from the first polynomial and multiplying it across the second polynomial. Be careful to watch the signs when distributing and to combine all like terms once you have performed the multiplication. Again, because this skill is probably such a natural process for you, it is most efficient to perform the distribution rather than look for a shortcut to the solution.

Practice Question

Which is the equivalent form of $(x - 3)(x^2 + 4x - 8)$?

F. $x^3 + x^2 - 20x + 24$
G. $x^3 + 7x^2 + 4x - 24$
H. $x^3 + 7x^2 + 20x - 24$
J. $x^3 + x^2 - 12x + 24$
K. $x^3 + x^2 + 4x + 24$

TIP

When multiplying a term from the first polynomial, be sure to take the sign of the coefficient as part of the term.

Solution/Explanation

(F) First multiply x through $(x^2 + 4x - 8)$ so that you are simply looking at $x(x^2 + 4x - 8) = x^3 + 4x^2 - 8x$. Then multiply -3 through $(x^2 + 4x - 8)$ so that you are simply looking at $-3(x^2 + 4x - 8) = -3x^2 - 12x + 24$ and then add your like terms. You have $x^3 + 4x^2 - 8x - 3x^2 - 12x + 24 = x^3 + x^2 - 20x + 24$.

REMEMBER

Factoring helps you find the expressions that can be multiplied together to equal the polynomial.

FACTORING POLYNOMIALS

Although you learned factoring in your first algebra class, you were most likely in your second algebra class before the procedure made sense. The elementary algebra problems on the ACT will ask you to factor quadratics that are relatively simple. That is to say, the leading coefficient is either 1 or a prime number. You may need to factor out a common term to notice the leading coefficient to be 1 or a prime number. For problems that have composite leading coefficients, you will find other strategies for factoring in the next chapter. Here, we will concentrate on simple factoring. Two types of problems that require factoring are those involving rational expressions and those involving quadratic equations.

To achieve a perfect score on the ACT, you must be able to factor quickly and correctly. You will need to call on this skill to aid you in solving more complex problems. In this chapter, however, the factoring will not be complex or difficult.

Simple Factoring

Let's review simple factoring! First, factor out a common term if possible. You ought to be left with a leading coefficient of either 1 or a prime number. Next, write two parentheses and place a binomial in each.

Given the expression $ax^2 + bx + c$ where a is equal to one, start filling in your factors with $(x_____)(x_____)$. Then consider two numbers whose product is c and whose sum is b (keeping the signs in mind). If c is negative, the two factors will have opposite signs; when you add the numbers together you will be adding a positive number and a negative number. If c is positive, the two factors will have the same sign (it may be positive or negative). When you add them together, you will find the sum of the numbers and keep the sign (watch the sign of b to determine the sign of the factors).

Here is an example to illustrate the concept. Give it a try.

Practice Question

Which of the following is the factored form of $x^2 - 7x + 10$?
A. $(x - 7)(x - 3)$
B. $(x + 4)(x + 3)$
C. $(x - 4)(x - 3)$
D. $(x - 5)(x - 2)$
E. $(x + 5)(x + 2)$

Solution/Explanation

(D) In this case, the leading coefficient is 1. You simply need to identify two factors of 10 whose sum is −7. The factors are −5 and −2. The factored form is $(x - 5)(x - 2)$.

Factoring with Prime Numbers

Now, let's review what this process will be like if *a* is a prime number. The factors will start out with $(ax_____)(x_____)$. This time, you will multiply *a* by *c* and determine which factors you are looking for. Find two factors of *ac* that add up to *b*. Then, work on the placement of factors of *c* (one will be multiplied by *a* and one will be multiplied by 1, and the resulting numbers will be added to equal *b*) so that the correct factors of *ac* add up to *b*. Try the following example. You will absolutely need to be able to factor expressions when simplifying rational expressions in the next chapter.

Practice Question

Which of the following is the factored form of the expression $3x^2 + 5x - 12$?
F. $(3x - 4)(x + 3)$
G. $(3x + 4)(x - 3)$
H. $(3x - 6)(x + 2)$
J. $(3x + 6)(x - 2)$
K. $(x - 4)(3x + 3)$

Solution/Explanation

(F) The leading coefficient is not equal to 1 and it is prime, so the first step is to establish that the factors will begin with $(3x_____)(x_____)$. Now, two factors of −36 whose sum is 5 are 9 and −4. You know that the two numbers placed in the parentheses must have a product of 12 and that you need your middle terms to be 9x and −4x to give you a sum of 5x. Using 3 and −4 as the

TIP

The ability to factor equations is essential to obtaining a perfect score.

factors of -12 and placing the 3 in the position that will be multiplied by the 3 in the first spot will give you 9. Placing these factors into the product of the binomials results in $(3x - 4)(x + 3)$. If you were to distribute this to check it, you would get $3x^2 + 9x - 4x - 12 = 3x^2 + 5x - 12$. Notice that the middle terms are $9x$ and $-4x$, which match the factors of $-36x$ and whose sum is $5x$.

Solving Quadratics

Once you have a quadratic equation set equal to zero and factored, the solution is simple. Problems that are categorized as elementary algebra will be in factored form already. For problems that are not yet factored, we will review strategies for solving non-linear equations in the next chapter. For now, let's review how to solve a factored equation that equals zero. Simply use the zero property of multiplication, which states that if the product of two or more terms equals zero then one or more of those terms must equal zero. If $x \times y \times z = 0$ then either x and/or y and/or z equal zero. So, when you have $(x - 7)(x + 4) = 0$ you know that either $x - 7 = 0$ (in which case $x = 7$) and/or $x + 4 = 0$ (in which case $x = -4$). The solution to the equation $(x - 7)(x + 4) = 0$ is $x = \{-4, 7\}$.

Practice Question

Which of the following is not a solution of $3(x - 8)(x - 3)(x + 4)(x + 7) = 0$?
F. -4
G. 0
H. 3
J. 8
K. -7

Solution/Explanation

(G) Since the equation is in factored form, you simply set each factor equal to zero and find the value of x that would make it true. $3 = 0$ cannot be true for any x. $x - 8 = 0$ is true when $x = 8$, $x - 3 = 0$ is true when $x = 3$, $x + 4 = 0$ is true when $x = -4$, and $x + 7 = 0$ is true when $x = -7$. So, the solutions are $x = \{8, 3, -4, -7\}$. 0 is not a solution of this equation.

Practice Set: Elementary Algebra

The following problems are all typical of the 24 elementary algebra problems on the ACT. These types of problems will occur most frequently at the beginning of the test, and some will be mixed in throughout the test. While practicing, challenge yourself to complete each problem in 30 seconds or less. Time yourself on the following 12 questions, and attempt to complete them in 6 minutes or less.

In the directions on the exam, you will be told to choose the correct answer and fill in the corresponding oval on the answer sheet. You will be reminded not to linger on problems that you are struggling to solve. In order to recognize when you are lingering, practice in a timed setting. You will be reminded that you are allowed to use a calculator on any problems but that it may not be the best choice every time. The directions will include a few final clarifying points, and then you will start the test.

You are not required to do the problems in any particular order. Moving through the test in chronological order will present you with a higher concentration of elementary algebra problems at the beginning, allowing you to move through the first part quickly and then take more time per problem as you continue through the test.

The directions and the test questions will be separated by a line across the page.

TIP

Don't linger over any one problem. Move on, then come back to it if you have time.

---

1. To increase the mean of 8 numbers by 5, by how much would the sum of the 8 numbers need to increase?
   A. 5
   B. 10
   C. 20
   D. 40
   E. 80

2. When $\frac{1}{7}n + 3 = \frac{-1}{5}(n - 20)$, what is the value of n?
   F. $\frac{1}{12}$
   G. $\frac{35}{12}$
   H. $\frac{12}{35}$
   J. 12
   K. 35

3. Cathy has a coupon for 10% off at her favorite CD store. When she arrives at the store she finds that the CDs are already on sale for 25% off. She would like to put an equation into her calculator to determine the cost of a CD after the 25% and additional 10% discounts. Using p for the original marked price, which of the following expressions will give her the discounted price?
   A. $p - .35p$
   B. $p - .35$
   C. $p - .325p$
   D. $p - .325$
   E. $p - .10p$

4. For all x, $(2x + 5)^2(-3x + 7) = ?$
   F. $-12x^2 + 70$
   G. $-6x^2 - x + 35$
   H. $4x^2 + 20x + 25$
   J. $4x^2 + 17x + 32$
   K. $-12x^3 - 32x^2 + 65x + 175$

5. The Key Club at the local high school is sponsoring an Easter egg hunt at the park. 250 children register for the hunt. The Key Club members decide that it is more fair if they separate the children into age groups. The children are divided into four age categories, as shown in the following table.

Age category	Under 2	2–5	6–10	Over 10
Number of children	25	53	125	47

70 eggs that have special prizes in them will be distributed proportionally to each age category. How many prizes will the club members award to the children in the 6–10 age range?

A. 18
B. 27
C. 32
D. 35
E. 53

6. The number 0.07 is 1000 times as large as which of the following numbers?

F. 0.7
G. 0.07
H. 0.007
J. 0.0007
K. 0.00007

7. Which of the following is equal to $\dfrac{\frac{3}{4}-\frac{1}{3}}{\frac{3}{4}+\frac{1}{3}}$?

A. $\dfrac{5}{12}$

B. $\dfrac{-5}{12}$

C. $\dfrac{-5}{13}$

D. $\dfrac{5}{13}$

E. $\dfrac{13}{5}$

8. Find the simplified form of $\dfrac{-10x^2 - 35x + 20}{3x^2 + 12x}$.

F. $\dfrac{-5(2x-1)}{3x}$

G. $\dfrac{-5}{3}$

H. $\dfrac{-5(2x^2 + 7x + 4)}{3x^2 + 12x}$

J. $-7x^2 - 23x + 20$

K. $\dfrac{-10}{3} - \dfrac{35}{12} + 20$

9. If $8 - 5x = -47$, then $2x = $?

A. 7.8
B. 15.6
C. 11
D. –11
E. 22

10. The formula $d = rt$ is called the distance formula. In this formula, d represents the distance traveled, r represents the rate of speed, and t represents the time traveled. If a person travels 90 miles in $2\frac{1}{2}$ hours, what is the value of r?

F. 36 mph
G. 45 mph
H. 72 mph
J. 180 mph
K. 225 mph

11. The product of $(-4x^6 y^7)(-2xy^3)$ is:

A. $8x^7 y^{10}$
B. $8x^6 y^{10}$
C. $8x^6 y^{21}$
D. $8x^7 y^{21}$
E. $-8x^6 y^{10}$

12. A bag contains 4 red gumballs, 7 green gumballs, 2 white gumballs, and 5 blue gumballs. How many additional white gumballs must be added to the 18 gumballs in the bag so that the probability of drawing a gumball that is not white is $\frac{2}{3}$?

F. 3
G. 4
H. 5
J. 6
K. 7

Solutions and Explanations

1. **(D)**
The sum of the 8 numbers would need to increase by 5 for each number, so multiply 5 by 8 to get 40.

2. **(G)**
Multiplying $\frac{1}{7}n + 3 = \frac{-1}{5}(n - 20)$ by 35 simplifies to $5n + 105 = -7(n - 20)$, which simplifies to $5n + 105 = -7n + 140$, which simplifies to $12n = 35$, which means that n must equal $\frac{35}{12}$.

3. **(C)**
A discount of 25% would leave 75% of the cost. Taking an additional 10% off the 75% remaining is equivalent to an additional 7.5% off the original price (10% of 75 is 7.5). 25% + 7.5% = 32.5% total discount. The original price minus 32.5% of the original price is the discounted price. 32.5% is equivalent to $\frac{32.5}{100} = 0.325$.

4. **(K)**
On the actual test, if you recognize that the answer should include a cubic, select the answer without solving. If you did not already solve it, solve it now and review the given solution.

$(2x + 5)^2(-3x + 7) = (4x^2 + 20x + 25)(-3x + 7) = -12x^3 - 60x^2 - 75x + 28x^2 + 140x + 175 = -12x^3 - 32x^2 + 65x + 175$

5. **(D)**
125 children in the 6–10 age group is $\frac{1}{2}$ of the 250 total runners. 35 prizes is half of the total of 70 prizes. Setting this up as a proportion would give you $\frac{125}{250} = \frac{x}{70}$ or $\frac{1}{2} = \frac{x}{70}$, which means that $x = 35$.

6. **(K)**
0.07/1000 = 0.00007

7. **(D)**
$$\frac{\frac{3}{4} - \frac{1}{3}}{\frac{3}{4} + \frac{1}{3}} = \frac{\frac{5}{12}}{\frac{13}{12}} = \frac{5}{12} \times \frac{12}{13} = \frac{5}{13}$$
Alternately, this can be solved by multiplying both the numerator and denominator by 12 as a first step.
$$\frac{12\left(\frac{3}{4} - \frac{1}{3}\right)}{12\left(\frac{3}{4} + \frac{1}{3}\right)} = \frac{9 - 4}{9 + 4} = \frac{5}{13}$$

8. **(F)**
$$\frac{-10x^2 - 35x + 20}{3x^2 + 12x} = \frac{-5(2x^2 + 7x - 4)}{3x(x + 4)}$$
$$= \frac{-5(2x - 1)(x + 4)}{3x(x + 4)}$$
$$= \frac{-5(2x - 1)}{3x}$$

9. **(E)**

$$8 - 5x = -47$$

$$-5x = -55$$

$$x = 11 \quad \text{so, } 2x = 22$$

10. **(F)**

$$d = rt$$

$$90 = r(2.5)$$

$$\frac{90}{2.5} = r$$

$$36 \text{ mph} = r$$

11. **(A)**

$$(-4x^6y^7)(-2xy^3) = -4(-2)x^{6+1}y^{7+3} = 8x^7y^{10}$$

12. **(J)**

There are 16 gumballs that are not white out of 18 total gumballs. 16 out of 24 would give you 2/3 probability of selecting a gumball that is not white. $18 + 6 = 24$, so you would need to increase the number of white gumballs by 6.

CHAPTER 9

Intermediate Algebra/ Coordinate Geometry

- Sequences and series
- Combinations and permutations
- Matrices
- Rational expressions and functions
- Conic sections

The questions in this category come from your Algebra 2 coursework (coordinate geometry is another way to say "graphing"). This category of questions will make up a subscore and will consist of 18 out of the 60 total questions (each topic will have 9 problems). These questions will be sprinkled in with the elementary algebra in the beginning of the test and show up with greater regularity as you move through the test.

If you have done well with the elementary algebra portion and averaged 30 seconds per question, you will have earned yourself 80 seconds for each question in this section. Some of the questions will be very easy and simply require that you find the slope or translate points. Others will be more difficult, requiring more thought and problem-solving skill. This is where you will have to decide whether a problem is best solved by graphing calculator, by hand, or if you should use another strategy for determining the solution more quickly. The key is to solve the easy problems and to use other strategies to determine solutions for the more difficult ones.

> ### INSIDE THE ACT 3G MIND
>
> The graphing calculator will come in handy for both coordinate geometry and intermediate algebra problems.

WHAT TO EXPECT

Coordinate geometry is simply another way of saying "graphing." Some of the problems in this section will be solved quickly and easily. These kinds of questions may simply ask you to translate points on the coordinate plane or to identify an even or odd function. In either of those cases, you will be able to select the answer from the choices quickly. Other problems will be more complicated, and it will take less time for you to solve them another way. In the case of more difficult problems, your deep understanding of the topic is what will make it possible for you to obtain a perfect score on the ACT mathematics section.

Intermediate algebra is generally all of the solving you have learned to do. The equations will include composite functions and rational expressions and converting from logarithmic to exponential, among other topics. All of these are topics you know well and you will excel at if you keep the time limit in mind.

Conic sections is a topic that you learned in Algebra 2 and is considered coordinate geometry, but you may not have spent much time on it in your class. If you are not comfortable with this topic, please see the fourth chapter of this section for an overview of conic sections. Once you have the basics down, you will be able to use your extensive knowledge of solving and graphing functions to solve problems involving conics.

This category has 18 problems, and they will be mixed throughout the exam with a heavier concentration in the latter part of the exam. Keep in mind that these problems should be solved in an average of 80 seconds each (give or take). When working through this chapter, try the examples on your own before reading the solution/explanation.

Let's start with the topics that may be a little less familiar, then go into the areas that you know better, and finish up with conic sections. Remember: There will only be nine questions from intermediate algebra on the ACT, so you will not necessarily see questions on each of the topics listed below. If you want a perfect score, however, you will need to be prepared for anything.

SEQUENCE AND SERIES

A sequence is simply an ordered list of numbers. A series is the sum of a given number of terms in a sequence.

TIP

A sequence can be arithmetic or geometric. An arithmetic sequence has a common difference between terms and is linear. A geometric sequence has a common ratio between terms and is exponential.

Arithmetic Sequence and Series

An arithmetic sequence has a common difference and is linear. It can be represented with your typical linear equation where y is the value of each term, m is the common difference (constant rate of change), x is the number of terms minus 1, and b is the value of the first term. For instance, if the sequence is 5, 9, 13, 17, 21, etc., then you can represent any term by the equation $y = 4x + 5$ where x is the number of terms minus 1. This is written in terms of sequence by using the explicit formula $a_n = a_1 + (n - 1)d$, where d is the common difference, n is the number of terms, and a_1 is the first term in the sequence. With this formula you can find the value of any variable in the formula given the values of the other variables. You may be asked to find the first term given the nth term, the common difference, and the value of n. Similarly, you may be given all but the common difference and asked to find that. Memorize this formula and you will be able to answer any arithmetic sequence problem quickly.

> ### ARITHMETIC SEQUENCE FORMULA
> $a_n = a_1 + (n - 1)d$, where d is the common difference, n is the number of terms, and a_1 is the first term in the sequence.

A series is the expression for the sum of a finite sequence (a set number of terms). For instance, given the finite sequence 5, 8, 11, 14, 17, 20 the corresponding series would be 5 + 8 + 11 + 14 + 17 + 20 with a value of 75. The sum of a finite sequence can be found using the formula $S_n = \dfrac{n}{2}(a_1 + a_n)$ where a_1 is the first term, a_n is the nth term, and n is the number of terms in the sequence. To use this formula you simply need to be given or to determine the values of the first and last terms in the sequence. You may need to use the formula given above for an arithmetic sequence in order to find the information necessary to determine the arithmetic series.

> ### ARITHMETIC SERIES FORMULA
> $S_n = \dfrac{n}{2}(a_1 + a_n)$, where a_1 is the first term, a_n is the nth term, and n is the number of terms in the sequence.

To solve the following problem, you will need to use the series formula to determine n and then use the sequence formula to determine d.

Practice Question

If the first term in an arithmetic series is 3 and the last term is 136, and the sum is 1390, what are the first four terms?

Solution/Explanation

$1390 = \dfrac{n}{2}(3 + 136)$, so $\dfrac{n}{2} = \dfrac{1390}{139} = 10$, which means that $n = 20$. Given that $n = 20$, and the first and last terms are 3 and 36, you can use the sequence formula to determine d. $136 = 3 + 19d$ or $133 = 19d$ or $7 = d$. This means that the first four terms are 3, 10, 17, and 24.

   As long as you know your formulas, problems like this one should not be too difficult for you.

TIP

Memorize the formulas listed throughout the mathematics section of this book!

Geometric Sequence and Series

A geometric sequence is exponential and can be recognized by the fact that it is non-linear. Upon more careful inspection, you will also notice a common ratio between terms in the sequence. Keep in mind: the *ratio* must be common. If a pattern does not have a common difference or a common ratio, it is simply a pattern and is not an arithmetic or a geometric sequence.

Examples of a geometric sequence: 4, 12, 36, 108 . . . or 100, 20, 4, 0.8 . . . Notice that it does not have to be increasing.

Similar to an arithmetic sequence or series, there are formulas for determining a given term in a geometric sequence and for determining a value of a geometric series. It is less likely that you will encounter a geometric series question on the ACT, but you should memorize the formula just in case you do. In the formulas for geometric sequence and series, r stands for the common ratio. In the two examples above, $r = 3$ for the first sequence and $r = 1/5$ for the second sequence.

> ### GEOMETRIC SEQUENCE FORMULA
> $a_n = a_1 \times r^{n-1}$, where r is the common ratio, n is the number term, a_n is the nth term in the sequence, and a_1 is the first term in the sequence.

You will want to be familiar with the sequence formula and the series formula.

> ### GEOMETRIC SERIES FORMULA
> $S_n = \dfrac{a_1(1 - r^n)}{1 - r}$, where r is the common ratio, n is the number term, and a_1 is the first term in the sequence.

COMBINATIONS AND PERMUTATIONS

Combinations and permutations are methods for determining the number of ways that different items can be grouped together. The main difference between the two is whether order matters or not. A great way to remember the difference between combinations and permutations is to think of the difference between ice cream scoops served in a bowl and ice cream served on a cone. If you have 10 flavors to choose from and you select 3 scoops to be served in a bowl, you could find the number of different combinations of the choices. If you were going to serve the scoops on a cone then the order would matter and you would find the number of different permutations of choices. Simply put, there are more permutations than combinations.

Combinations (Order Does Not Matter)

TIP

Once you know whether the problem places significance on the order of the results or not, your calculator can do the rest. Use MATH, then PRB to find the formula.

In the case of combinations, you have a number of something and you want to know the number of ways that you can select some of that whole set. You will use the formula $_nC_r = \dfrac{n!}{r!(n-r)!}$ for $0 \le r \le n$. In this formula, n is the total number of choices and r is the number you are selecting from that total. You will not be told whether a problem is a combination problem or a permutation problem so you will have to recognize it as such.

Here's an example of a combination problem: There are 15 children in a class and 5 will be selected to perform classroom jobs this week. How many different ways can the children be chosen?

$$_{15}C_5 = \frac{15!}{5!(15-5)!} = \frac{15 \cdot 14 \cdot 13 \cdot 12 \cdot 11 \cdot 10 \cdot 9 \cdot 8 \cdot 7 \cdot 6 \cdot 5 \cdot 4 \cdot 3 \cdot 2 \cdot 1}{5 \cdot 4 \cdot 3 \cdot 2 \cdot 1 \cdot 10 \cdot 9 \cdot 8 \cdot 7 \cdot 6 \cdot 5 \cdot 4 \cdot 3 \cdot 2 \cdot 1}$$

$$= \frac{15 \cdot 14 \cdot 13 \cdot 12 \cdot 11}{5 \cdot 4 \cdot 3 \cdot 2 \cdot 1} = 3003$$

This calculation can be done simply on your graphing calculator. Type 15, then press MATH, select PRB, 3: $_nC_r$, then type 5 and ENTER to receive the same result of 3003.

> ### COMBINATION FORMULA
>
> $$_nC_r = \frac{n!}{r!(n-r)!} \text{ for } 0 \le r \le n.$$

Permutations (Order Does Matter)

In the case of permutations, order does matter and the calculation is a little different. It still involves factorials ($n!$) and division, and it can still be done quite simply on the calculator. For permutations the formula is $_nP_r = \dfrac{n!}{(n-r)!}$ for $0 \le r \le n$.

Again, n is the total number of choices and r is the number that you are selecting from that total. For an example of where order matters, let's use a horse race. There are 10 horses running and you need to determine the number of ways that 1st, 2nd, and 3rd place can be arranged. Whenever order matters, the calculation is a permutation and not a combination.

$$_{15}P_3 = \frac{10!}{(10-3)!} = \frac{10 \cdot 9 \cdot 8 \cdot 7 \cdot 6 \cdot 5 \cdot 4 \cdot 3 \cdot 2 \cdot 1}{7 \cdot 6 \cdot 5 \cdot 4 \cdot 3 \cdot 2 \cdot 1} = 10 \cdot 9 \cdot 8 = 720$$

You will find the same result by using your graphing calculator. Type 10, then MATH, select PRB, select 4: $_nP_r$, then type 3 and ENTER.

> ### PERMUTATION FORMULA
>
> $$_nP_r = \frac{n!}{(n-r)!} \text{ for } 0 \le r \le n.$$

MATRICES

A matrix is an array of numbers. A matrix is described by its dimensions by stating the number of rows by the number of columns. Addition, subtraction, and scalar multiplication can be performed on matrices. Matrices can also be cross multiplied.

TIP

Unless you are very comfortable with matrices and your graphing calculator, don't use them to perform geometric transformations or to solve systems of equations.

On the ACT, matrices can be used to solve a system of equations. They can also be used to determine coordinates of a geometric figure following a transformation.

If you are very comfortable with matrices and like to use them for geometric transformations and/or solving equations, go for it. If you are not comfortable with them and cannot use your calculator to solve them quickly don't try it. Use other, more familiar strategies for performing geometric transformations and/or solving systems.

You should review basic operations involving matrices in case you run into a problem on the ACT. It pays to be prepared.

Adding and subtracting matrices can be done with like-dimensioned matrices. You simply add or subtract corresponding elements (elements in the same position as each other).

For example:

$$\begin{bmatrix} 5 & 7 & -3 \\ 2 & -1 & 4 \\ 1 & 3 & -2 \end{bmatrix} + \begin{bmatrix} 6 & -2 & -1 \\ -2 & 3 & 5 \\ -6 & 2 & 2 \end{bmatrix} = \begin{bmatrix} 11 & 5 & -4 \\ 0 & 2 & 9 \\ -5 & 5 & 0 \end{bmatrix}$$

or

$$\begin{bmatrix} 5 & 7 & -3 \\ 2 & -1 & 4 \\ 1 & 3 & -2 \end{bmatrix} - \begin{bmatrix} 6 & -2 & -1 \\ -2 & 3 & 5 \\ -6 & 2 & 2 \end{bmatrix} = \begin{bmatrix} -1 & 9 & -2 \\ 4 & -4 & -1 \\ 7 & 1 & -4 \end{bmatrix}$$

Scalar multiplication is when a constant is multiplied by a matrix. In this case, the constant is multiplied by each element and the resulting matrix has the same dimensions as the original matrix.

For example:

$$3\begin{bmatrix} -2 & 5 \\ -3 & -1 \end{bmatrix} = \begin{bmatrix} -6 & 15 \\ -9 & -3 \end{bmatrix} \quad \text{or} \quad -2\begin{bmatrix} 3 \\ -1 \\ 2 \end{bmatrix} = \begin{bmatrix} -6 \\ 2 \\ -4 \end{bmatrix}$$

TIP

Operations on matrices are most efficiently done in your head.

These operations are most quickly done by hand even though they can also be done using a graphing calculator. If you have a problem with addition, subtraction, or scalar multiplication of matrices, examine the problem and perform the operation in your head as you look for the answer among the answer choices.

RATIONAL EXPRESSIONS AND FUNCTIONS

A rational expression is simply a fraction involving variables. In order to simplify it, you will need to remember your rules of exponents. You will also need to factor quadratics and simply factor common terms out.

RULES OF EXPONENTS

Product Rule $x^m \cdot x^n = x^{m+n}$

Quotient Rule $\dfrac{x^m}{x^n} = x^{m-n}$

Power Rule $(x^m)^n = x^{mn}$

For example, $\dfrac{2x^4 y^3}{3x^9} \cdot \dfrac{-9x^2}{5y} = \dfrac{-6y^2}{5x^3}$

Most often with rational expressions, the problem will involve polynomials, which must be factored in order to be simplified.

For example, $\dfrac{x^4}{x^2 + 2x + 1} \Big/ \dfrac{5x^2}{x^2 - 1} = \dfrac{x^4}{(x+1)(x+1)} \cdot \dfrac{(x+1)(x-1)}{5x^2} = \dfrac{x^2(x-1)}{5(x+1)}$

A function is rational when the simplified form contains a variable in the denominator. What makes these functions unique is the fact that there are values of x for which the function is undefined. Any value of x that would make the denominator of the simplified form equal to zero is undefined and will show up on the graph as an asymptote. Knowing where that will occur is an excellent way to narrow your solution choices. In order to determine this you must simplify the rational function using factoring. A much faster way is to graph the function on your calculator and play with your window until you can match the given function to the solution choice. If the value of x would make both the denominator and the numerator zero, it will show up as a hole in the graph rather than an asymptote.

LOGARITHMIC AND EXPONENTIAL FUNCTIONS

Logarithmic and exponential functions are inverses of each other. Be sure that you commit the properties of both to memory. Many problems involving these functions can be solved by converting to the opposite function and using the properties of both.

Converting Between Logarithmic and Exponential Functions

On the ACT, the most likely use of either exponential equations or logarithmic equations will be in solving an equation involving the opposite function. For instance, if you are solving an exponential equation in which the variable is in the exponent, you will use logs to bring it down. If you are solving a logarithmic equation in which x cannot be isolated, you will use an exponential function to solve.

> If $y = b^x$, then $\log_b y = x$ and vice versa.

Logarithmic Functions

Three things to have in your toolbox when working with logarithms are the conversion from logarithmic to exponential, the properties of logarithms, and the change of base formula.

Regardless of the base you are working in, you can use the properties of logarithms to simplify an equation or expression.

> **PROPERTIES OF LOGARITHMS**
>
> Product Property $\log_b MN = \log_b M + \log_b N$
>
> Quotient Property $\log_b \dfrac{M}{N} = \log_b M - \log_b N$
>
> Power Property $\log_b M^x = x\log_b M$

 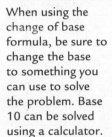

TIP

When using the change of base formula, be sure to change the base to something you can use to solve the problem. Base 10 can be solved using a calculator.

When you are dealing with a logarithmic equation that is neither common nor natural, you will simplify it and then either convert it to an exponential equation to solve for *x* or use the change of base formula to convert it to a common logarithm, which can be solved on your calculator.

> **CHANGE OF BASE FORMULA**
>
> $$\log_b M = \frac{\log_c M}{\log_c b}$$
>
> (This formula will convert from any base to any base.)

Exponential Functions

An exponential function has the variable in the exponent. The graph of the function increases or decreases exponentially and cannot cross the *x* axis since there is no value of *x* that will make the function equal 0. You can solve an exponential equation by expressing both sides of the equation in the same base so that the exponents can be set equal and you can solve for the variable.

When you cannot express each side of the equation in terms of an equivalent base, use logarithms to solve the equation. Exponential and logarithmic functions are inverses of each other. One can be used to undo the other and vice versa. Also the graphs are inverses of each other. If you can convert from exponential to logarithmic, you can use logs to solve exponential equations.

TIP

If you can express both sides of the equation using the same base, the exponents can be set equal to each other. *bx = by* means that *x = y*.

> If $y = b^x$, then $\log_b y = x$ and vice versa.

You can use your graphing calculator to graph both exponential and logarithmic functions. Be sure to mind your window. Remember that finding an *x* for a given value of the function simply means determining the *x* value that corresponds to the given *y*. You can do this using the TRACE key and tracing the graph of the function to the given *y*. This may be quicker than solving the equation, assuming the equation is already written in *y =* or *f(x) =* form.

GRAPHING LINEAR FUNCTIONS AND INEQUALITIES

You can graph a line or an inequality using your graphing calculator. However, this may not always be the fastest way to solve the problem. If the equation/inequality is written in standard form ($ax + by = c$) then determine the x and y intercepts and find the corresponding graph from the answer choices. If the equation/inequality is written in slope-intercept form ($y = mx + b$) then plug it into your calculator, double-check the window settings, and graph.

SYSTEMS OF EQUATIONS AND INEQUALITIES

A system can be solved using substitution, elimination, or graphing. If you are given one equation and a value for either x or y, the fastest way to solve it is by using substitution. Simply substitute the value you are given into the equation to find the value of the other variable and find the point of intersection in the answer choices. If the equation is written in standard form, you will have to decide whether it is fastest to solve for y and use your calculator, or to use elimination to find the value of one variable and then use substitution for the second variable. If the equation is written in $y =$ form, then the graphing calculator is absolutely the fastest way to solve it. Simply plug the equations into $y =$, graph them, and calculate the intersection.

QUADRATIC FUNCTIONS

Graphing, factoring, and solving quadratic functions should be almost second nature for you. To save time on the ACT, consider the fastest way to solve a quadratic. You will have your graphing calculator for the entire test. Does it take more time to factor and solve or to graph and calculate x intercepts? In most cases, graphing is faster. In cases where the roots are irrational or imaginary, solving using the quadratic formula is fastest.

QUADRATIC FORMULA

If $ax^2 + bx + c = 0$, then $\dfrac{-b \pm \sqrt{b^2 - 4ac}}{2a}$ where $a \neq 0$

TIP

The discriminant b2 - 4ac can be used to *quickly* determine the nature of the roots of a quadratic equation.

As you know, a quadratic function may have one real solution, two real solutions, or non-real solutions. This classification can be determined quickly by using only the discriminant of the quadratic formula. If $b^2 - 4ac$ is equal to zero, there is one real solution; if it is less than zero, there are imaginary or complex solutions; and if it is positive, there are two real solutions.

FUNCTION NOTATION

$F(x) =$ is synonymous with $y =$. With function notation you may be asked to substitute for x by finding f(a given number). You may also be asked to perform operations on functions (addition, subtraction, multiplication, and division), which is as simple as having each function in parentheses and simplifying.

Composition of functions is different than operations on functions. With composition of functions, you are being asked to find f of g of x, which can be written as $f(g(x))$ or $(f \circ g)(x)$.

$$\text{Given that } f(x) = 2x^2 + 9 \text{ and } g(x) = -3x, (f \circ g)(x)$$
$$= 2(-3x)^2 + 9 = 2(9x^2) + 9 = 18x^2 + 9$$

Operations on those functions are different. $F(x) + g(x)$ is simply $2x^2 - 3x + 9$.

In most cases you will be asked to find the value of the resulting function for a given x. You should perform the operation or composition using the variables, then substitute the value of x into the resulting function.

TIP

Operations on functions can be written as $f(x) + g(x)$ or $(f + g)(x)$. The operation is the same; the notation is the only difference.

CONIC SECTIONS

Conic sections result when a plane intersects a double cone. If you slice a double cone (where the points meet in the center), you get one of four shapes: a parabola, a circle, an ellipse, or a hyperbola. You have probably worked extensively with parabolas because they are the graph of a quadratic function. If you consider the vertex form of the equation of a quadratic and all that you know about that form, you can easily transfer your knowledge to circles, ellipses, and hyperbole (plural of *hyperbola*).

PARABOLA

$$y = a(x - h)^2 + k$$

where (h,k) is the vertex and a determines the orientation and width of the resulting graph.

Use your understanding of the vertex form of a parabola to understand the vertex form of the equations for circles, ellipses, and hyperbola. In all four cases, (h,k) is an important point. In a parabola, (h,k) is the vertex. In a circle, (h,k) is the center point. In an ellipse, (h,k) is the point that is equidistant from the extremes in x and the extremes in y. In a hyperbola, (h,k) is the point that is between the two vertices of the graph.

With a quadratic equation, you can complete the square in order to write the equation in vertex form. Similarly, completing the square in both x and y will give you the standard form of the equations of a circle, an ellipse, or a hyperbola. With 60 questions in 60 minutes, you do not have time to do extensive work with each problem. In the case of conic sections, recognize which conic you are dealing with and be ready to go from an equation in standard form to a graph or vice versa. More explanation and examples of graphs are included in the final chapter of the mathematics section of this text. For now, review the standard form of each equation.

TIP

You do not have time to complete the square in both variables on this test.

CIRCLE

$$(x - h)^2 + (y - k)^2 = r^2$$

where (h,k) is the center and r is the radius of the circle.

ELLIPSE

$$\frac{(x-h)^2}{a^2} + \frac{(y-k)^2}{b^2} = 1$$

where (h,k) is the center, a is the distance from the center in x, and b is the distance from the center in y.

HYPERBOLA

$$\frac{(x-h)^2}{a^2} - \frac{(y-k)^2}{b^2} = 1$$

where (h,k) is the center, a is the distance from the center in x, and b is the distance from the center in y.

The topics in this chapter are familiar to you, and your first instinct may be to go on autopilot and solve every problem. But don't forget about your timing—80 seconds can fly by. Use your graphing calculator whenever it is quickest. The last chapter of the mathematics section will include a graphing calculator review and conic section explanation. Review these items carefully and memorize the formulas. To obtain the perfect score, timing will be everything!

Practice Set: Intermediate Algebra/Coordinate Geometry

The following problems are all typical of the 18 intermediate algebra/coordinate geometry problems on the ACT. These types of problems will be sprinkled among the beginning test questions and then make up about half of the questions toward the end of the test. While practicing, challenge yourself to complete each problem in 80 seconds or less. In order to accomplish this, you will need to make a split-second decision about your strategy and then move full-speed ahead. Time yourself on these 12 questions and attempt to complete them in 16 minutes or less.

In order to improve your time, set a timer and work through the problems in the allotted time without guessing. When the time has ended, finish the questions in an alternate color and track the amount of time you take to finish. Check your answers. The key is to establish efficiency—to choose the correct answers as quickly as possible. Guessing will not earn you a perfect score.

The directions and the test questions on the exam will be separated by a line across the page.

---

1. What is the real value of x in the equation,
   $\log_2 80 - \log_2 5 = \log_3 x$?
   A. 8
   B. 48
   C. 75
   D. 64
   E. 81

2. In the standard (x,y) coordinate plane, the midpoint of $\overline{AB}$ is $(8,-5)$ and B is located at $(12,-1)$. If (x,y) are the coordinates of A, what is the value of $x + y$?
   F. -8
   G. -7
   H. -5
   J. 7
   K. 8

3. A function F is defined as follows:

   for $x > 0$, $F(x) = x^6 - x^3 - 17x - 17$

   for $x < 0$, $F(x) = -x^6 - x^3 + 17x - 17$

   What is the value of $F(-1)$?
   A. -34
   B. -2
   C. 0
   D. 2
   E. 34

4. For $i^2 = -1$, $(1 - 3i)^3 = ?$
   F. -26
   G. -8
   H. $-10 + 30i$
   J. $-26 + 18i$
   K. $10 + 18i$

5. The sum of the real numbers x and y is 17. Their difference is 3. What is the value of xy?
   A. -140
   B. -60
   C. 11
   D. 70
   E. 140

6. What are the real solutions of $2|x|^2 + 4|x| - 6 = 0$?
   F. $\{1\}$
   G. $\{-1,1\}$
   H. $\{1,-3\}$
   J. $\{1,3\}$
   K. $\{-3,3\}$

7. Tickets to the annual Follies Show at Littleton High School are $4 for adults and $2.50 for students. There is a cost of $750 to produce the show. If the x axis represents the number of adult tickets sold and the y axis represents the number of student tickets sold, which graph represents all the possible combinations of ticket sales that allow the junior class to at least cover the cost of the show?

A.

B.

C.

D.

E.

8. For all $x > 5$, $\dfrac{5x^2 - x^3}{x^2 - x - 20} = ?$

F. $\dfrac{-x^2}{x + 4}$

G. $\dfrac{x^2}{x + 4}$

H. $\dfrac{-5 + x}{20}$

J. $\dfrac{5x - x^2}{x - 19}$

K. $\dfrac{-5x + x^2}{x - 19}$

9. A circle in the standard (x,y) coordinate plane has center $(5,-3)$ and radius 4 units. Which of the following equations represents this circle?

A. $(x + 5)^2 + (y - 3)^2 = 4$
B. $(x - 5)^2 + (y + 3)^2 = 4$
C. $(x + 5)^2 + (y - 3)^2 = 8$
D. $(x - 5)^2 + (y + 3)^2 = 16$
E. $(x + 5)^2 + (y - 3)^2 = 16$

10. Consider the functions $f(x) = \sqrt{x}$ and $g(x) = x^2 - b$. In the standard (x,y) coordinate plane, $y = f(g(x))$ passes through the point $(3,5)$. What is the value of b?

F. 16
G. 4
H. -2
J. -4
K. -16

11. For what value of k does $4x^2 + kx + 25 = 0$ have exactly one real solution for x?

A. 5
B. 10
C. 15
D. 20
E. 25

12. What is the slope of the line through $(-3,7)$ and $(2,5)$ in the standard (x,y) coordinate plane?

F. $\dfrac{-5}{2}$

G. $\dfrac{-2}{5}$

H. undefined

J. $\dfrac{2}{5}$

K. $\dfrac{5}{2}$

Solutions and Explanations

1. **(E)** Given the problem $\log_2 80 - \log_2 5 = \log_3 x$, you must simplify before converting logarithmic to exponential to solve. To simplify, recall that subtraction of logs is equivalent to the log of the quotient (and vice versa). So, $\log_2 80 - \log_2 5 = \log_3 x$ is equivalent to $\log_2 \dfrac{80}{5} = \log_3 x$, which is equivalent to $\log_2 16 = \log_3 x$, which can be converted to exponential by writing $2^{\log_3 x} = 16$. Since $16 = 2^4$, you have $2^{\log_3 x} = 2^4$, which means that $\log_3 x = 4$ or $3^4 = x$, so $x = 81$.

2. **(H)** A midpoint has coordinates that are the average of the coordinates of the endpoints. For this problem, that means that $\dfrac{12 + x}{2} = 8$ and $\dfrac{-1 + y}{2} = -5$, which simplify to the point $(4,-9)$. You were not asked to find the endpoint but rather the sum of the coordinates of the endpoint, which would be $4 - 9 = -5$.

3. **(A)** Since the value of x is -1, you must substitute this value into the equation for x values < 0. When you substitute -1 in for x in the function $F(x) = -x^6 - x^3 + 17x - 17$, you have $-(-1)^6 - (-1)^3 + 17(-1) - 17$ or $-1 + 1 - 17 - 17 = -34$.

4. **(J)** In order to solve $(1 - 3i)^3 = ?$, you will need to FOIL, simplify, and then FOIL and simplify again. $(1 - 3i)(1 - 3i)(1 - 3i)$ simplifies to $(1 - 6i + 9i^2)(1 - 3i)$. Remembering that $i^2 = -1$, you know that $(1 - 6i + 9i^2)(1 - 3i) = (1 - 6i - 9)(1 - 3i) = (-8 - 6i)(1 - 3i)$, which simplifies to $-8 + 18i + 18i^2 = -8 + 18i - 18 = -26 + 18i$.

5. **(D)** This problem poses a system of the equations $x + y = 17$ and $x - y = 3$. Solving this by elimination, you find that $2x = 20$ and $x = 10$. You substitute 10 in for x in either equation to find that $y = 7$. You were asked to find the product xy, so $10 \times 7 = 70$.

6. **(G)** In order to solve this equation, you will first treat it as if the absolute value symbols are not included. For the simple quadratic $2x^2 + 4x - 6 = 0$ you will factor out 2 and factor to get $2(x - 1)(x + 3) = 0$. Solving this quadratic gives you the solutions 1 and -3. This is where the absolute value comes back into play. You have $|x| = 1$ or $|x| = -3$. Since the absolute value cannot equal a negative number, you eliminate the choice -3. Now you have $|x| = 1$, which means that $x = 1$ or $x = -1$ leaving you with the solution $\{-1,1\}$.

7. **(C)** In order to solve this problem, you must first develop the inequality $4x + 2.5y \geq 750$, then solve for y to find that $y \geq \dfrac{-8}{5}x + 300$, and then use your graphing calculator to graph the equation. Or you could simply find the x and y intercepts to be $(0,300)$ and $(187.5,0)$ and select the graph with those intercepts and the shading indicating greater than or equal to.

8. **(F)** Factor both the numerator and the denominator in order to simplify. $\dfrac{5x^2 - x^3}{x^2 - x - 20} =$ $\dfrac{x^2(5 - x)}{(x - 5)(x + 4)} = \dfrac{-x^2(x - 5)}{(x - 5)(x + 4)}$ For the last step, factoring out a negative sign helps you to see that you have $(x - 5)$ in both the numerator and the denominator. This can be simplified to $\dfrac{-x^2}{x + 4}$.

9. **(D)** For a circle with center point $(5,-3)$ and radius 4, you simply plug the corresponding values into the standard form of a circle equation $(x - h)^2 + (y - k)^2 = r^2$ where the center is (h,k) and the radius is r. Therefore, $(x - 5)^2 + (y + 3)^2 = 16$.

10. **(K)** $F(g(x)) = \sqrt{x^2 - b}$, and when the point $(3,5)$ is substituted into this equation, you have $5 = \sqrt{3^2 - b}$ or $5 = \sqrt{9 - b}$. In order to eliminate the radical, you square both sides, resulting in $25 = 9 - b$, which simplifies to $16 = -b$ or $-16 = b$.

11. **(D)** To determine the possible values for k such that the quadratic has exactly one root, you use the discriminant $b^2 - 4ac = 0$. If $\sqrt{b^2 - 4ac}$ equals zero, the solution of the quadratic will simply be $\dfrac{-b}{2a}$. In this case you have $k^2 - 4(4)(25) = 0$ or $k^2 - 400 = 0$, meaning that $k^2 = 400$ and k can equal either -20 or 20. Since only 20 is a choice, it is the value choice for which there is exactly one solution to the quadratic.

12. **(G)** $m = \dfrac{y_2 - y_1}{x_2 - x_1} = \dfrac{7 - 5}{-3 - 2} = \dfrac{2}{-5} = \dfrac{-2}{5}$

CHAPTER 10

Plane Geometry/ Trigonometry

- Angles
- Properties of circles, triangles, and quadrilaterals
- Right triangles
- Trigonometric functions

The questions in this category come from your geometry coursework as well as some Algebra 2 or trigonometry. This category of questions will make up a subscore and will consist of 18 problems (14 geometry problems and 4 trigonometry problems) out of the total 60 questions. These questions will be sprinkled in with the elementary algebra in the beginning of the test and show up with greater regularity as you move through the test.

Most of this portion of the test is based on your geometry coursework. You will be required to solve problems that involve the properties of polygons, circles and angles, transformations of shapes, area, surface area and volume, and reasoning and proof. Grouping your review of these concepts into big ideas will help you recall the many things you know well. Many of the problems in this category will involve more complex problem-solving and some thought beyond surface knowledge of properties. Review the topics and problems discussed in this chapter very carefully. Use your reasoning skills to pull your knowledge together and solve the problems as efficiently as possible.

A very small part of the overall exam (4 problems out of 36) will be based on trigonometry. This could include using trigonometry to solve right triangles, unit circle, graphs of trigonometric functions, and using trigonometric identities to solve equations involving trigonometric identities. If you have not had a full course on trigonometry, you can still work toward a perfect score on the ACT. Simply review the mini-lesson in the next chapter and try your hand at the sample problems here. You may also ask your current mathematics teacher for an overview of these topics. The key will be to know enough about the topics to use your graphing calculator and solve the problems quickly and correctly.

ANGLES AND RELATIONS AMONG PARALLEL AND PERPENDICULAR LINES

Perpendicular lines meet at a right angle, which measures 90 degrees. This fact will come up in many problems involving angles. A problem may state that the sides are perpendicular rather than indicating the angle size. Perpendicular lines tend to appear in problems involving triangles, where you will need to use either the

Pythagorean theorem or right triangle trigonometry. You will be expected to know that the height of a triangle meets the base at a right angle, the diagonals of a kite are perpendicular, and a tangent to a circle meets the radius at a right angle. These angles will be used to form right triangles that you will be asked to solve.

PYTHAGOREAN THEOREM
$$a^2 + b^2 = c^2$$

The Pythagorean theorem may be used to solve for a side length of a right triangle or to determine whether a triangle is a right triangle or not.

For example, you may be asked whether or not a triangle with side lengths 5, 8, and 11 is a right triangle.

Use the Pythagorean theorem with 5 and 8 as the lengths of the legs and 11 as the length of the hypotenuse. Since $25 + 64 \neq 121$, this is not a right triangle.

Parallel lines will come up in problems involving quadrilaterals and problems involving parallel lines cut by a transversal. Everything you know about parallels cut by a transversal can be applied to quadrilaterals involving parallel sides (or parallelograms which include rectangles, rhombi, squares, and trapezoids).

Lines *l* and *m* are parallel and lines *j* and *k* are parallel. The $m \angle 2 = 73°$, find the measure of the other 11 angles.

- Angles 2 and 6 and 2 and 10 are corresponding and therefore congruent.

- Angles 2 and 3, 6 and 7, and 10 and 11 are vertical and therefore congruent.

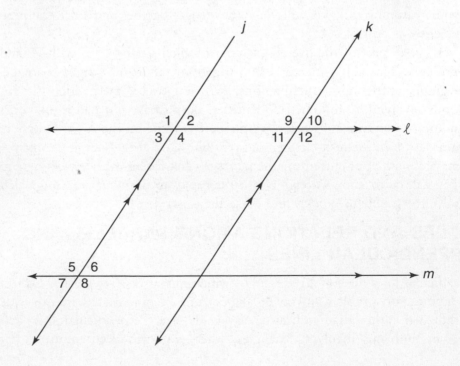

- Angles 2 and 1, 2 and 4, 6 and 5, 6 and 8, 10 and 9, and 10 and 12 are linear pairs and therefore supplementary.

The ACT may replace angle names with variable expressions, requiring you to find the value of the variable as an additional step.

TIP

Corresponding and vertical angles are congruent and linear pairs are supplementary.

PROPERTIES OF CIRCLES

Everything your teacher taught you about circles is fair game: chords, arcs, semicircles, inscribed and central angles, tangents and the angles they form with a radius.

Key things to remember:

- Central angle occurs at the center and cuts the circle at an arc whose measure is equivalent to the measure of the angle.

- An inscribed angle is half the measure of the corresponding central and arc measure.

- A line tangent to the circle will meet the radius of the circle at a 90° angle.

- The diameter is the longest chord, and it divides the circle into two semicircles.

- The area of a sector of the circle can be found by multiplying the area of the entire circle by the fraction of the circle the sector includes.

- The area of a segment of a circle can be found by determining the area of the sector and subtracting the area of the triangle.

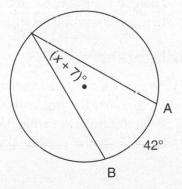

Find x.

Solution: Since the inscribed angle is half of the arc measure, $(x + 7)° = 21°$ and $x = 14°$.

SOLVING FOR ANGLES IN TWO-DIMENSIONAL SHAPES

Problems requiring you to find angle measures are assessing your knowledge of properties and theorems. You will need to call on your knowledge of linear pairs, vertical angles, exterior angles, sum of angles, and many other concepts.

For example, find the exterior angle *x* for a regular hexagon.

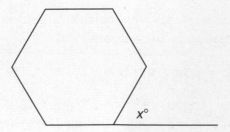

The sum of the angles in a hexagon can be found by using the formula $(n-2)180°$ where $n = 6$. $4(180°) = 720°$. Since this hexagon is regular, each interior angle is congruent and measures 120°. Angle *x* is a linear pair with an interior angle and therefore measures 60°.

Properties of Triangles

Triangle properties will come up when you are working with almost any shape, reasoning and proof, angles, circles, area, and volume. You will need to know triangle congruence in order to use the information from one triangle to find angles and side lengths in another. You will use properties of isosceles triangles to find area and perimeter of regular polygons.

The height of an isosceles or equilateral triangle can be found by using the Pythagorean theorem if you know the length of the base and the side. Triangle properties can also be used to solve problems involving a kite (the diagonals of a kite meet at a right angle). Triangle sum and the reflexive property are also key properties to keep in mind when solving problems involving triangles.

Properties of Quadrilaterals

A rectangle, square, and rhombus are special parallelograms. Recalling the properties of parallelograms and then the properties that make these quadrilaterals special will be an easy way to keep all of the information straight in your mind. Be sure to review both general trapezoids and isosceles trapezoids. Also review the properties of a kite.

When reviewing all properties, be sure to note congruence of angles, supplementary angles, properties of diagonals, and parallel sides. Knowledge of the properties of quadrilaterals will help you solve angle problems and proof problems. Triangles may be placed within a quadrilateral, and the properties of the quadrilateral will give you clues to side lengths and angle measures of the triangle. Remember that angle relationships of a set of parallel sides being crossed by a transversal apply when you have a problem involving a parallelogram.

> ## PROPERTIES OF QUADRILATERALS
>
> **Parallelogram**: opposite sides parallel and congruent
>
> **Rectangle**: a parallelogram with four 90° angles
>
> **Rhombus**: a parallelogram with four congruent sides
>
> **Square**: a parallelogram with four 90° angles and four congruent sides
>
> **Trapezoid**: exactly one set of parallel sides
>
> **Isosceles trapezoid**: one set of parallel bases and two congruent sides
>
> **Kite**: two sets of consecutive congruent sides

TRANSFORMATIONS

Transformation is the general term for translations, reflections, and rotations. All of these transformations can occur on the coordinate plane but are not restricted to it. A rotation of a two-dimensional figure may produce a three-dimensional figure.

A translation moves the figure on the coordinate plane. You will find the resulting figure by changing each coordinate by the prescribed amount. For instance, if the figure is to move right 5 and down 3, you will add 5 to the x coordinate of each vertex and subtract 3 from the y coordinate of each vertex. By plotting the new vertices and connecting them, you will have the translated figure.

A rotation moves a figure about a fixed point by a given angle. A rotation of 360 degrees will result in the original figure. A rotation of 180 degrees results in the reflection of the figure. A rotation of 20 degrees simply turns the figure about the point of rotation by 20 degrees.

A reflection results in the mirror image of the figure about a given line. To find the resulting figure you need only to imagine that the line of reflection is a mirror and either imagine or plot what the reflection would be on the opposite side of the line.

REASONING AND PROOF

When you solve problems that involve multiple steps and require you to recall properties of geometric shapes, you are using your reasoning skills. You use your reasoning skills in a more formal way when you are required to perform a proof. On the ACT, the questions are all multiple choice. That means that the proof questions will be restricted to things that can be done within the constraints of the multiple-choice format.

Some ways that you may encounter proofs on multiple-choice questions are:

• Select which statement is true based on the given information.

• Which statement is not true based on the given information?

• Which reason is accurate for the given statement?

• Which statement is accurate for the given reason?

These are only examples of what you may run into on the ACT. In any case, you will be required to recall properties of geometric figures along with the reflexive property, triangle congruence, and of course CPCTC (corresponding parts of congruent triangles are congruent).

> ## TRIANGLE CONGRUENCE
> SAS, SSS, and ASA are each sufficient for
> proving that two triangles are congruent.

TIP

The volume of a pyramid is $\frac{1}{3}$ times the area of the base times the height. The volume of a cone is $\frac{1}{3}$ times the area of a circular base times height.

VOLUME

Volume is simply the area of the base times the height of the object. Properties of triangles and the Pythagorean theorem or right triangle trigonometry may be required to determine the information you will need to use in the formula.

Volume of an oblique three-dimensional shape is equivalent to the volume the shape would have if it were not oblique. You must be sure to use the actual height of the object and not the length from the base to the top on the outside of the object.

SPECIAL RIGHT TRIANGLES

There are two special right triangles. One is the 30-60-90 triangle and the other is the 45-45-90 triangle. The 30-60-90 triangle is half of an equilateral triangle, and the 45-45-90 triangle is half of a square. Knowing the relationship between the side lengths of these two triangles may save you time on the test. You can discover these relationships by using variables for the side lengths (with the 30-60-90, the shorter leg is half the length of the hypotenuse, and with the 45-45-90, the two legs are congruent) and using the Pythagorean theorem to solve for each variable.

TIP

Height always hits the base at a 90° angle.

> ## 30-60-90 TRIANGLE
> If you use h for the hypotenuse, the short leg $= \frac{1}{2}h$ and the long leg $= \frac{h}{2}\sqrt{3}$.
>
> ## 45-45-90 TRIANGLE
> Using h for the hypotenuse, each leg $= \frac{\sqrt{2}}{2}h$.

RIGHT TRIANGLE TRIGONOMETRY

Right triangle trigonometry is basically summed up by the acronym SOH-CAH-TOA. When working with right triangles, the sine of an angle is equivalent to the length of the opposite side (to the angle) divided by the length of the hypotenuse (SOH). The cosine of an angle is equivalent to the length of the adjacent side (to the angle) divided by the hypotenuse (CAH). The tangent of an angle is equivalent to the length of the opposite side (to the angle) divided by the adjacent side (TOA). These formulas allow you to solve for all side lengths and all angles given that you have either two sides or a side and an angle value.

A right triangle is typically labeled with capital letters naming the angles and corresponding lowercase letters naming the sides. Note the general right triangle here.

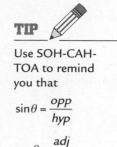

TIP

Use SOH-CAH-TOA to remind you that

$$\sin\theta = \frac{opp}{hyp}$$

$$\cos\theta = \frac{adj}{hyp}$$

$$\tan\theta = \frac{opp}{adj}$$

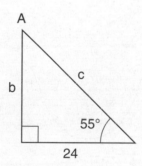

For example, find the values of all side lengths and angles in triangle *ABC*.

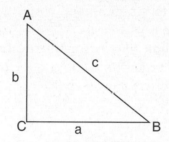

To find side *b*, use tangent and the opposite and adjacent sides. To find side *c*, use cosine and the adjacent and hypotenuse sides. To find angle *A*, use the complementary nature of the two non-right angles in a right triangle.

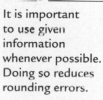

TIP

It is important to use given information whenever possible. Doing so reduces rounding errors.

$$\tan 55 = \frac{b}{24}, b = 24 \tan 55, b = 34.2756 \text{ or } 34$$

$$\cos 55 = \frac{24}{c}, \ c = \frac{24}{\cos 55}, c = 41.8427 \text{ or } 42$$

Angle $A = 90° - 55° = 35°$

VALUES OF TRIGONOMETRIC FUNCTIONS

The value of a trigonometric function can be found quickly and easily using your graphing calculator. It happens to correspond to the x and y coordinates of points along the unit circle as a ray is extended from the origin at the given angle. The relationship to the unit circle helps you understand the trigonometric function, but that understanding is not required for a perfect score on the exam. You need to be able to use your graphing calculator and be familiar with the range of values and behavior of the graph of the function. This will allow you to check the answer obtained on the calculator.

Graphing Trigonometric Functions

A graphing calculator will graph a trigonometric function quickly. The key is to set the window appropriately and to set the mode correctly to radians or degrees, depending on the form the angle is written in.

When a graphical representation of a trigonometric function is the problem, knowing the parent functions and transformations on the trigonometric graphs will allow you to quickly select the correct answer choice.

Know your parent functions:

$$f(x) = \sin(x)$$

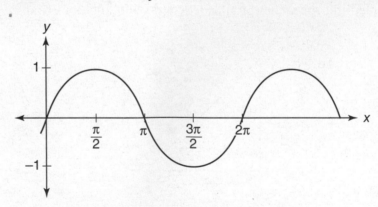

$$f(x) = \cos(x)$$

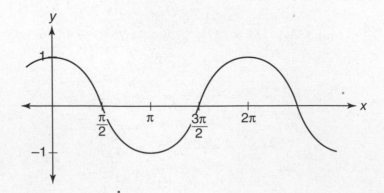

$$f(x) = \tan(x)$$

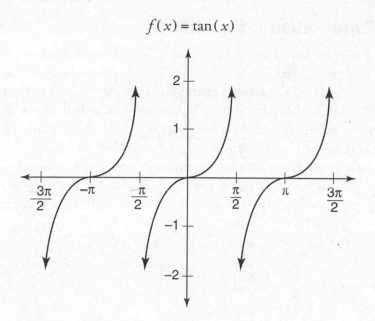

In the general form $f(x) = a \sin b (x - h) + k$, $|a|$ is the amplitude, $\dfrac{2\pi}{b}$ is the period (assuming x is in radians and b is greater than zero), h is the horizontal shift, and k is the vertical shift.

Use of Trigonometric Identities

Trigonometric identities are ways of representing trig functions in terms of one another. These allow you to substitute one function (in an expression) for another. This is helpful when you have an equation involving more than one trig function and you do not have the value of the angle. Review the list of common trig identities in the next chapter. You may run into a problem involving trig identities on the ACT but they do not appear on every test. The most common or basic is $\sin \theta = \sqrt{1 - \cos^2 \theta}$ or $\cos \theta = \sqrt{1 - \sin^2 \theta}$. These identities can be used to replace either $\sin \theta$ or $\cos \theta$ with an expression involving the other.

For example, simplify the expression $(1 + \sin \theta)(1 - \sin \theta)$.

To simplify this, you will first multiply it out to get $1 - \sin^2 \theta$, which is equivalent to $\cos^2 \theta$.

Solving Trigonometric Equations

Solving trigonometric equations is very similar to solving any other equation. You will want to isolate the variable and solve. When you are solving for an angle, you will have to isolate the entire trigonometric function and then use the inverse function to find the angle measure. When the inverse function is taken, it is taken of both sides of the equation. You may be required to use a trigonometric identity to simplify the equation of one function in order to isolate and solve.

With a complicated equation that requires multiple steps to isolate the variable, it may be quicker to use your calculator to check the solutions. Find the value of each side of the equation with a given solution choice and check to see the two sides are equal.

Practice Set: Plane Geometry/Trigonometry

The following problems are typical of the 18 plane geometry/trigonometry problems on the ACT. These types of problems are sprinkled among the beginning test questions and make up about half of the questions toward the end of the test. While practicing, challenge yourself to complete each problem in 80 seconds or less. In order to accomplish this, you will need to make a split-second decision around strategy and then move full speed ahead. Time yourself on these 12 questions and attempt to complete them in 16 minutes or less.

In order to improve your time, set a timer and work through the problems in the allotted time without guessing. When the time has ended, finish the questions in an alternate color and track the amount of time you take to finish. Check your answers. The key is to establish efficiency—to select the correct answers as quickly as possible. Guessing will not earn you a perfect score.

In the directions on the exam you will be told to choose the correct answer and fill in the corresponding oval on the answer sheet. You will be reminded not to linger on problems that you are struggling to solve. (In order to know when you are lingering, you will want to practice in a timed setting.) You will be reminded that you are allowed to use a calculator on any problem but that it may not be the best choice every time. (You'll know from your practice when the use of a calculator is most appropriate.) The directions will include a few final clarifying points, and then you will begin.

1. Which of the following is not a property of a parallelogram?
   A. Opposite sides are congruent.
   B. Consecutive angles are supplementary.
   C. Diagonals are congruent.
   D. Opposite sides are parallel.
   E. The sum of the angles is 360°.

2. Find the x value for which l is parallel to m.

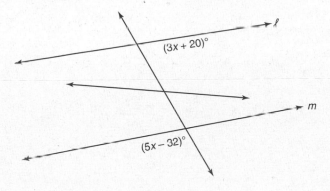

   F. 6
   G. 16
   H. 20
   J. 24
   K. 26

3. Which is the equation of the trigonometric function graphed here?

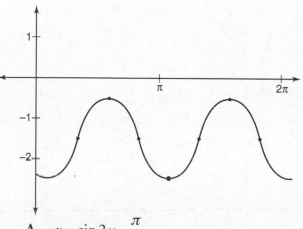

   A. $y = \sin 2x - \dfrac{\pi}{3}$

   B. $y = \sin 2\left(x + \dfrac{\pi}{3}\right)$

   C. $y = \sin 2\left(x - \dfrac{\pi}{3}\right)$

   D. $y = \sin 2\left(x - \dfrac{\pi}{3}\right) - \dfrac{3}{2}$

   E. $y = \sin 2\left(x + \dfrac{\pi}{3}\right) - \dfrac{3}{2}$

4. Which of the following are the dimensions of a right triangle?
   F. 0.6, 0.8, 0.12
   G. 2, 3, 4
   H. 9, 12, 15
   J. 9, 13, 21
   K. 18, 23, 25

5. Find the volume of a cone with a slant height of 15 inches and a base with a 16-inch diameter.
   A. 271π
   B. 320π
   C. 960π
   D. 1280π
   E. 3248π

6. Find the coordinates of point $A(-7,3)$ when it is reflected about the line $y = x$.
   F. $(-7, -3)$
   G. $(-3, 7)$
   H. $(3, -7)$
   J. $(3, 7)$
   K. $(7, 3)$

7. Find x.

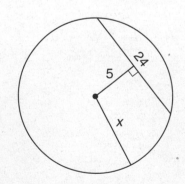

   A. 7
   B. 11
   C. 12
   D. 13
   E. 15

8. Solve for x, given that the area is 120.

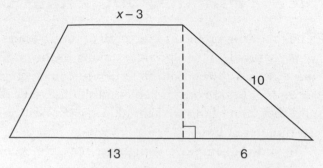

   F. 7
   G. 11
   H. 12
   J. 14
   K. 15

9. When constructing wheelchair ramps, the ramp must not rise more than 1 inch for every foot of ramp. What is the maximum angle the ramp can make with the ground for a 3-foot ramp?
   A. 4.8°
   B. 14.34°
   C. 14.47°
   D. 19.47°
   E. 90°

10. By which postulate or theorem are triangle *ABC* and triangle *DBC* congruent?

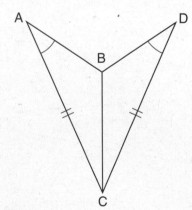

   F. SAS
   G. SSS
   H. AAS
   J. ASA
   K. There is not enough information to determine congruence.

11. Find x.

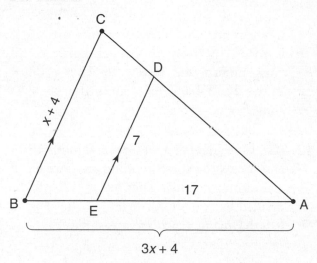

A. 2.16
B. 3
C. 4.33
D. 5
E. 10

12. Find the arc measure of the arc cut by one side of a circumscribed regular hexagon.

F. 30°
G. 60°
H. 120°
J. 180°
K. 240°

Solutions and Explanations

1. (**C**) While diagonals are congruent when the parallelogram is a rectangle, this is not necessarily true for all parallelograms.

2. (**J**) When l is parallel to m, the two angles are supplementary because each is congruent to the linear pair of the other. Since they are supplementary, $5x - 32 + 3x + 20 = 180$, $8x - 12 = 180$, $8x = 192$, and $x = 24$.

3. (**D**) The graph has a period of 2, and it is translated $\frac{\pi}{3}$ to the right and $\frac{3}{2}$ down. The period of 2 means that the curve completes a cycle between 0 and π. Translating right and down translates each point right and down.

4. (**H**) To determine whether or not a triangle is a right triangle, substitute the values into the Pythagorean theorem and check to be sure the sentence is true. $9^2 + 12^2 = 15^2$, $81 + 144 = 225$.

5. (**A**) The slant height and the diameter can be used with the Pythagorean theorem to find the height of the cone. $15^2 - 8^2 = 161$, and the square root of 161 is approximately 12.6885. This height along with the radius can be used in the formula for the volume of a cone $\left(\frac{1}{3}\pi r^2 h\right)$ to find that the volume is approximately 270.69π or 271π.

6. (**H**) When reflecting about $y = x$, use the y coordinate of the original point to determine the x coordinate and the x coordinate of the original point to determine the new y coordinate. This is the same as graphing the point and the line $y = x$, then folding the graph along the line $y = x$ and drawing a point where the original point lands.

7. (**D**) The segment from the center perpendicular to a chord bisects the chord. If the radius is drawn to meet the endpoint of the chord, a right triangle will be formed with legs measuring 5 and 12 and hypotenuse of x. Use the Pythagorean theorem to find that the hypotenuse measures the square root of the sum of 12^2 and 5^2, which is 13.

8. **(J)** Use the Pythagorean theorem to find that the height of the trapezoid is 8. Then use the formula for the area of a trapezoid, $A = \frac{1}{2}(b_1 + b_2)h$, to get $120 = \frac{1}{2}(19 + x - 3)8$, which means that $120 = 4(16 + x)$, $30 = 16 + x$, and $x = 14$.

9. **(A)** The ratio of height to hypotenuse (ramp length) is constant at 1 inch to 12 inches. You may choose to use 3 inches to 36 inches for this problem. Either way, use the sine function to determine the angle, $\sin\theta = \frac{1}{12}$. Then, taking the inverse sine of both sides will give you the answer of 4.8°.

10. **(K)** $BC \cong BC$ by the reflexive property and $\angle A \cong \angle D$ and $AC \cong CD$ are given. Even though you are given three pieces of information, they are not in the correct order to provide sufficient evidence to determine congruence. When there are two sides and an angle congruent, the angle must fall between the two sides to be sufficient evidence that the triangles are congruent.

11. **(E)** Triangles *ABC* and *AED* are similar because all angles are congruent. Since the triangles are similar, $x + 4$ is to 7 as $3x + 4$ is to 17. Setting up the proportion and cross multiplying results in $17x + 68 = 21x + 28$. Solving for x gives you $40 = 4x$ and $10 = x$.

12. **(G)** One angle of a regular hexagon is 120°, and it cuts the corresponding arc to result in a measure of 240°. That leaves 120° to be divided by two chords that are equivalent in length, making each arc measure 60°.

Mini-Lessons As Review

CHAPTER 11

- Conic sections
- Trigonometry
- Graphing calculator

The math section of the ACT includes content that is familiar to most juniors in the United States. What is challenging about obtaining a perfect score is the time constraint. By familiarizing yourself with the content, vocabulary, and formulas that will appear on the test, and armed with your graphing calculator, you will increase your pace while taking the exam.

Depending on the coursework you have completed, you may need a deeper explanation of conic sections and trigonometry. A mini-lesson on each of these topics is included in this chapter. These mini-lessons are intended to give greater context to the information you studied already in previous chapters. Also in this chapter, we will review how to use a graphing calculator on the ACT.

Remember that reading through this book once is not sufficient studying for a perfect score on the exam. You should have marked the book along the way with highlights and notes. Be sure to go back through the math section and study those topics that were unfamiliar or difficult for you the first time through. Give yourself some time away from the text and then come back with fresh eyes and read through it again, practicing the problems again as well. Good luck!

Mini-Lesson: Conic Sections

Conic sections are slices of a cone and can be a parabola, circle, ellipse, or hyperbola. This is a complex topic, but our goal is simply to give you enough information to solve problems on the ACT. The general form of the equation can be determined by completing the square on each variable. The general form of the equation will tell you which transformation to make on the graph of the parent function.

Circles and Ellipses

Circles have the general equation of $(x - h)^2 + (y - k)^2 = r^2$ where (h,k) is the center and r is the radius.

For example, $x^2 + y^2 = 9$ is a circle centered at $(0,0)$ with a radius of 3.

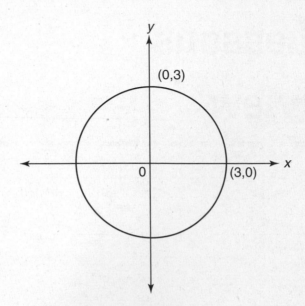

Ellipses are very similar to circles. The difference is that they extend a different amount in *x* and in *y*. So, instead of being shaped like a circle, they are shaped like an oval. In the equation this shows up as denominators under the *x* and *y* expression, and the equation equals 1 instead of a radius squared. The general equation for an ellipse is $\dfrac{(x-h)^2}{a^2} + \dfrac{(y-k)^2}{b^2} = 1$, where (h,k) is the center, *a* is the amount that the ellipse extends horizontally from the center, and *b* is the amount that the ellipse extends vertically.

For example, $\dfrac{x^2}{25} + \dfrac{y^2}{49} = 1$ is an ellipse centered at $(0,0)$, which extends to -5 and 5 on the *x* axis, and to 7 and -7 on the *y* axis.

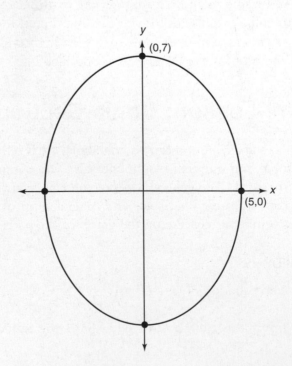

Hyperbolas

Hyperbolas are a bit trickier than circles and ellipses, but the nice thing is that they are easy to spot in a graph or an equation. The equation of a hyperbola is very similar to that of an ellipse. The difference is that, instead of a sum, it is a difference. There are two possibilities, one where the y term is subtracted from the x term, and the reverse. There will be a reference point at (h,k), a will tell you about the horizontal distance from the reference point, and b will tell you about the vertical distance from the reference point. A difference is that these references describe a box that lies between the points that make up the solution of the equation and the graph. In this case, a picture is worth a thousand words. Examine the graphical representations of the following:

$$\frac{(x-h)^2}{a^2} - \frac{(y-k)^2}{b^2} = 1$$

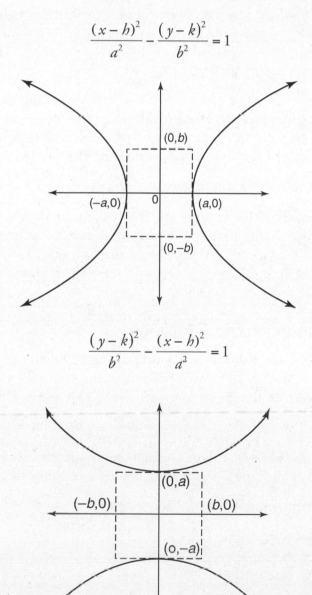

$$\frac{(y-k)^2}{b^2} - \frac{(x-h)^2}{a^2} = 1$$

The key points to remember about a hyperbola are the subtraction sign in the equation, and the general characteristics of the graph based on (h,k), a, and b.

Mini-Lesson: Trigonometry

The topic of trigonometry makes up a very small portion of the test and really works to separate the excellent students from the rest. Students who are not working toward a perfect score may be inclined to skip the four problems that involve trigonometry. For those (like you!) who seek a perfect score, no topic in this category is beyond comprehension. These can be four easy problems for you. The problems can come from any of the following topics, but it is unlikely that all four topics will be included. At the very least, you should expect to come across a right triangle trigonometry question.

Right Triangle Trigonometry

Right triangle trigonometry is used to find side lengths and angle values in right triangles. Specifically, angles and side lengths of right triangles can be found using sine, cosine, and tangent functions. As you know, right triangles have sides called legs and a hypotenuse (The longest side, which is opposite the right angle). Use SOH-CAH-TOA to remind you that $\sin\theta = \dfrac{opp}{hyp}$, $\cos\theta = \dfrac{adj}{hyp}$, and $\tan\theta = \dfrac{opp}{adj}$.

Solving these equations for an angle will require you to take the inverse function of each side in order to eliminate the function. This is done easily on your calculator. Try it now by taking $\sin^{-1}(\sin 30)$. Notice that the angle is in degrees, so you will want to be sure your calculator is set to degrees. The inverse sine of the sine of 30 equals 30.

Graphs of Trigonometric Functions

The graphs of sine, cosine, and tangent functions can be found using your graphing calculator. Use the TRACE key on your calculator to examine characteristics of the graphs of each of these functions. You will notice that there is no value for the tangent of $\dfrac{\pi}{2}$, $\dfrac{3\pi}{2}$, and all the multiples of those angles. This is because the value of the adjacent side (x value) at those locations along the unit circle is zero. As you know, the result of dividing by zero is undefined. Looking more specifically at sine and cosine, you will notice key characteristics at x values of 0, $\dfrac{\pi}{6}$, $\dfrac{\pi}{4}$, $\dfrac{\pi}{3}$, and multiples of these angles.

Trigonometric Transformations

In the chapter on plane geometry and trigonometry, you examined the parent functions of sine, cosine, and tangent. The period for a parent function of sine or cosine is 2π, and the range is from -1 to 1. As with the other functions, (h,k) shifts the parent function by $-h$ horizontally and k vertically. So, examining the general equation of a sine function, $f(x) = a \sin b(x - h) + k$, $|a|$ is the amplitude (affects the range), $\dfrac{2\pi}{b}$ is the period (notice that when b is 1 the period is 2π), h is the horizontal shift, and k is the vertical shift. Set the graphing window on your calculator and explore how changes to the equation affect the graph of the function. Before you examine the graph, try predicting what you think will occur on the basis of the change you make to the equation

Trigonometric Identities

For the purposes of the ACT, you will focus on three trigonometric identities in one. Consider a right triangle where the hypotenuse is 1 (think "unit circle"). You have the length of one leg (along the x axis) valued at $\cos\theta$ and the length of the other leg (along the y axis) valued at $\sin\theta$. Using the Pythagorean theorem, you find that $\sin^2\theta + \cos^2\theta = 1^2$ or $\mathbf{\sin^2\theta + \cos^2\theta = 1}$. This is the basic trigonometric identity. Using this identity, you can solve for either $\sin^2\theta$ or $\cos^2\theta$ by simply subtracting. This gives you two more identities to use: $\mathbf{\sin^2\theta = 1 - \cos^2\theta}$ and $\mathbf{\cos^2\theta = 1 - \sin^2\theta}$. Each of these identities can be solved further by taking the square root of both sides. These identities are especially helpful when you are trying to solve an equation involving both sine and cosine. You can use either equation to substitute in for either $\sin(x)$ or $\cos(x)$, which will allow you to work with one trig function.

Mini-Lesson: Graphing Calculator

Your graphing calculator will help you tremendously if you know how to use it for the different types of problems on the ACT. Briefly review the following topics concerning your graphing calculator.

Computation

- Fractions. Remember that you may need to tell your calculator to give you the answer in the form of a fraction so that it matches the answer choices.

- Exponents. The x^2 key is handy, but you may also need to use the $\wedge$ symbol when working with a different power.

- Roots. Square roots are easy, but be sure to locate the key for finding a cube root as well.

- Logarithms. Base 10 and base e (ln) are readily available. Be sure you know the change of base formula and practice changing bases to base 10 and solving with your calculator.

- Trigonometry (radians or degrees). Know whether the problem involves radians or degrees and practice changing from one to the other. You may encounter problems that are set up using radians and degrees throughout the exam.

Statistics

- Lists. A list will only be useful if you are very fast and accurate at filling it in and you are using it for something that you can't do faster without a list. Be sure your lists are all empty before you start the test.

- Basic statistics. If you decide to enter data into a list, you can use your calculator to find the mean, median, and standard deviation of your data.

Graphing

- Window settings. Your window settings will depend on the graph in question. You will need to estimate the window required and set your calculator accordingly.

- TRACE and CALCULATE. TRACE can be used to find points along the graph, and CALCULATE is especially helpful when locating intercepts and maximums or minimums.

Know when to use your graphing calculator. It may be that the most efficient way to solve a problem is *without* the calculator *at all*. For areas that you are weak in, speed is less important than accuracy—use the calculator. Sometimes you will use the calculator to check the answer choices rather than to solve the problem itself.

Practice making these decisions and working within time limits on the practice math test that follows. You may even want to code your test by writing a "c" next to the problems you use your calculator for and then reviewing that code once you have completed the practice test.

Now that you've reviewed all the math concepts tested on the ACT, it's time to take a full-length practice test to see how well you do. Good luck!

KEYS TO ACHIEVING MATH PERFECTION

You selected this particular preparation book because you believe in yourself. You have read through the chapters and have a good idea of the content you will encounter on the ACT. Use this book as your reference tool and your classroom as your practice gym. Remember what you have learned here:

⚷ Seek Out Word Problems

Whether your teacher assigns them or not, solve word problems at every opportunity. Whenever possible, draw and label a diagram that depicts the situation in the math problem. This is an efficient way to gather key information from the word problem so that you can pull that information quickly into your formula or an equation.

⚷ Practice Using Your Graphing Calculator

Practice using your graphing calculator often and in a variety of ways. Use it to solve problems when appropriate to the topic in class. Also use it to determine a ballpark estimate in order to practice this crucial strategy.

⚷ Get Accustomed to the Time Crunch

When working on homework that is review (material you have previously learned), set a timer for the number of problems times 80 seconds per problem. Solve the problems as efficiently as you can and switch pen colors when the timer goes off. This is a stiff time limit when you are not able to practice the strategies related to multiple choice. It is still great practice and will help you get used to the pressure of the timed testing environment.

⚷ Seek Additional Help

Seek additional help from your teacher on content that seems least familiar to you. If you do not have much experience with conic sections, for example, ask your teacher to loan you a book that has good explanations, and practice problems in it. You know what areas you need extra help in, and it is up to you to get it.

With your intelligence and education along with the strategies in this book, the perfect score in math is within your reach!

Answer Sheet

MATH PRACTICE TEST

Directions: Mark one answer only for each question. Make the mark dark. Erase completely any mark made in error. (Additional or stray marks will be counted as mistakes on the actual ACT.)

1 Ⓐ Ⓑ Ⓒ Ⓓ Ⓔ	16 Ⓕ Ⓖ Ⓗ Ⓙ Ⓚ	31 Ⓐ Ⓑ Ⓒ Ⓓ Ⓔ	46 Ⓕ Ⓖ Ⓗ Ⓙ Ⓚ
2 Ⓕ Ⓖ Ⓗ Ⓙ Ⓚ	17 Ⓐ Ⓑ Ⓒ Ⓓ Ⓔ	32 Ⓕ Ⓖ Ⓗ Ⓙ Ⓚ	47 Ⓐ Ⓑ Ⓒ Ⓓ Ⓔ
3 Ⓐ Ⓑ Ⓒ Ⓓ Ⓔ	18 Ⓕ Ⓖ Ⓗ Ⓙ Ⓚ	33 Ⓐ Ⓑ Ⓒ Ⓓ Ⓔ	48 Ⓕ Ⓖ Ⓗ Ⓙ Ⓚ
4 Ⓕ Ⓖ Ⓗ Ⓙ Ⓚ	19 Ⓐ Ⓑ Ⓒ Ⓓ Ⓔ	34 Ⓕ Ⓖ Ⓗ Ⓙ Ⓚ	49 Ⓐ Ⓑ Ⓒ Ⓓ Ⓔ
5 Ⓐ Ⓑ Ⓒ Ⓓ Ⓔ	20 Ⓕ Ⓖ Ⓗ Ⓙ Ⓚ	35 Ⓐ Ⓑ Ⓒ Ⓓ Ⓔ	50 Ⓕ Ⓖ Ⓗ Ⓙ Ⓚ
6 Ⓕ Ⓖ Ⓗ Ⓙ Ⓚ	21 Ⓐ Ⓑ Ⓒ Ⓓ Ⓔ	36 Ⓕ Ⓖ Ⓗ Ⓙ Ⓚ	51 Ⓐ Ⓑ Ⓒ Ⓓ Ⓔ
7 Ⓐ Ⓑ Ⓒ Ⓓ Ⓔ	22 Ⓕ Ⓖ Ⓗ Ⓙ Ⓚ	37 Ⓐ Ⓑ Ⓒ Ⓓ Ⓔ	52 Ⓕ Ⓖ Ⓗ Ⓙ Ⓚ
8 Ⓕ Ⓖ Ⓗ Ⓙ Ⓚ	23 Ⓐ Ⓑ Ⓒ Ⓓ Ⓔ	38 Ⓕ Ⓖ Ⓗ Ⓙ Ⓚ	53 Ⓐ Ⓑ Ⓒ Ⓓ Ⓔ
9 Ⓐ Ⓑ Ⓒ Ⓓ Ⓔ	24 Ⓕ Ⓖ Ⓗ Ⓙ Ⓚ	39 Ⓐ Ⓑ Ⓒ Ⓓ Ⓔ	54 Ⓕ Ⓖ Ⓗ Ⓙ Ⓚ
10 Ⓕ Ⓖ Ⓗ Ⓙ Ⓚ	25 Ⓐ Ⓑ Ⓒ Ⓓ Ⓔ	40 Ⓕ Ⓖ Ⓗ Ⓙ Ⓚ	55 Ⓐ Ⓑ Ⓒ Ⓓ Ⓔ
11 Ⓐ Ⓑ Ⓒ Ⓓ Ⓔ	26 Ⓕ Ⓖ Ⓗ Ⓙ Ⓚ	41 Ⓐ Ⓑ Ⓒ Ⓓ Ⓔ	56 Ⓕ Ⓖ Ⓗ Ⓙ Ⓚ
12 Ⓕ Ⓖ Ⓗ Ⓙ Ⓚ	27 Ⓐ Ⓑ Ⓒ Ⓓ Ⓔ	42 Ⓕ Ⓖ Ⓗ Ⓙ Ⓚ	57 Ⓐ Ⓑ Ⓒ Ⓓ Ⓔ
13 Ⓐ Ⓑ Ⓒ Ⓓ Ⓔ	28 Ⓕ Ⓖ Ⓗ Ⓙ Ⓚ	43 Ⓐ Ⓑ Ⓒ Ⓓ Ⓔ	58 Ⓕ Ⓖ Ⓗ Ⓙ Ⓚ
14 Ⓕ Ⓖ Ⓗ Ⓙ Ⓚ	29 Ⓐ Ⓑ Ⓒ Ⓓ Ⓔ	44 Ⓕ Ⓖ Ⓗ Ⓙ Ⓚ	59 Ⓐ Ⓑ Ⓒ Ⓓ Ⓔ
15 Ⓐ Ⓑ Ⓒ Ⓓ Ⓔ	30 Ⓕ Ⓖ Ⓗ Ⓙ Ⓚ	45 Ⓐ Ⓑ Ⓒ Ⓓ Ⓔ	60 Ⓕ Ⓖ Ⓗ Ⓙ Ⓚ

Math Practice Test

Directions: You have 60 minutes to complete 60 questions. Time yourself—that's important! Read and solve each problem.

If a problem is difficult, move to the next problem and come back to the skipped problem after you have gone through the entire math section of the exam. Your calculator can be used on any problem you choose.

Keep your pacing and strategies in mind. You should be able to work more quickly at the beginning of the test because it includes a greater concentration of elementary algebra questions. This also means that the strategy for most of the beginning questions will be to solve the problem. As you move through the test, you will want to use different strategies, and the problems will take more time.

Do not linger over problems that take too much time. Solve as many problems as you can, then return to the others in the time you have left.

Remember that figures are not drawn to scale. You must rely on the explanation in the problem for relative conditions on the illustration (congruence, similarity, etc.).

DO YOUR FIGURING HERE

1. What is the equation of a circle that includes a point at $(1, 2)$ and is centered at $(4, 2)$?
   A. $(x - 4)^2 + (y - 2)^2 = 5$
   B. $(x - 4)^2 + (y - 5)^2 = 2$
   C. $(x + 4)^2 + (y + 2)^2 = 5$
   D. $(x - 4)^2 + (y - 5)^2 = 25$
   E. $(x - 4)^2 + (y - 2)^2 = 25$

2. Simplify $(4x^2 + 2x^2 - 3(x - 7)) - (-2x^4 - 2x^2 + 3x - 5)$.
   F. $10x^2 - 6x + 26$
   G. $6x^4 + 4x^2 + 26$
   H. $6x^4 + 4x^2 - 6x + 26$
   J. $2x^4 + 8x^2 - 6x + 26$
   K. $2x^4 - 6x + 26$

DO YOUR FIGURING HERE

3. Find $2x(x - 3y) + 2y^2$ when $x = -6$ and
   $y = 3$.
   A. -9
   B. 54
   C. 81
   D. 126
   E. 198

4. Bennett is twice as old as his daughter
   Alissa, who is three years younger than her
   brother Neal. If the sum of their ages is 63,
   how old is Neal?
   F. 15
   G. 18
   H. 20
   J. 23
   K. 30

5. When Corina performs in a cheerleading
   competition she makes 2 mistakes in every
   3 minutes of performance. If she performs
   for a total of 18 minutes in the competition
   tonight, how many mistakes will she make?
   A. 12
   B. 15
   C. 16
   D. 27
   E. 30

6. Each student in the choir must earn $2500
   to attend a performance in Ireland this
   summer. To earn the funds they are selling
   candy bars and t-shirts. For each candy bar
   sold, the singer earns $1 credit, and for
   each t-shirt the singer earns $5.75. Which
   equation represents the number of candy
   bars (x) and t-shirts (y) that must be sold
   by each singer to ensure that he/she can
   attend the performance?
   F. $(x + 1) + (y + 5.75) \geq 2500$
   G. $5.75x + y \geq 2500$
   H. $x + 5.75y \geq 2500$
   J. $6.75xy \geq 2500$
   K. $6.75 (x + y) \geq 2500$

DO YOUR FIGURING HERE

7. Quadrilateral *ABCD* is a kite. Which of the following cannot be determined?

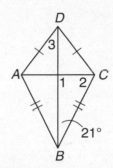

    A. m∠3 = 21°
    B. m∠1 = 90°
    C. m∠2 = 69°
    D. $AD \cong CD$
    E. $AB \cong CB$

8. Which of the following is the factored form of $2x^2 - 3x - 9$?
    F. $(2x - 3)(x - 9)$
    G. $(2x - 9)(x + 3)$
    H. $(3x + 2)(x - 3)$
    J. $(2x + 3)(x - 3)$
    K. $(x + 3)(2x - 3)$

9. Madison surveyed the student body and found that 3 out of 7 students go by a nickname. In a class of 35 students, how many students can Madison predict will go by a nickname?
    A. 8
    B. 10
    C. 15
    D. 21
    E. 28

10. What is a value of *x* if $|x - 7| = 5$
    F. −35
    G. −12
    H. −2
    J. 12
    K. 35

DO YOUR FIGURING HERE

11. Which of the following is equivalent to $(3x - 7)(x + 4)$?
    A. $12x^2 - 10x - 7$
    B. $3x^2 + 5x - 28$
    C. $3x^2 - 3x - 28$
    D. $3x^2 - 28$
    E. $4x - 3$

12. Which three-dimensional figure is formed by rotating a right triangle about a leg?
    F. prism
    G. sphere
    H. cone
    J. cylinder
    K. pyramid

13. Find $33 + (4 - 3^2) - 24 \div 8$.
    A. 7/4
    B. 5/2
    C. 7
    D. 25
    E. 31

14. Which of the following is a solution of $-7\sqrt[2]{3x - 8} + 3 = -4x + 7$ for x.
    F. -8
    G. -0.18
    H. 0.18
    J. 8
    K. no real solution

15. Determine the expression that represents $m\angle R$ in triangle PQR given that side $PQ = 7$, side $QR = 9$, and $m\angle P = 110$.

    (Note: The law of sines states that the ratio of the side lengths to the sines of the opposite angle are equal for any triangle.)

    A. $\sin^{-1}\left(\dfrac{7 \sin 110°}{9}\right)$
    B. $\sin^{-1} 63 \sin 110°$
    C. $\sin^{-1}\left(\dfrac{\sin 110°}{63}\right)$
    D. $\dfrac{7 \sin 110°}{9}$
    E. $\dfrac{\sin 110°}{63}$

DO YOUR FIGURING HERE

16. On Crazy Hair Day, 17% of the girls dyed their hair pink, but not one boy dyed his hair pink. If 39% of the total student body are girls, what percent of the total student body wore pink hair on Crazy Hair Day?
    F. 2.3%
    G. 6.6%
    H. 10.4%
    J. 17%
    K. 22%

17. Simplify $\dfrac{3x^5 y^3 z}{x^2 yz^4} \times x^3 y^3 z$
    A. $3x^8 y^6 z^2$
    B. $\dfrac{3x^4}{z^3}$
    C. $\dfrac{3x^3 y^2}{z^3}$
    D. $\dfrac{3x^6 y^5}{z^2}$
    E. $\dfrac{3x^9 y^6}{z^2}$

18. List $\dfrac{2}{3}$, $\sqrt{2}$, 0.7, $\dfrac{7}{4}$, and 1.5 in order from least to greatest.
    F. $\dfrac{2}{3}, 0.7, \sqrt{2}, 1.5, \dfrac{7}{4}$
    G. $\dfrac{2}{3}, \sqrt{2}, 0.7, \dfrac{7}{4}, 1.5$
    H. $\dfrac{2}{3}, \sqrt{2}, 0.7, 1.5, \dfrac{7}{4}$
    J. $\dfrac{2}{3}, 0.7, \sqrt{2}, \dfrac{7}{4}, 1.5$
    K. $\dfrac{2}{3}, 0.7, \dfrac{7}{4}, 1.5, \sqrt{2}$

19. Find $(2 + 4i)(3 - 2i) + (-3i)(5i)$.
    A. $-17 + 8i$
    B. $13 + 8i$
    C. $13 + 16i$
    D. $29 + 8i$
    E. $29 + 16i$

20. The quadratic formula states that

$x = \dfrac{-b \pm \sqrt{b^2 - 4ac}}{2a}$. Find x given that

$a = 2$, $b = 4$, and $c = 2$.

F. $-1 \pm \sqrt{2}$
G. -1
H. 0
J. 1
K. $1 \pm \sqrt{2}$

21. Quadrilateral *ABCD* has point *B* located at $(2, -1)$. Find the new coordinates of *B* once the quadrilateral is translated $(4, -7)$.

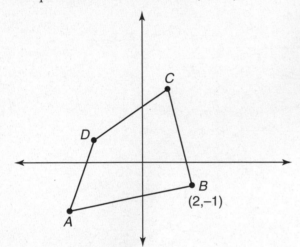

A. $(4, -8)$
B. $(4, -7)$
C. $(4, 6)$
D. $(6, 6)$
E. $(6, -8)$

22. Solve $\dfrac{3}{4}n + \dfrac{2}{5}n = 46$ for n.

F. 2
G. 13.5
H. 16.7
J. 40
K. 184

DO YOUR FIGURING HERE

23. Find the equation of a parabola with maximum at (3, 4) that goes through (5, 2).

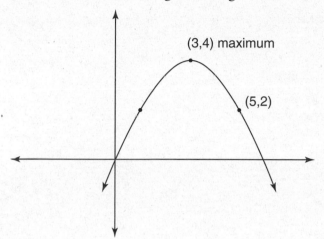

(3,4) maximum

(5,2)

  A. $f(x) = \dfrac{-1}{32}(x+3)^2 + 4$

  B. $f(x) = \dfrac{3}{32}(x+3)^2 - 4$

  C. $f(x) = \dfrac{-1}{2}(x-3)^2 + 4$

  D. $f(x) = \dfrac{3}{2}(x-3)^2 - 4$

  E. $f(x) = -1(x-3)^2 + 4$

24. Jack is a newborn baby who spends 60% of his time sleeping. Out of the other 40% of his time, 60% is spent either eating, burping, or having his diaper changed. What percent of Jack's total time is left for playing?

  F. 0%
  G. 16%
  H. 20%
  J. 24%
  K. 40%

25. Solve $\dfrac{-2}{x^2 - 2} = \dfrac{2}{x - 4}$.

  A. $\{-6, 2\}$
  B. $\{-3, 4\}$
  C. $\{-3, 2\}$
  D. $\{-2, 6\}$
  E. $\{3, 2\}$

26. Given that $a = b$, which of the following reflects the multiplicative property?

   F. $ac = bc$
   G. $b = c \Rightarrow a = c$
   H. $a + c = b + c$
   J. $ab = 1$
   K. $a^m = b^m$

27. Determine the volume of a cone with a circular base of area 9π and a height of $7x$.

   A. $\dfrac{3}{7}\pi x$
   B. $21\pi x$
   C. $9\pi \times 7x$
   D. $63\pi x$
   E. $567\pi x$

28. Express $\sin\theta$ in terms of $\cos\theta$.

   F. $\dfrac{1}{\cos\theta}$
   G. $\sqrt{\cos\theta}$
   H. $1 - \cos\theta$
   J. $1 - \cos^2\theta$
   K. $\pm\sqrt{1 - \cos^2\theta}$

29. Which expression represents the pattern in the table?

1	2	3	4	5	n
3	0	-3	-6	-9	

   A. $-3n$
   B. $-3n + 6$
   C. $n + 2$
   D. $3n$
   E. $6n - 3$

DO YOUR FIGURING HERE

30. At Frank's Pizza a medium pizza is priced at $12.95 and a large pizza is priced at $15.95. A medium pizza has a diameter of 6 inches and a large pizza has a diameter of 8 inches. Carlos would like to buy the pizza that costs the least per square inch. Select the expression that represents the difference in areas of the large and medium pizzas.

   F. $\dfrac{15.95}{64\pi} - \dfrac{12.95}{36\pi}$

   G. $\dfrac{15.95}{16\pi} - \dfrac{12.95}{9\pi}$

   H. $8\pi - 6\pi$

   J. $16\pi - 9\pi$

   K. $64\pi - 36\pi$

31. Which of the following is equivalent to $(3x^3y^4)(-2x^2y^5)^3$?

   A. $-216x^{216}y^{729}$
   B. $-24x^9y^{19}$
   C. $-24x^{18}y^{60}$
   D. $-18x^9y^{19}$
   E. $24x^{16}y^{60}$

32. Find the greatest common factor of $116x$ and 128.

   F. 2
   G. 4
   H. 32
   J. $116x$
   K. $128x$

33. Determine the slope of a line perpendicular to $-3x + 5y = 20$.

   A. -4

   B. $\dfrac{-5}{3}$

   C. $\dfrac{-3}{5}$

   D. $\dfrac{-1}{4}$

   E. $\dfrac{3}{20}$

34. The student council is going to hire a DJ for the winter dance. Each board member is responsible for getting a quote from a DJ and providing an equation that reflects the quote so that the council can select the best quote. Alex talks with Sound Machine and is told that they will charge a set-up fee of $35 and an additional $20 per hour. Which equation represents the cost for x hours?

F. $35 - 20x$

G. $15x$

H. $20x + 35$

J. $35x + 20$

K. $(20 + 35)x$

35. Find the perimeter of

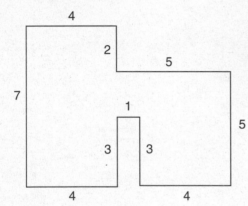

A. 25

B. 32

C. 35

D. 38

E. 63

DO YOUR FIGURING HERE

36. Select the graph of $\dfrac{(x-4)^2}{25} + \dfrac{(y-9)^2}{4} = 1$.

F.

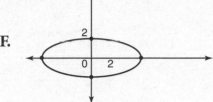

G.

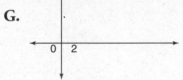

H.

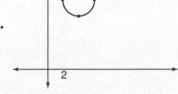

J.

K.

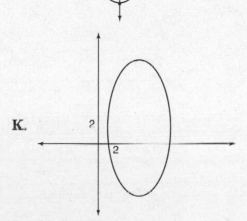

37. A bag contains 4 red marbles, 7 white marbles, and 3 blue marbles. If Sue pulls one marble from the bag, what is the probability that the marble will be blue?

A. $\dfrac{1}{14}$

B. $\dfrac{1}{11}$

C. $\dfrac{3}{14}$

D. $\dfrac{3}{11}$

E. $\dfrac{11}{14}$

38. Which of the following is the solution set of x values for $3x^3 - 15x^2 - 42x = 0$?

F. $\{-2, 21\}$
G. $\{-2, 7\}$
H. $\{-2, 3, 7\}$
J. $\{-2, 0, 7\}$
K. $\{-2, 0, 21\}$

39. Determine the equation of the line that contains the points $(-2.5, 4)$ and $(5, -2)$.

A. $6x + 7.5y = 2$
B. $6x - 7.5y = 2$
C. $12x - 15y = -4$
D. $12x + 15y = -4$
E. $12x + 15y = 30$

40. Find the area of a right triangle with hypotenuse of 10 and side of 8.

F. 5
G. 24
H. 40
J. 48
K. 80

DO YOUR FIGURING HERE

41. Find x, given that $|5x - 9| - 8 = -1$.

   A. no solution

   B. $\dfrac{8}{5}$

   C. $\dfrac{16}{5}$

   D. $\left\{2, \dfrac{8}{5}\right\}$

   E. $\left\{\dfrac{2}{5}, \dfrac{16}{5}\right\}$

42. Find the volume of a regular hexagonal pyramid with a base of side length 4 and a height of 9.

   F. $12\sqrt{3}$

   G. $36\sqrt{3}$

   H. $72\sqrt{3}$

   J. $144\sqrt{3}$

   K. $216\sqrt{3}$

43. Find the height a 17-foot ladder can reach on the side of a building when it hits the ground at a 65° angle.

   A. 7.2 ft
   B. 15.4 ft
   C. 36.5 ft
   D. 48 ft
   E. 224 ft

44. The diameter of a circle is 34 cm and a chord in that same circle is 30 cm. What is the distance from the center of that circle to the chord?

   F. 4 cm
   G. 8 cm
   H. 8.5 cm
   J. 16 cm
   K. 26 cm

45. Find *x*.

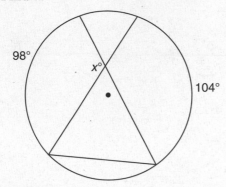

   A. 49°
   B. 52°
   C. 79°
   D. 98°
   E. 101°

46. If the first term in an arithmetic series is $\frac{8}{3}$ and the last term is $\frac{40}{3}$, and the sum is 72, what are the first four terms?

   F. $\frac{8}{3}, \frac{12}{3}, \frac{16}{3}, \frac{20}{3}$

   G. $\frac{8}{3}, \frac{14}{3}, \frac{20}{3}, \frac{26}{3}$

   H. $\frac{8}{3}, \frac{16}{3}, \frac{24}{3}, \frac{32}{3}$

   J. $\frac{8}{3}, \frac{16}{3}, \frac{32}{3}, \frac{40}{3}$

   K. $\frac{8}{3}, \frac{20}{3}, \frac{28}{3}, \frac{40}{3}$

47. If $3x\sqrt{50} - \sqrt{32x^2} = \sqrt{18}$, find *x*.

   A. $-8\sqrt{2}$

   B. 0

   C. $\frac{3}{11}$

   D. $\frac{1}{3}$

   E. $\frac{12}{11}$

DO YOUR FIGURING HERE

48. If $-2(x - 7) + (x - 6) = 23$, find x.
  F. -31
  G. -15
  H. -5
  J. -3
  K. -1

49. Find the area of an equilateral triangle with a side length of 12.
  A. $6\sqrt{3}$
  B. $18\sqrt{3}$
  C. $36\sqrt{3}$
  D. $72\sqrt{3}$
  E. not enough information

50. Determine the point of intersection of the following system of equations.
$$y = -\frac{1}{2}x + \frac{13}{4}$$
$$-2x + 3y = 8$$
  F. $(0, -3)$
  G. $(0, 3)$
  H. $(0.5, 3)$
  J. $(8.5, -3)$
  K. $(8.5, 3)$

51. Which of the following is not true for a kite?

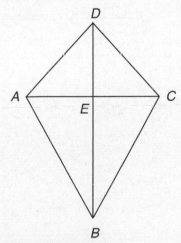

  A. $AE \cong CE$
  B. $DE \cong BE$
  C. $\angle ABE \cong \angle CBE$
  D. $\angle E = 90°$
  E. $\angle ADB \cong \angle CDB$

DO YOUR FIGURING HERE

52. Tony has an A average in his math class and there is one test left. In order to keep the A, he will have to maintain an average test score that is at least 90%. He has completed 5 of the 6 tests and his current average is 91%. Which of the following scores is the lowest he can earn while still maintaining his A?

  F. 80%
  G. 85%
  H. 89%
  J. 90%
  K. 91%

53. Determine the number of real solutions there are for $9x^2 - 12x + 18 = 0$.

  A. no real solutions
  B. 1 real solution
  C. 2 real solutions
  D. 3 real solutions
  E. not enough information

54. Find the perimeter of the quadrilateral that circumscribes this circle.

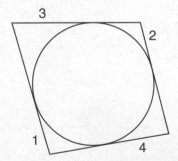

  F. 10
  G. 12
  H. 15
  J. 17
  K. 20

55. Find $f(-3)$ given that $f(x) = -2x(x^2 - 8x + 4) - 3x^2 - 2$.

  A. −258
  B. 31
  C. 193
  D. 247
  E. 258

DO YOUR FIGURING HERE

56. Find point *B* of segment *AB* if *A* is located at (−3, 7) and the midpoint of *AB* is located at (1, 3).
   F. (−2, 10)
   G. (−1, 5)
   H. (3, −7)
   J. (5, −1)
   K. (10, 2)

57. Which function has an amplitude of 4 and a period of 8?
   A. $y = -4\sin\theta$

   B. $y = \sin\dfrac{\pi}{8}\theta$

   C. $y = 4\sin\dfrac{\pi}{8}\theta$

   D. $y = 4\sin\dfrac{\pi}{4}\theta$

   E. $y = \sin\dfrac{\pi}{4}\theta$

58. Find the measure of the exterior angle of a regular dodecagon.
   F. 15°
   G. 30°
   H. 36°
   J. 144°
   K. 150°

59. Select the equation that reflects the coordinates in the table.

x	0	1	2	3
y	2	6	18	54

   A. $y = 3x + 2$
   B. $y = 3x + 3$
   C. $y = 2^x$
   D. $y = 3^x$
   E. $y = 2(3^x)$

60. Find angle *x* in this isosceles trapezoid.

F. 22°
G. 56°
H. 68°
J. 102°
K. 112°

Answer Key

1. E	11. B	21. E	31. B	41. E	51. B
2. J	12. H	22. J	32. G	42. H	52. G
3. E	13. D	23. C	33. B	43. B	53. A
4. G	14. J	24. G	34. H	44. G	54. K
5. A	15. A	25. C	35. D	45. E	55. C
6. H	16. G	26. F	36. G	46. F	56. J
7. A	17. D	27. B	37. C	47. C	57. D
8. J	18. F	28. K	38. J	48. G	58. G
9. C	19. D	29. B	39. E	49. C	59. E
10. J	20. G	30. J	40. G	50. H	60. K

Solutions and Explanations

1. (E) To determine the radius, use the distance formula to find the distance between the point on the circle and the center point. The distance formula is $d = \sqrt{(x_2 - x_1)^2 + (y_2 - y_1)^2}$, which in this case equals $\sqrt{(4-1)^2 + (2--2)^2}$, which equals $\sqrt{3^2 + 4^2} = \sqrt{9+16} = \sqrt{25} = 5$. Now you have the radius and the center point, which is all you need to write the equation of the circle. The general form of the equation is $(x - h)^2 + (y - k)^2 = r^2$. With the center and radius for this particular circle, we have $(x - 4)^2 + (y - 2)^2 = 25$.

2. (J) The first round through you will have $6x^2 - 3x + 21 + 2x^4 + 2x^2 - 3x + 5$. Then, combining like terms and writing in descending order results in $2x^4 + 8x^2 - 6x + 26$.

3. (E) For this problem you can choose to either simplify and then substitute or to substitute and then calculate. Simplifying first results in $2x^2 - 6xy + 2y^2$. With values for x and y substituted into the simplified expression, you have $2(-6)^2 - 6(-6)(3) + 2(3)^2 = 2(36) + 36(3) + 2(9) = 72 + 108 + 18 = 198$.

Substituting in first is fastest because you can enter the values in parentheses and exponents directly into your calculator. $2 \times -6 \times (-6 - 3 \times 3) + 2 \times (3)^2 = 198$.

4. (G) If you set Alissa's age to x, then Bennett is $2x$ and Neal is $x + 3$. The sum of x, $2x$, and $x + 3$ is 63, so $4x + 3 = 63$. Solving for x, you find that Alissa (x) is 15 and so Neal is 18 (3 years older than Alissa).

5. **(A)** Using a proportion to solve, we note that $\frac{mistakes}{minutes} = \frac{2}{3}$. Knowing that she performs for a total of 18 minutes, we can use $\frac{2}{3} = \frac{x}{18}$. Since 3 times 6 is 18, and 2 times 6 is 12, we find that Corina makes 12 mistakes in 18 minutes.

6. **(H)** Every candy bar earns \$1, so x represents the number of dollars earned from candy bars. Every t-shirt earns \$5.75, so $5.75y$ represents the number of dollars earned from t-shirts. The sum of all money earned $(x + 5.75y)$ must be greater than or equal to \$2500 (the amount required to pay for the trip).

7. **(A)** Diagonals of a kite meet at a right angle. Angle 2 and angle CBD are complementary, making $m\angle 2 = 69°$. The two congruency statements are indicated on the diagram. There is not enough information on the diagram to indicate the measure of angle 3.

8. **(J)** In order to have a middle term of $-3x$, there must be an outer and inner product that adds to $-3x$; in this case that is $-6x$ and $3x$. Distributing this answer out will give us the first term of $2x^2$, the middle term of $-6x$, and the last term of -9.

9. **(C)** This is a proportion problem where $\frac{students\ with\ nickname}{total\ students} = \frac{3}{7} = \frac{x}{35}$. Since 7 times 5 is 35, we multiply 5 by 3 to find that 15 out of 35 students will go by a nickname.

10. **(J)** Since $|x - 7| = 5$ we know that $x - 7 = -5$ OR $x - 7 = 5$. To find all possible solutions, we must solve both cases. The first case, $x - 7 = -5$, results in $x = 2$. The second case, $x - 7 = 5$, results in $x = 12$. So the solution is $x = 2$ or 12 because either would result in a true statement.

11. **(B)** Distribute $3x$ across $(x + 4)$ and then -7 across $(x + 4)$ to give $3x^2 + 12x - 7x - 28$, which simplifies to $3x^2 + 5x - 28$.

12. **(H)** A right triangle being rotated around one leg causes the base of the triangle to form a circle and the hypotenuse to slope from the circle to a point that describes a cone.

13. **(D)** With $33 + (4 - 9) - 24 \div 8$, the parentheses and division come before addition and subtraction, resulting in $33 - 5 - 3 = 33 - 8 = 25$.

14. **(J)** This problem can be solved by isolating the radical, squaring both sides, setting the equation equal to zero, and using the quadratic formula. You will

get two real solutions, 8 and 1.5625. However, this process is much more time-consuming than the one you should use on the exam, which is to plug each value into the equation and find the one that makes the sentence true (the one in which the sides of the equation are equal). The only solution choice that makes the equation true is 8.

15. **(A)** Begin by sketching triangle PQR. Using the law of sines enables you to set $\dfrac{\sin 110°}{9}$ equal to $\dfrac{\sin R}{7}$. Multiplying both sides by 7 gives you $\dfrac{7\sin 110°}{9} = \sin R$. In order to isolate R, you must take the inverse sine of both sides, giving you $R = \sin^{-1}\left(\dfrac{7\sin 110°}{9}\right)$.

16. **(G)** This is determined simply by taking 17% of 39%, or $0.17 \times 0.39 = 0.0663$ (6.6%).

17. **(D)** First simplify $\dfrac{3x^5 y^3 z}{x^2 yz^4}$ by dividing (find the difference of the powers) and you get $\dfrac{3x^3 y^2}{z^3}$. Then multiply that by $x^3 y^3 z$ to get $\dfrac{3x^6 y^5}{z^2}$.

18. **(F)** Use your knowledge of the fractions and the decimals and check the value of $\sqrt{2}$ on your calculator. The value of $\sqrt{2}$ is .707, which makes it larger than .7.

19. **(D)** Distribute $(2 + 4i)$ across $(3 - 2i)$ to get $6 - 4i + 12i - 8i^2$ and add the product of $-3i$ and $5i$, which is $-15i^2$. Recalling that i^2 is equivalent to -1, you get $6 + 8i + 8 + 15$, which simplifies to $29 + 8i$.

20. **(G)** Substitute the values of a, b, and c into the quadratic formula to get $\dfrac{-4 \pm \sqrt{4^2 - 4(2)(2)}}{2(2)} = \dfrac{-4 \pm \sqrt[2]{16 - 16}}{4} = \dfrac{-4}{4} = -1$.

21. **(E)** Simply add 4 to the x coordinate and -7 to the y coordinate to get $(2 + 4, -1 + -8)$, which simplifies to $(6, -8)$.

22. **(J)** To quickly eliminate all fractions, multiply through both sides of the equation by 20. You will be left with $15n + 8n = 920$. Collecting like terms results in $23n = 920$, and dividing by 23 on both sides reveals that $n = 40$.

23. **(C)** The general equation for a parabola is $f(x) = a(x - h)^2 + k$. You can substitute the coordinates of the maximum for h and k and the coordinates of the point for x and $f(x)$. These substitutions give you $2 = a(5 - 3)^2 + 4$, which simplifies to $2 = 4a + 4$, which simplifies to $-2 = 4a$ and $-\frac{1}{2} = a$. Once you have the value of a, write the equation of the line by leaving $f(x)$ and x variables and replacing a, h, and k with the values specific to this function.

24. **(G)** If 60% of 40% of Jack's time is spent doing anything but playing, then 40% of 40% is left for playing. 40% of 40% is 16%.

25. **(C)** Multiply across the equation by $(x^2 - 2)(x - 4)$ to eliminate denominators. This leaves you with $-2(x - 4) = 2(x^2 - 2)$, which distributes out to $-2x + 8 = 2x^2 - 4$. Bringing all terms to the right and setting the equation equal to zero gives you $0 = 2x^2 + 2x - 12$. By factoring out a 2, you have a quadratic equation with a leading coefficient of one. $0 = 2(x^2 + x - 6)$ factors to $0 = 2(x + 3)(x - 2)$, giving you the solutions of x as -3 and 2. You must check to make sure that neither of these x values would cause the original equation to be undefined. They do not, so the solution is $\{-3, 2\}$.

26. **(F)** The multiplicative property of equality says that when you multiply two equivalent expressions by the same non-zero term, the resulting expressions are also equivalent.

27. **(B)** The volume of a cone is $\frac{1}{3}$ the volume of the cylinder with the equivalent base and height. Since the area of the base is 9π and the height is $7x$, the volume is $\frac{1}{3} \cdot 9\pi \cdot 7x$ or $21\pi x$.

28. **(K)** $\sin^2\theta + \cos^2\theta = 1$, and subtracting $\cos^2\theta$ from both sides leaves you with $\sin^2\theta$ in terms of cosine. The problem states that you are to find the value of sine in terms of cosine, so you must take the square root of both sides, which results in $\sin\theta = \pm\sqrt{1 - \cos^2\theta}$.

29. **(B)** Each term is decreasing at the constant rate of negative 3, which gives you $-3n$. The next step is to determine the value of the rule when n is zero (what we would call the y intercept if we were finding an equation in terms of x and y). To do that, we use any value of n and the corresponding value of the rule. Since $-3(1) +$ zero value $= 3$, we find that the zero value equals 6. Given the constant rate and the value at $n = 0$, we are able to write the rule of $-3n + 6$.

30. **(J)** The problem gives you diameters of the medium and large pizzas. The formula for the area of a circle is πr^2. To find the radius, simply take half of the diameter. The area of the large pizza is 8 divided by 2 squared and multiplied

by π, or 16π, and the area of the medium pizza is 6 divided by 2 squared and multiplied by π, or 9π. The difference in the areas is simply $16\pi - 9\pi$.

31. (B) Raising a power to a power requires that you raise the coefficient to that power and multiply each power by the power (in this case 3). Raising $-2x^2y^5$ to the 3rd equals $-8x^6y^{15}$. Then multiply that result by $3x^3y^4$ to get $-24x^9y^{19}$.

32. (G) The greatest number that divides evenly into both $116x$ and 128 is 4. This can be found by first dividing by two and then dividing by two again. The factors left are 29 and 32. Since 29 is prime and is not a factor of 32, you have found that the greatest common factor is 2^2, or 4.

33. (B) The slopes of perpendicular lines are negative reciprocals of each other. To find the slope of the line perpendicular to $-3x + 5y = 20$, find the slope of this line either by using $\dfrac{-B}{A}$ or by solving for y. The slope of this line is $\dfrac{3}{5}$, and the negative reciprocal of $\dfrac{3}{5}$ is $\dfrac{-5}{3}$.

34. (H) The DJ charges $35 for showing up regardless of the number of hours and then $20 per hour of service. $20x$ represents the cost for x hours and $+ 35$ represents the base charge. $20x + 35$ is the total cost of hiring a DJ for the dance.

35. (D) Be sure to write all of the side lengths on the diagram. Once you have done that, add them up to find 38 as the perimeter.

36. (G)

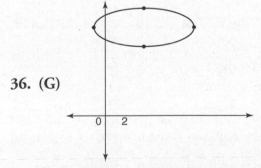

The equation represents an ellipse with the center point at (4, 9) and extended 5 in x and 2 in y. The graph for choice G shows the ellipse translated from the origin to the right 4 and up 9. It extends 5 horizontally in both directions and 2 vertically in both directions.

37. (C) There are a total of 14 marbles, and 3 of them are blue. The probability of choosing a blue marble is 3 out of 14.

38. (J) Factoring out a $3x$ leaves you with a quadratic with a leading coefficient of 1. Factoring $x^2 - 5x - 14$ gives you $(x - 7)(x + 2)$. So, all together you have

$3x(x - 7)(x + 2) = 0$, which means that either $3x$ and/or $(x - 7)$ and/or $(x + 2)$ must equal zero. Taking them one at a time, x must equal either 0 and/or -2 and/or 7, which is written as $\{-2, 0, 7\}$.

39. **(E)** Use the two points to find the slope, $\dfrac{6}{-7.5}$, and then use one point and the slope in the slope intercept equation to find $b = 2$. Once you have the slope intercept form, multiply through by -7.5 and move x to the left side. Multiply through by -2 to get the equation in standard form (positive x coefficient and no decimals or fractions).

40. **(G)** The area of a triangle is $\dfrac{1}{2}$ base times height. The base and height must meet at a 90° angle. For this problem, you are given the hypotenuse and a leg, which do not meet at a right angle. The first step is to determine the length of the second leg so that you have the information you need to determine area. Using the Pythagorean theorem, you find that the square root of $100 - 64$ is 6. Using the area formula, the area is $\dfrac{1}{2}(6)(8) = 24$.

41. **(E)** Solving an equation involving absolute value requires that you first isolate the absolute value and then solve for both cases that make the equation true. In this case you have $|5x - 9| = 7$, which means that $5x - 9 = \pm 7$. If $5x - 9 = 7$ then $x = \dfrac{16}{5}$, and if $5x - 9 = -7$ then $x = \dfrac{2}{5}$.

42. **(H)** The volume of a pyramid is $\dfrac{1}{3}$ of the area of the base times the height. In this case, the base is a regular hexagon with side length of 4. To find the area of a regular polygon, you can use the formula $A = \dfrac{1}{2}ap$, where a is the apothem (height of an interior triangle) and p is the perimeter. To find the apothem you must consider that a regular hexagon is made up of six equilateral triangles, making the height of each $\dfrac{1}{2}s\sqrt{3}$. The area of this hexagon is $\dfrac{1}{2}(4)(2\sqrt{3}) = 4\sqrt{3}$. Take that area and multiply it by 1/3 and the height of 9, and you find that the volume of the pyramid is $72\sqrt{3}$.

43. **(B)** The ladder meets the ground at a 65° angle and is 17 feet long. This forms a right triangle with the building. The triangle has a hypotenuse of 17 feet, and you are asked to find the height it reaches against the building. To find the height, given the hypotenuse and the angle opposite the height, use the sine

function. In this case, $\sin 65° = \dfrac{x}{17}$. Multiplying both sides by 17 will give you the value of x, which is 15.4.

44. **(G)** A diameter of the circle can be drawn to have an endpoint in common with the chord. The distance from the center to the chord is the perpendicular bisector of the chord. Drawing the distance, the chord and the diameter will construct a right triangle with a hypotenuse of 17 cm and a leg that is 15 cm. Finding the distance is as simple as finding the square root of the difference between 17 squared and 15 squared, which is 8.

45. **(E)** The arc lengths of 98° and 104° give you the inscribed angle measures of 49° and 52°. These inscribed angle measures are two angles in a triangle. The third angle is 79°, and $x = \dfrac{98+104}{2}$ and measures 101°.

46. **(F)** This problem involves two steps. The first is to use the series formula to determine the number of terms included in the sum. Using the formula, you find that $72 = \dfrac{n}{2}\left(\dfrac{8}{3}+\dfrac{40}{3}\right)$, which results in $n = 9$. Once you know that $\dfrac{40}{3}$ is in fact the 9th term, you can use the sequence formula to determine the common difference. Using the sequence formula, you find that $\dfrac{40}{3} = \dfrac{8}{3} + (8)d$ and $d = \dfrac{4}{3}$. Knowing the common difference and the first term in the sequence, you will simply add $\dfrac{4}{3}$ to each term to find the next.

47. **(C)** Simplifying each radical, the equation simplifies to $15x\sqrt{2} - 4x\sqrt{2} = 3\sqrt{2}$. Adding like terms on the left side of the equation gives you $11x\sqrt{2} = 3\sqrt{2}$, and dividing both sides by $11\sqrt{2}$ results in the solution $x = \dfrac{3}{11}$.

48. **(G)** Distribute −2 across $(x - 7)$, add like terms, solve for x, and you find that $x = -15$.

49. **(C)** To determine the height of the equilateral triangle, you can remember the special right triangle and know that the height is $6\sqrt{3}$. Or you can drop a segment from the vertex perpendicular to the base and use the Pythagorean theorem to find the height, given that the hypotenuse is 12 and the base in this case would be half that, or 6. Once you have determined the height, use the triangle area formula to find that the area is $\dfrac{1}{2}(12)\left(6\sqrt{3}\right) = 36\sqrt{3}$.

50. (**H**) One way to solve is to write each equation in standard form and use elimination. Another way to solve is to substitute the value of y which is $-\frac{1}{2}x + \frac{13}{4}$ for y in the second equation, solve for x, and then substitute back in for y. The most efficient way to solve this system is to solve the second equation for y, put both equations into the graphing calculator, graph them, and find the point of intersection.

51. (**B**) The diagonals in a kite meet at a perpendicular angle; AC is bisected but DB is not bisected. The diagonals also bisect angles D and B but do not bisect A and C.

52. (**G**) Currently Tony has a total of 455 points (91 times 5), and in order to keep an A he must have a total of 540 points (90 times 6) after the next test. That is a difference of 85 points, so Tony must earn at least 85 points, on the next test to maintain his A average.

53. (**A**) The discriminant of the quadratic formula, $b^2 - 4ac$, tells you the value of the part of the formula that is under the square root symbol. Taking the square root of a negative number will result in imaginary solutions or no real solutions. In this case, $144 - 4(9)(18)$—or if you divide through by 3 first, $16 - 4(3)(6)$—are both negative, resulting in no real solutions.

54. (**K**) From each vertex to the point tangent to the circle, the two segments are congruent. So, the perimeter is $3 + 2 + 2 + 4 + 4 + 1 + 1 + 3 = 20$.

55. (**C**) To find $f(-3)$, substitute -3 in for each x and use order of operations. Doing so will give you $6(9 + 24 + 4) - 27 - 2 = 6(37) - 29 = 193$.

56. (**J**) The midpoint is made up of coordinates that are the average of the coordinates of the endpoints. In this case you can find x and y by using the midpoint formula with one endpoint and using (x, y) as the second endpoint. For instance, $\frac{-3 + x}{2} = 1$ and $\frac{7 + y}{2} = 3$. Solving each equation for the variable results in an x value of 5 and a y value of -1, indicating that the missing endpoint occurs at $(5, -1)$.

57. (**D**) The amplitude change is determined by the coefficient on the function. The period change is determined by the coefficient on the angle. Recall that $\frac{2\pi}{b}$ is the period, so setting 8 equal to $\frac{2\pi}{b}$ and solving for b gives you $\frac{\pi}{4}$.

58. (**G**) A dodecagon has 12 sides and the sum of the interior angles is 1800°, making each interior angle 150°. The interior and exterior angle pairs are supplementary, making the exterior angle measure 30°.

59. (**E**) The pattern is increasing at an exponential rate, in this case meaning that each term is three times the last term. This growth indicates that 3 must be raised to the x power. It does not tell you everything, though. You must still evaluate the expression at $x = 0$ to determine the rest. When $x = 0$, $3^x = 1$, but the value of y is 2, indicating that 3^x must be multiplied by 2, making the equation $y = 2(3^x)$.

60. (**K**) In an isosceles trapezoid, the two angles at each base are congruent to each other. Since a trapezoid has two parallel sides, the side crossing those parallel sides is a transversal and results in consecutive interior angles being supplementary. With those two relationships, the result is that x and 68° are supplementary, making $x = 112°$.

READING

Balancing Efficiency and Accuracy

CHAPTER 13

- Reading strategies
- Identifying the main idea
- Taking notes

Many movies begin with what is called an establishing shot—a shot that reveals the expanse of the setting. When approaching the ACT reading test for the first time, it's helpful to pretend you have a movie camera in hand so that you, too, can shoot an establishing shot and then zoom in on more specific information.

READING: A VISUAL METAPHOR

Pretend you're aiming a camera at the test. Zoom all the way out and what do you see? Four passages and 40 questions. Zoom in one notch further. The passages come in one of four categories: prose fiction, social science, humanities, and natural science. At this point, you have two options: zoom in on the passage or pan over to the questions.

Start with the passage. Zoom in on one: social science. You notice a citation and seven or eight paragraphs. When you look at the citation, what knowledge does it trigger? Does it look like a government document? A piece of investigative journalism? A biographical essay? Now zoom in on the paragraphs. Do they look bulky, wordy, sparse? All the information you're registering can work to your advantage. Zoom to the first paragraph. It either introduces a topic, provides some necessary background, or offers an idea to refute in the second paragraph. Look at the body of the essay. It offers examples and explanations that support the central idea of the essay. Point your camera at the last paragraph. It offers a conclusion that reasserts the central idea or question, maybe spinning the essay in some new, imaginative direction. Focus on the transitions. All paragraphs fit together into an organized, discernable whole, like links in a chain. Zoom back out for the big picture, imagining tone or theme. Is the tone cynical? Reverent? Ironic? Didactic? What's the main point or central idea? What's the author trying to say about the topic?

Now focus in on the questions. Quickly, you realize that some questions offer specific line number references and contain eye-catching terms such as proper nouns. That helps! You notice, as you zoom in and begin examining the wording of particular questions, that some ask you to recall details, some ask you to infer ideas based on details, and some ask about the central purpose, idea, or tone of the essay. Occasionally, you might spot a contextual vocabulary question. With a little more critical eye, you might notice that questions jump around in the passage. Question 3 might ask about line 79, while question 7 asks about line 4.

In a moment of revelation, you realize something else: the correct answers are right in front of you! You only need to weed out the incorrect ones! Usually, you'll be able to eliminate two or three right away, which gives you, in essence, the equivalent of a true/false question.

Balancing Accuracy and Efficiency

The movie camera analogy shows that there is a tremendous amount you know about the passage before even reading it. You'll become a more efficient reader if you approach the reading test in terms of the camera analogy, which allows you to zoom in and out, refocus, and reframe in the blink of an eye.

INSIDE THE ACT 36 MIND

The ACT reading section is about balancing efficiency and accuracy. You don't need to skim, but you also can't luxuriate in the content or style of the passage. Based on clues the test offers, you will know when to look at the big picture and when to focus on details, when to look at the passage and when to look at the questions. Eventually, you'll know how to avoid a useless piece of information without missing something important. That's the key. Eight minutes per passage is not a lot of time, but it's enough if you work wisely.

READING STRATEGIES

The chapters on reading, besides supplying you with lots of practice, will cover the following strategies:

It's All in the Timing

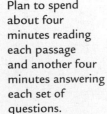

TIP

Plan to spend about four minutes reading each passage and another four minutes answering each set of questions.

When you're working on a homework assignment or a final exam, you often have as much time as you need to read and answer questions. Not this time. To prepare for the reading test, you'll need to adopt time-saving strategies. More students run out of time on the reading section of the ACT than on any other section. On a very general level, you want to spend about four minutes reading each passage and four minutes answering each set of questions, which leaves you three minutes of leeway at the end of the test. Timing is the key to success.

Before Reading

Zoom Out and See the Big Picture

Take a few seconds to look at the passage as a whole. How many paragraphs does it contain? What size are the paragraphs? How many lines long is the passage?

Mentally get a picture of the size and even the structure of the passage. Do you notice multiple lines of dialogue? Are some of the paragraphs longer than others? By gaining a broader perspective of the passage, you prepare your mind to read in more detail.

Clear Your Mind and Preheat Your Brain

These strategies sound simple, but they are easy to overlook when time is a factor. Remove all mental clutter. Think only about your background knowledge of the topic and the words in front of you. Forget about any mental distractions that might cause you to lose focus as you read. Zoom in on the passage's citation, thinking briefly about the topic and glancing at key words in the passage. Spend a few seconds identifying what you already know about the topic. Your brain needs to be primed to accept the new information. Skimming the questions for key words, line numbers or dates may also help you focus your reading, but don't spend more than a few seconds doing so. Reading the questions prior to reading the passage is NOT recommended; there is not enough time to do this.

While Reading

Identify Main Idea and Tone

Once you've "preheated your brain," use the first paragraph to begin identifying the main idea and tone of the passage. Early on in your reading, consider the purpose of the passage. A first paragraph of a fictional passage may introduce the main character and conflict within a story. A social science passage may begin by exploring the dynamics of Socialist Russia. Think about the author's attitude, the tone of the passage. How does the author feel about the subject or topic? Normally, you'll be able to tell within a paragraph or two. As you continue beyond paragraphs 1 and 2, read to absorb the big ideas, knowing you can look up the details later.

"Indexing" the Passage: The Key to Balancing Efficiency and Accuracy!

No strategy will help you identify important details more efficiently than this one. Don't get bogged down in detailed note taking or text marking, but do follow this quick but *invaluable* three-step process, which works best when executed paragraph by paragraph.

Indexing 101:

1. **Read the paragraph**, trying to focus on its main argument or claim. Non-fiction paragraphs will almost always have one. The main argument will be a combination of the topic *and* the author's opinion on the topic. Avoid getting bogged down in detail as much as you can, but don't skim either—reading for the main argument lies somewhere in between.

2. **Summarize the main argument** of the paragraph in your head, *in your own words*. Each paragraph will have a central argument or angle. Some might have more than one major idea that feels important, but try your best to narrow your summary.

3. **Choose a key word or short phrase to write in the margin** before moving on to the next paragraph. The word only needs to make sense to you, as its sole purpose is to trigger your short-term memory if and when a question relates to this paragraph.

Now, try the strategy using a sample paragraph:

1. **Read.**

   Soon the governments of the United States and its allies enthusiastically pursued a "peace dividend," slashing military budgets and manpower levels in order to reduce taxes or divert resources to other pursuits. By the late 1990s sobering international challenges had taken the bloom off, however; the enduring complexities of national security were apparent to many. Indeed, although the stakes were never as high as they had been during the potential life-or-death struggle with the Soviet Union, American armed forces found their operational tempo of deployment to distant theaters and into harm's way greater than it had been since the Vietnam War.

2. **Summarize the main argument in your head.** Once you have sifted through bizarre phrases such as "had taken the bloom off" and "operational tempo," your summary will probably sound something like the following:

   "Governments cut military budgets after the Cold War but eventually realized that they were still deploying forces for other challenges."

3. **Write a key word or phrase in the margin.** Your key phrase might be something like *"still deploying,"* but it can be anything as long as it is brief and reminds you of the paragraph's central claim.

Of course, the more you practice this strategy, the more efficient and effective you'll become at it. There are two reasons this strategy works. First, since indexing forces you to focus on the main argument of a paragraph and to quickly commit the argument to memory before you move on, it makes you more efficient when determining answers to questions. Second, indexing helps you break the passage up into manageable sections. By spotlighting one chunk of text at a time, you will feel less overwhelmed and more focused as you move through the test.

TIP

Transitions are the links that hold the essay together, so be sure to note them as you index a passage.

Take Note of Transitions

As you read, consider how the passage is structured. Notice the major transitions. In a traditional essay, an intro will precede the supporting paragraphs, which will precede a conclusion. Many ACT passages fit this mold. As you index the passage, pause to consider (for just a second) how paragraphs connect. After quickly reading the passage in three to four minutes, you should have a good idea about how the entire passage is organized. When it comes to tracking down details, knowing how paragraphs fit together is as important as knowing the contents of each paragraph.

After Reading

Guess First, Then Find the Answer

Especially when questions ask you to infer the main point, the tone, or the definition of a word in context, treating the question as though it were a "short answer" question can help immensely. Guessing the correct answer first may help eliminate some answer options or help identify which options sound similar to your initial response. If none of the answer options are close to your initial guess, then you will probably need to spend more time looking for the answer to that question. These indicators can help you search your index to locate the answer within the text. A key phrase from the question stem probably falls into one of the categories listed in your index. Your understanding of the organizational structure will be helpful as well, as are dates. For example, if you see the year *1938* in the question, chances are it's somewhere in the passage, too. Skip over your index and go directly to the passage to find the date. All of these strategies can get you close to an answer before you even consider the four answer choices.

TIP

To find the correct answer look for line numbers, key words, and dates within the question.

QUESTION TYPES

Essentially, the ACT gives you three types of reading questions:

1. Questions that ask you to find a detail in the passage

2. Questions that ask you to make an inference or judgment about the passage

3. Questions that test your knowledge of vocabulary in context (least common)

Knowing that you'll only be required to do three different things when you answer questions can be comforting when you're pressed for time.

READING IS THE KEY!

Whatever you do, master the skills in this section. If you can handle the reading portion of the exam, you will be at a huge advantage when it comes to at least three quarters of the ACT, as science and English—and even mathematics, to a degree— require many of these skills. Good luck, and remember to let your camera work for you.

Fiction: Are You a Good Judge of Character?

CHAPTER 14

- Staying focused
- Working efficiently
- The four pillars of fiction

Many students find the fiction passage to be the easiest passage in the reading section. Why? Because, if you're like many high school students, teachers have fed you a steady diet of fiction for years. You understand its central elements—plot, character, conflict, theme—the way a dog knows its favorite corner. You've circled around and around these elements, settled into them, wandered away, returned. What's more, you likely require very little time with a new piece of imaginative literature before you've become accustomed to its author's particular rhythms and tendencies. In short, you're already a fiction pro. Even if you prefer to read nonfiction, you feel at ease—or at least not totally bewildered—when you sit in front of a work of fiction.

STAYING FOCUSED

For you, the biggest challenge may be to stay focused and, in a sense, not let yourself enjoy or analyze the reading too much.

INSIDE THE ACT 36 MIND

Remember. You are reading fiction *only* to answer multiple-choice questions on the ACT. You are not reading for enjoyment. You are not reading to wow your teacher with your ability to analyze similes, symbols, and syntax. You're reading for points, and points alone!

The purpose of this chapter is to teach you to read fiction in a way that maximizes its value to you as a test-taker. You have 8 minutes to read a 900–1000-word passage and answer 10 questions. You won't have time to luxuriate and enjoy the story, and you won't have time to analyze the significance of the color red as it applies to feminist discourse. If you want to pick up "easy" points on the fiction passage, focus on working as efficiently as possible. Move on as quickly as you can to the non-fiction passages, where you will see 75 percent of the points.

Work Accurately but Efficiently

Know *why* you're reading! Here are two approaches to avoid if you want to save time:

1. *Don't* **read for enjoyment.** Reading because you love the words will hurt you, as relaxed reading is seldom goal-oriented reading.

   Skilled readers, even when they read with no goal in mind, are constantly making connections. Mostly semiconsciously, they wonder about things, remember other books and events, notice structure, repair confusion, and marvel at expert writing. For now, set aside the expansive mind-wandering that makes reading enjoyable.

2. *Don't* **read as though you're eventually going to write an essay.** Although more closely related to your goal, reading the way you've been taught to read in English class doesn't work well either. Reading for the perfect essay topic isn't focused enough. When doing so, you tend to troll the passage for every possible minute detail, analyzing a work of fiction to death in the hope that you'll discover something "original" to say.

   If you enjoy searching for subtle arguments, the ACT is not calibrated for you. It's easier! Focus on four pillars of analysis: characterization, overview, structure, and tone. The first letters of these categories spell "COST," and it will cost you time and accuracy if you fail to focus on these simple tenets.

> **REMEMBER**
>
> Reading fiction on the ACT is very different from reading for your English class or for pleasure. On the exam, you're reading for points only!

COST: THE FOUR PILLARS OF FICTION

A writer of traditional fiction can only develop so much in 75 to100 lines. Fiction passages, therefore, are almost always brief studies in character. They describe one to three characters, their relationships, and their inner or outer conflicts. Fiction passages also tend to present some sort of general theme, so reading with a sense of the main idea is a must. Besides understanding characterization and acquiring a general sense of the passage, strive to understand the passage's structure. Using the movie camera metaphor as a reminder (see the introduction), internalize an outline of the passage. Finally, gain a sense of the narrator's attitude toward her surroundings and a feel for the mood the author establishes.

Characterization

As almost all fiction passages are character-driven, understanding the subtleties of character will help you immensely. Ask yourself the following questions as you read, and you should know all you need to know to answer even the most challenging ACT question:

- How many central characters are there?

- From whose point of view is the passage told?

- How do the central characters look, think, feel, and act?

- How would you characterize the relationships among central characters?

- What conflicts exist among central characters?

- What conflicts exist within the minds of central characters?

Practice enough and you'll be able to do this kind of simple analysis in the time it takes to read the passage quickly.

Overview

Read to identify the theme, *big picture*, or main idea—whichever term makes you most comfortable. Having a general sense of the passage will help you answer detail and inference questions and will allow you to answer big-picture questions before you even look at the answer choices.

Structure

Zoom out to observe the paragraph sequence, and determine each paragraph's role in the passage as a whole. Essentially, create a brief index or summary of the passage as you go. The most efficient way to internalize the structure of a passage is to write a one- to three-word summary of each paragraph in the margins. Why one to three words? Anything more takes up too much time, and anything less decreases your ability to recall the paragraph when you refer back to it, which you'll have to do when asked a question about detail.

TIP

Restrict your index to one to three words per paragraph.

Tone and Mood

Tone in fiction is the narrator's attitude toward the subject. Mood is the emotion or feeling that you, the reader, are supposed to receive from the passage as a whole. Getting the feel for these "voice" elements will position you for success on many ACT questions.

That's it. All ACT fiction questions will be variations on one of these literary elements. No Christ figures, esoteric literary devices, or Freudian analysis, just crisp, clear, focused reading. Let's try a couple questions about *Dracula*, by Bram Stoker.

EXERCISE #1

What I saw was the Count's head coming out from the window. I did not see the face, but I knew the man by the neck and the movement of his back and arms. In any case I could not mistake the hands, which I had had so many opportunities of studying. I was at first interested and somewhat amused, for it is wonderful how small a matter will interest and amuse a man when he is a prisoner. But my very feelings changed to repulsion and terror when I saw the whole man slowly emerge from the window and begin to crawl down the castle wall over the dreadful abyss, face down with his cloak spreading out around him like great wings. At first I could not believe my eyes. I thought it was some trick of the moonlight, some weird effect of shadow, but I kept looking, and it could be no delusion. I saw the fingers and toes grasp the corners of the stones, worn clear of the mortar by the stress of years, and by thus using every projection and inequality move downwards with considerable speed, just as a lizard moves along a wall.

What manner of man is this, or what manner of creature, is it in the semblance of man? I feel the dread of this horrible place overpowering me. I am in fear, in awful fear, and there is no escape for me. I am encompassed about with terrors that I dare not think of.

Practice Questions

1. Which of the following details is NOT included in the narrator's description of the Count?
   A. his winglike cloak
   B. his terrifying facial expression
   C. his nimble fingers and toes
   D. his inverted body position

2. It can be inferred from the passage that the narrator witnesses the actions of the Count with a mixture of:
   F. respect and nostalgia.
   G. anxiety and arrogance.
   H. impatience and amusement.
   J. curiosity and fear.

Discussion

Question 1: This question asks about detail, and you may notice that one of the pillars of fiction is *not* attention to detail. Confused? Don't be. Two strategies are on your side. First, if you paid attention to the characterization of Count Dracula, you know that he is depicted crawling facedown wearing a cloak. Rule out answer A. Now think about structure. In most passages, you'll have several paragraphs with which to contend. If you have a sense of the focus of each paragraph, you know that paragraph 1 contains a detailed description of the Count. Take a few seconds to scan the paragraph, finding references to his fingers and toes and his inverted body position. C and D are out, leaving you with answer B. If you require further proof, note that lines 1 and 2 state clearly that the narrator can't "see the face" and therefore can't read a facial expression. **Answer: (B).**

Question 2: A sense of tone and mood is critical to this question. It could be argued that the narrator respects the Count, but nowhere is there proof that he feels a longing for the past. Rule out option F. Next, the narrator feel anxious, but he feels more helpless than arrogant; therefore, option G is incorrect. H and J are the best answers, as it could be said that the narrator feels impatient in the sense that most prisoners feel impatient, and he does mention early in paragraph 1 that he is "amused." But look at the scope of the passage. What's missing? Doesn't the overriding tone have more to do with fear than impatience or amusement? The narrator's amusement is passing, and his impatience has little to do with his observations of the Count. Fear drives the tone of this passage. Be wary of "out of scope" answers such as answer H. These kinds of answer choices are prevalent in the ACT Reading section, and often appear correct, especially when you're pressed for time. **Answer: (J).**

EXERCISE #2

Read the following passage and respond to the questions listed below it. The passage is an excerpt from Lewis Carroll's *Alice in Wonderland*.

"You ought to be ashamed of yourself," said Alice, "a great girl like you," (she might well say this), "to go on crying in this way! Stop this moment, I tell you!" But she went on all the same, shedding gallons of tears, until there was a large
Line pool all round her, about four inches deep and reaching half down the hall.
(5) After a time she heard a little pattering of feet in the distance, and she hastily dried her eyes to see what was coming. It was the White Rabbit returning, splendidly dressed, with a pair of white kid gloves in one hand and a large fan in the other: he came trotting along in a great hurry, muttering to himself as he came, "Oh! the Duchess, the Duchess! Oh! won't she be savage if I've kept
(10) her waiting!" Alice felt so desperate that she was ready to ask help of any one; so, when the Rabbit came near her, she began, in a low, timid voice, "If you please, sir—" The Rabbit started violently, dropped the white kid gloves and the fan and skurried away into the darkness as hard as he could go.

• How many central characters are there?

_____

_____

_____

- From whose point of view is the passage told?

  _____

  _____

  _____

- How would you describe the way central characters look, think, feel, and act?

  _____

  _____

  _____

- How would you characterize the relationships among central characters?

  _____

  _____

  _____

- What conflicts exist among central characters?

  _____

  _____

  _____

- What conflicts exist within the minds of central characters?

  _____

  _____

  _____

Practice Questions

Now, answer these multiple-choice questions about the passage.

1. When Alice stops talking to herself and addresses the rabbit, her attitude goes from:
   A. timid about her crying to angry.
   B. nervous about the rabbit to timid.
   C. critical of herself to hesitant.
   D. decisive about her situation to indecisive.

2. All of the following details convey the rabbit's hurried state EXCEPT:
   F. "a little pattering of feet" (line 5).
   G. "The rabbit started violently" (line 12).
   H. "'won't she be savage if I've kept her waiting!'" (lines 9–10).
   J. "scurried away into the darkness" (line 13).

Discussion

Question 1: Knowledge of both characterization and structure will help you in question 1. Furthermore, this question presents opportunity to employ the "guess first, then answer" strategy. In reading the short passage, it should become clear to you that one central character, from whose point of view the story is told, has a surprise run-in with another character. The change in the central character's attitude—one state before the encounter, another state after the encounter—becomes the focus of the passage. Alice reproaches herself for crying before the rabbit appears and timidly asks for help after he appears, her desperation overpowering her self-reproach for just a moment. So, you might guess that her attitude shifts from self-reproach to cautiousness. Now look at the answer choices. Option A, "timid about her crying to angry," makes little sense given your reading. Alice may seem angry at herself in the first half of the passage, but once the rabbit appears, she focuses on trying to get help. If anything, the attitudes are reversed. Rule out A. The phrase "nervous about the rabbit" should allow you to rule out option B, because nowhere in the text does it suggest that Alice might be nervous about the rabbit before the rabbit appears. In fact, the passage suggests that the rabbit arrives unexpectedly, that Alice hasn't considered his existence until he enters the scene. Option C matches your initial guess fairly well: "self-reproach" sounds like "critical of herself," and "cautiousness" is in the same family as "hesitant." Consider option D: Alice does not seem decisive about her situation at the outset of the passage. If anything, she seems somewhat lost and confused. So, even though she appears somewhat "indecisive" once the rabbit appears, option D can't be correct because she is never decisive in the beginning of the passage. **Answer: (C).**

TIP

Watch for changes in a character's attitude over the course of a passage.

Question 2: In order to answer this one correctly, you have to have a sense of how details in fiction convey characterization and mood. You probably realized the rabbit was in a hurry when you read the passage. Now determine which three of the four details make him appear rushed. Option F, "a little pattering of feet," is an auditory image that represents someone in a hurry. Option G, "the rabbit started violently," is in the spirit of the rabbit's jumpy personality but really represents his surprise at meeting Alice more than his rushed state. Option H, a piece of dialogue indicating that the rabbit does not want to keep the duchess waiting, refers directly to his hurried state. Option J, "scurried away into the darkness," again depicts the rabbit in a rush. The rabbit's reaction in option G does not necessarily imply that he is in a hurry. **Answer: (G).**

EXERCISE #3

Read the following passage. In the margin next to each paragraph write down a one- to three-word summary. If you see dialogue or extremely short paragraphs, it may be in your best interest to "bundle," or summarize several short paragraphs at once.

The following is an excerpt from *The Adventures of Tom Sawyer* by Mark Twain.

"TOM!"

No answer.

"TOM!"

Line   No answer.

(5)   "What's gone with that boy, I wonder? You TOM!"

No answer.

The old lady pulled her spectacles down and looked over them about the room; then she put them up and looked out under them. She seldom or never looked THROUGH them for so small a thing as a boy; they were her state pair, the

(10)   pride of her heart, and were built for "style," not service—she could have seen through a pair of stove-lids just as well. She looked perplexed for a moment, and then said, not fiercely, but still loud enough for the furniture to hear:

"Well, I lay if I get hold of you I'll—"

She did not finish, for by this time she was bending down and punching

(15)   under the bed with the broom, and so she needed breath to punctuate the punches with. She resurrected nothing but the cat.

"I never did see the beat of that boy!"

She went to the open door and stood in it and looked out among the tomato vines and "jimpson" weeds that constituted the garden. No Tom. So she

(20)   lifted up her voice at an angle calculated for distance and shouted:

"Y-o-u-u TOM!"

There was a slight noise behind her and she turned just in time to seize a small boy by the slack of his roundabout and arrest his flight.

"There! I might 'a' thought of that closet. What you been doing in there?"

(25)   "Nothing."

"Nothing! Look at your hands. And look at your mouth. What IS that truck?"

"I don't know, aunt."

"Well, I know. It's jam—that's what it is. Forty times I've said if you didn't

(30)   let that jam alone I'd skin you. Hand me that switch."

The switch hovered in the air—the peril was desperate—

"My! Look behind you, aunt!"

The old lady whirled round, and snatched her skirts out of danger. The lad fled on the instant, scrambled up the high board-fence, and disappeared over it.

(35)   His aunt Polly stood surprised a moment, and then broke into a gentle laugh.

"Hang the boy, can't I never learn anything? Ain't he played me tricks enough like that for me to be looking out for him by this time? But old fools is the biggest fools there is. Can't learn an old dog new tricks, as the saying is. But my goodness, he never plays them alike, two days, and how is a body to

(40) know what's coming? He 'pears to know just how long he can torment me before I get my dander up, and he knows if he can make out to put me off for a minute or make me laugh, it's all down again and I can't hit him a lick. I ain't doing my duty by that boy, and that's the Lord's truth, goodness knows. Spare the rod and spile the child, as the Good Book says. I'm a laying

(45) up sin and suffering for us both, I know. He's full of the Old Scratch, but laws-a-me! he's my own dead sister's boy, poor thing, and I ain't got the heart to lash him, somehow. Every time I let him off, my conscience does hurt me so, and every time I hit him my old heart most breaks. Well-a-well, man that is born of woman is of few days and full of trouble, as the Scripture

(50) says, and I reckon it's so. He'll play hookey this evening,* and I'll just be obleeged to make him work, to-morrow, to punish him. It's mighty hard to make him work Saturdays, when all the boys is having holiday, but he hates work more than he hates anything else, and I've GOT to do some of my duty by him, or I'll be the ruination of the child."

(55) Tom did play hookey, and he had a very good time. He got back home barely in season to help Jim, the small colored boy, saw next-day's wood and split the kindlings before supper—at least he was there in time to tell his adventures to Jim while Jim did three-fourths of the work.

POSSIBLE STRUCTURAL INDEX OF THE PASSAGE

Lines 1–6: Woman calls repeatedly for "Tom"—no answer.

Lines 7–12: Description of glasses—woman can't see well.

Lines 13–21: Continues to express frustration while looking for Tom.

Lines 22–31: Woman finds Tom eating jam in the closet and threatens to beat him.

Lines 32–35: Tom escapes.

Lines 36–54: Woman, "Aunt Polly," ponders her parenting skills and her ambivalent feelings about Tom—characterized as a kind, upstanding, concerned parent.

Lines 55–58: Tom is characterized as unabashedly mischievous.

TIP

For passages with dialogue or very short paragraphs, try "bundling" several paragraphs together in your index.

The above notes are more developed than yours should be. They have been expanded in order to illustrate this strategy for you. Your notes need only be long enough to trigger your short-term memory—no more than one or two words per section.

---

*Southwestern for "afternoon"

Practice Questions

Answer these three questions about the passage. If it's helpful, use your index to help you answer.

1. The line stating that Aunt Polly's spectacles are "built for 'style,' not service—she could have seen through a pair of stove-lids just as well" (lines 10–11) illustrates the idea that Aunt Polly:
   A. doesn't see very well through her glasses.
   B. is not very attractive in her glasses.
   C. is frustrated by Tom's behavior.
   D. is prideful regarding her parenting.

2. In lines 1–21, the narrative is interrupted by brief lines of dialogue. It could be argued that this technique serves all of the following purposes EXCEPT:
   F. to highlight Aunt Polly's confusion.
   G. to illustrate that Aunt Polly looks in more than one place for Tom.
   H. to allow the reader to witness Aunt Polly's threatening tone.
   J. to characterize Tom Sawyer as lazy.

3. The primary function of lines 36–54 is to:
   A. characterize Aunt Polly as an angry surrogate parent.
   B. depict Aunt Polly as a caring but confused guardian.
   C. illustrate that Aunt Polly can see again after finding her glasses.
   D. demonstrate Tom's mischievous, playful nature.

Discussion

Question 1: This question is subtle, because it requires you to sense the narrator's ironic tone. The easiest way to answer a question like this is to translate it into your own words: "Guess, then try to find the answer." Based on your index and the line number reference, you know to focus on a specific section of text. Now translate the passage. The phrase "built for 'style,' not service" indicates that the glasses are more a show item than a functional one. The phrase, "she could have seen through a pair of stove lids just as well" equates Aunt Polly's ability to see through her glasses with her ability to see through a piece of metal, indicating that she can't see through them very well. Scanning the answers, answer A seems to make the most sense. Answer B is not within the scope of the question: Aunt Polly may or may not be attractive, but lines 10–11 neither refute nor support the claim. Aunt Polly is clearly frustrated by Tom, but lines 10–11 don't refer to her frustration, so rule out answer C. Aunt Polly's pride is mentioned just before the quotation, but again, the quotation itself doesn't refer to her pride or her parenting. When the ACT gives you a specific quotation, read it carefully; it will provide you with the answer. **Answer: (A).**

Question 2: Here's another subtle question that requires a good deal of analysis. The phrase "it could be argued" is your best friend here; it tells you that you only need to find the one implausible answer. Aunt Polly's repeated attempts to call for Tom could indicate that she is confused, so answer F is *plausible*. At times when Aunt Polly pauses, she seems to be in a different place than she has been previously; therefore, answer G is *plausible*. Answer H is also reasonable: The choppy rhythm of the passage along with Aunt Polly's dialogue allow the reader to sense her irritated tone and frustration with Tom's behavior. Answer J is implausible, based on lines 1–21. We have no clues about Tom's character other than his name and the idea that he frustrates Aunt Polly. There is no evidence to prove or disprove his laziness. Again, it is essential that you base your answers only on the text. Background knowledge of Tom Sawyer and his tendency to laze around and allow others to work for him—as implied in the final section of the passage—is a trap here. **Answer: (J).**

Question 3: Because you've indexed the passage, you know the central concern of lines 36–54: Aunt Polly's mixed feelings about taking care of Tom. The monologue in question depicts a woman who wants to raise Tom well but hasn't figured out how to do so. The paragraph depicts her as more exasperated than angry, so disregard option A. Option B matches the index of the paragraph: Aunt Polly's character can be described as caring and confused. Option C is illogical if you read the entire passage and would only tempt a reader who had skimmed so fast that he wasn't able to remember the structure of the passage. Since you've indexed, you know that Twain only mentions Aunt Polly's vision early in the passage—definitely not in lines 36–54. Twain alludes to Tom's devilish nature in this paragraph, but the characterization of Aunt Polly is its "primary function." **Answer: (B).**

FOUR KEYS TO SUCCESS IN FICTION READING

1. Remember: It's only eight minutes of the test. Use your time wisely!

2. Read with purpose. Don't lose focus by letting your imagination wander.

3. Stay at the appropriate level of analysis. Don't over-think, and don't read as though you were about to write an essay.

4. Focus on *COST*.
   - Characterization: Look for physical or emotional depiction, relationships, and inner and outer conflicts.
   - Overview: Think "theme," "main idea," or "generalization."
   - Structure: Know how the passage is built, the purpose of each paragraph and each transition.
   - Tone and mood: Note the narrator's attitude and the general emotional feel of the passage.

FINAL PRACTICE

Using the strategies outlined in this chapter, read the following passage and answer the ten questions that follow it. The passage comes from *My Antonia* by Willa Cather.

Last summer I happened to be crossing the plains of Iowa in a season of intense heat, and it was my good fortune to have for a traveling companion James Quayle Burden—Jim Burden, as we still call him in the West. He and

Line
(5)
I are old friends—we grew up together in the same Nebraska town—and we had much to say to each other. While the train flashed through never-ending miles of ripe wheat, by country towns and bright-flowered pastures and oak groves wilting in the sun, we sat in the observation car, where the woodwork was hot to the touch and red dust lay deep over everything. The dust and heat, the burning wind, reminded us of many things. We were

(10)
talking about what it is like to spend one's childhood in little towns like these, buried in wheat and corn, under stimulating extremes of climate: burning summers when the world lies green and billowy beneath a brilliant sky, when one is fairly stifled in vegetation, in the color and smell of strong weeds and heavy harvests; blustery winters with little snow, when the whole

(15)
country is stripped bare and gray as sheet-iron. We agreed that no one who had not grown up in a little prairie town could know anything about it. It was a kind of freemasonry, we said.

Although Jim Burden and I both live in New York, and are old friends, I do not see much of him there. He is legal counsel for one of the great

(20)
Western railways, and is sometimes away from his New York office for weeks together. That is one reason why we do not often meet. Another is that I do not like his wife.

When Jim was still an obscure young lawyer, struggling to make his way in New York, his career was suddenly advanced by a brilliant marriage.

(25)
Genevieve Whitney was the only daughter of a distinguished man. Her marriage with young Burden was the subject of sharp comment at the time. It was said she had been brutally jilted by her cousin, Rutland Whitney, and that she married this unknown man from the West out of bravado. She was a restless, headstrong girl, even then, who liked to astonish her friends. Later, when

(30)
I knew her, she was always doing something unexpected. She gave one of her town houses for a Suffrage headquarters, produced one of her own plays at the Princess Theater, was arrested for picketing during a garment-makers' strike, etc. I am never able to believe that she has much feeling for the causes to which she lends her name and her fleeting interest. She is handsome, ener-

(35)
getic, executive, but to me she seems unimpressionable and temperamentally incapable of enthusiasm. Her husband's quiet tastes irritate her, I think, and she finds it worth while to play the patroness to a group of young poets and painters of advanced ideas and mediocre ability. She has her own fortune and lives her own life. For some reason, she wishes to remain Mrs. James Burden.

(40) As for Jim, no disappointments have been severe enough to chill his naturally romantic and ardent disposition. This disposition, though it often made him seem very funny when he was a boy, has been one of the strongest elements in his success. He loves with a personal passion the great country through which his railway runs and branches. His faith in it and his knowledge of it

(45) have played an important part in its development. He is always able to raise capital for new enterprises in Wyoming or Montana, and has helped young men out there to do remarkable things in mines and timber and oil. If a young man with an idea can once get Jim Burden's attention, can manage to accompany him when he goes off into the wilds hunting for lost parks

(50) or exploring new canyons, then the money which means action is usually forthcoming. Jim is still able to lose himself in those big Western dreams. Though he is over forty now, he meets new people and new enterprises with the impulsiveness by which his boyhood friends remember him. He never seems to me to grow older. His fresh color and sandy hair and quick-chang-

(55) ing blue eyes are those of a young man, and his sympathetic, solicitous interest in women is as youthful as it is Western and American.

During that burning day when we were crossing Iowa, our talk kept returning to a central figure, a Bohemian girl whom we had known long ago and whom both of us admired. More than any other person we remembered, this girl

(60) seemed to mean to us the country, the conditions, the whole adventure of our childhood. To speak her name was to call up pictures of people and places, to set a quiet drama going in one's brain. I had lost sight of her altogether, but Jim had found her again after long years, had renewed a friendship that meant a great deal to him, and out of his busy life had set apart time enough to enjoy

(65) that friendship. His mind was full of her that day. He made me see her again, feel her presence, revived all my old affection for her.

"I can't see," he said impetuously, "why you have never written anything about Antonía."

1. As it is used in the passage, the term "freemasonry" (line 17) refers to:
   A. a trade organization.
   B. a common bond.
   C. an ancient brotherhood.
   D. a set of rituals.

2. All of the following details describing Jim Burden's wife refer to her personal qualities EXCEPT:
   F. "she is handsome, energetic, executive" (lines 34–35)
   G. "she was a restless, headstrong girl" (lines 28–29)
   H. "she had been brutally jilted by her cousin" (line 27)
   J. "she was always doing something unexpected" (line 30)

3. A reasonable description of Jim Burden, based on the passage, could contain all of the following adjectives EXCEPT:
   A. young-at-heart.
   B. impulsive.
   C. adventurous.
   D. temperamental.

4. The title of the novel, *My Antonía*, probably refers to:
   F. the narrator.
   G. the Bohemian girl.
   H. Jim's Burden's wife.
   J. Rutland Whitney.

5. Which of the following choices best describes the narrator's attitude toward Jim Burden and his wife, respectively?
   A. indignant toward him and surprised by her
   B. soothed by him and admiring of her
   C. complimentary of him and critical of her
   D. shocked by him and disapproving of her

6. The passage establishes that the narrator and Jim have all of the following traits in common EXCEPT:
   F. an interest in legal matters.
   G. an established life in New York City.
   H. an intimate knowledge of the Great Plains region.
   J. a common fondness for a woman in their past.

7. The central purpose of this passage is to:
   A. establish two characters caught in a bad marriage.
   B. assess the intelligence of a powerful attorney.
   C. provide a vivid description of Nebraska.
   D. establish two characters linked by past experiences.

8. The primary function of the first paragraph is to:
   F. establish a tone that is later contradicted.
   G. lay groundwork for the passage's central conflict.
   H. establish setting and mood.
   J. describe the pleasures of train travel.

9. The narrator would probably agree with which of the following statements about Jim Burden?
   A. He is a solid husband but a careless businessman.
   B. He has achieved success but has forgotten his past.
   C. He is an amusing man who has planned his life carefully.
   D. He is a romantic individual who has retained his youthfulness.

10. All of the following details suggest that Genevieve and Jim do not have a close marriage EXCEPT:
   F. separate sources of income.
   G. separate interests.
   H. differing levels of enthusiasm for projects.
   J. Jim's interest in other women.

Answers and Explanations

1. **(B)** This question asks you to define a word given a certain context. While knowledge of the word helps, paying close attention to context and substituting a word of your own may be more efficient. The lines immediately above line 17 establish the context of the word *freemasonry* in the passage: "We agreed that no one who had not grown up in a little prairie town could know anything about it" (lines 15–16). These lines suggest that "growing up in a little prairie town" is a secret understanding that can only be had by people who actually lived the experience. The connection between the narrator and Jim establishes the context for the word *freemasonry*. Next, substitute your own word for the word *freemasonry*. It [growing up in a little prairie town] was a kind of special *connection*. Option A makes little sense unless you associate the word *mason*, which refers to a type of trade, with a trade group. Option B fits well given the idea that the two characters share a common "bond" or understanding of growing up in a small prairie town. Option C refers to the word in its historical sense; the Freemasons are indeed a longstanding fraternal organization. However, the term is not used literally in this context; the narrator uses the term figuratively to emphasize her bond with Jim Burden. Option D alludes to the rituals associated with Freemasons, which, although accurate in a sense, don't relate to the word as it is used here.

2. **(H)** This question really is as easy as it looks. Because you have every line reference in front of you, you may not even need to look back at the passage. Simply determine for yourself which line *does not* seem to represent a personal quality. *Handsome*, *energetic*, and *executive* do refer to personal qualities, as do *restless* and *headstrong*, so rule out options F and G. Option H refers to the character being jilted by her cousin. Whether or not you can define *jilted* is irrelevant here. Although it helps to know that *jilted* is another word for "dumped," realizing that the action is completed by someone other than Jim Burden's wife is enough to tell you that the phrase does not refer to her personal qualities. Anyone can be jilted, regardless of personality. Option H makes sense. Option J refers to Jim Burden's wife's impulsive nature: a personal characteristic. Rule out J.

3. **(D)** This one is tough because it requires you to prove three separate aspects of Jim's character, just so you can disprove one. Consider saving this question until you have finished all other questions for this passage. Whatever you do,

don't spend inordinate amounts of time on it. If your general sense of his character helps you, use it to your advantage. The phrase "he never seems to me to grow older" (lines 53–54) alludes to his being young at heart, so rule out option A. Lines 52–53 refer to Jim's impulsiveness, and lines 49 and 50 refer to his adventurous spirit by depicting him as he "goes off into the wilds hunting for lost parks or exploring new canyons." These details disprove options B and C. Line 35 refers to Jim's wife as temperamental, but nowhere do we get the idea that Jim shares this quality.

4. **(G)** Two simple inferences should help you narrow this question down in a hurry. First, the narrator mentions the name *Antonía* to Jim immediately following a paragraph where she states her affection for a "bohemian girl." This juxtaposition suggests that the last line of dialogue refers to the same girl. Second, the term *My* placed before *Antonía* in the title implies a certain amount of affection for her held by either the narrator, Jim, or both. Option F makes little sense, because the narrator refers to Antonía directly in the final line of the passage. Option G makes sense given the previous inferences. Option H is unlikely: Because Jim Burden's wife is depicted as unsympathetic, it is unlikely that the narrator would attach an affectionate term like *my* when referring to her. Rutland Whitney, option J, has a different name altogether and therefore is an illogical choice.

5. **(C)** This question has two-sided answer choices, so narrow your options by looking at one side first. The left-hand adjectives refer to the narrator's opinion of Jim: *indignant, soothed, complimentary,* and *shocked.* The narrator shows neither angry disbelief nor shock at Jim, so rule out options A and D. Now address the leftover options on the right side, which refer to the narrator's opinion of Jim's wife: *admiring* and *critical.* Because the narrator states that she dislikes Jim's wife and spends nearly two full paragraphs criticizing her, rule out *admiring.*

6. **(F)** This detail question requires you again to prove three options correct in order to disprove one. Option F is shaky: While Jim is an attorney, nowhere does it state that the narrator has an interest in the law. Line 18, which states, "Jim Burden and I both live in New York," helps rule out option G. Lines 9–17 refer to both characters' intimate knowledge of Nebraska, part of the Great Plains, which allows you to rule out option H. The final two paragraphs of the section disprove option J, as both characters clearly feel affectionate toward a woman in their past.

7. **(D)** This "main point" question requires you to have a general sense of the passage, the "O" in the "COST" acronym. Option A is unlikely to be the answer: Although Jim's marriage seems questionable, the narrator mentions nothing of her own. Aside from a slight inkling that the narrator has feelings for Jim, the reader can glean no proof that her marriage is in trouble. While

the narrator alludes to Jim's talents as an attorney (option B), this information is merely a character detail and not the main idea. The description of Nebraska (option C) establishes setting and mood but falls short of being a "main point" of the passage. Option D, "establish two characters linked by past experiences," makes sense. The bulk of the passage describes these two characters, their long friendship, and their common interests and affections.

8. **(H)** Understanding the literary elements of tone, conflict, and mood is important when answering this question. Tone in fiction refers to the narrator's attitude. Although her friendly, approving attitude—at least toward Jim—is established in paragraph 1 (option F), it stays consistent throughout the passage. Option G, although it may seem reasonable at first, is not the answer because paragraph 1 does little to set up the central conflict in the passage, which is the narrator's dislike of Jim's wife. Mood refers to the emotional feel of the passage. The detail about the geography of Nebraska in paragraph 1 establishes the setting. This vivid description also creates mood with phrases such as "burning summers," "stifled in vegetation," "stripped bare," and "gray as sheet-iron." While the passage mentions train travel (option J), describing the pleasures of the train ride is not the primary purpose of the paragraph.

9. **(D)** This question requires you to make an inference based on your understanding of the narrator. Luckily, the entire passage is told from the narrator's point of view, so you have plenty of evidence with which to work. If you can establish that the narrator's attitude toward Jim is positive, that she admires and is even a little smitten with him, then you can assume that her statements about him would fit the same mold. Would she call him *careless* (option A)? Probably not—in fact she clearly admires his business acumen. The first and last paragraphs both disprove option B; the narrator clearly sees Jim as one who reveres and even yearns for his past. The narrator's characterization of Jim as impulsive (line 53) refutes option C. The narrator calls Jim "naturally romantic" (line 41) and also states that he "never seems to me to grow older" (lines 53–54).

10. **(H)** This question also asks you to draw a conclusion based on specific details. Genevieve has "her own fortune" (line 38), which could suggest that their marriage is distant in the financial sense. Rule out option F. Jim and his wife seem to live separate lives, with differing interests and schedules (option G), which could also suggest a marriage that isn't close. Both Jim and Genevieve take on projects with energy and enthusiasm—this trait really doesn't differ in them—which makes option H seem like the answer. Paragraph 4 refers to Jim's "solicitous" interest in women (lines 55–56), a characteristic that could strain his marriage. This tendency, coupled with his demonstrative affection for Antonía, suggest that he might not be completely loyal to his wife. Rule out option J.

The Nuances of Nonfiction

> - Nonfiction reading strategies
> - Types of passages and questions

Three of the four passages on the reading test will qualify as nonfiction, chosen from three different disciplines: humanities, social science, and natural science. These passages test your reading ability with texts seen at the college level. Contrary to most high school English curriculums, the world consists mostly of nonfiction.

STRATEGIES FOR APPROACHING NONFICTION PASSAGES

It's All in the Timing

Many students try the same strategy they use when assigned a textbook reading and questions at the end of a chapter: They read the questions first and then hunt for answers as they read. The ACT Reading test does not allow enough time for this strategy. It is more important to gain a solid understanding of the main ideas and structure of the passage *before* reading the questions. Spend about four minutes reading the passage and four minutes answering the questions. This timing strategy will leave you about three minutes of leeway at the end of the test.

    With one brief glance at the section, you will gain a sense of which passage will be the most difficult for you. Practice will also reveal which topics make you the most comfortable. Once you determine which subjects you tend to like the most, choose one of two strategies and stick with it. Your first option is to go from easiest to hardest, which might give you a few extra minutes at the end of the test for the passage that you consider the most challenging. This strategy maximizes the amount of time you focus on passages with which you are comfortable; "rushed" time at the end is spent on difficult questions you might have missed anyway. Your other option is to start with the most difficult passage first and get it out of the way. If you begin with the most challenging passage, watch the clock closely. Don't spend more than eight minutes on the passage before moving on to the next one. You can always come back to it at the end.

TIP

In nonfiction passages, the key is to identify the topic, decipher the main idea, understand the passage's structure, and locate supporting details.

Regardless of the order you choose, keep these two points in mind.

1. You *do* have the freedom to complete the questions in any order you'd like!

2. A balanced approach maximizes your score. In other words, it is better to guess on a question or two at the end of a passage for the sake of getting to the next one than it is to miss an entire passage or most of it at the end of the testing period.

See the Big Picture

Consider the camera metaphor at the beginning of Chapter 13. When approaching a nonfiction passage, gain a broad perspective by zooming all the way out. Look at the length of the passage. Prepare to read by counting the number of paragraphs and noting the number of lines. Next, tell yourself, *I have four minutes to read this passage.* Your brain needs to see the passage as a whole before you begin, and it needs to understand the time constraints involved. Because reading doesn't normally involve such ridiculous time limitations, your brain needs to prepare for the challenge of efficient reading. If you don't prepare mentally, your brain will read in the same way it always does. It will take the time to reread the confusing parts, it will decipher confusing vocabulary using context clues, and it will take extra time focusing in on details that, within the confines of the ACT, just aren't important.

Zoom In and Preheat Your Brain

Prepare to read quickly and actively by attuning your mind to the topic. What is the passage about? The brain stores new information by "linking" it to information it already contains. If you are unable to connect the new information to something you already know, then you won't remember any new information. You need to "preheat" your brain. Zoom in on the citation of the passage and note the title, if there is one; then, read the first few sentences of the passage. What is the passage about? The moon? The Harlem Renaissance? The history of the samurai sword? What do you already know about the topic? Make a connection to what you already know—even if it is incorrect or obscure. You may think, *The only thing I remember about the samurai sword is that my favorite childhood cartoon character used one while fighting evil sorcerers and demons.* Well, that information is enough to "preheat" your brain. The new information about the samurai sword will now be stored in your brain next to your favorite childhood cartoon character. Even though the organizational system sounds odd, the "preheating" process works.

Clear Your Mind

This strategy may sound contradictory considering that you were just told to fill your mind with connections to the topic. Keep your connections intact, but clear your mind of tangential topics that might distract you from the task at hand. Mental distractions hinder your ability to remain "in the zone" while reading the passages. Your mind will wander to the baseball game on TV that you aren't watching because you are studying for the ACT. You might think about your new boyfriend and whether or not he wants to date someone smarter than he is. Sometimes more serious and emotional tangents will invade your mental space while you read.

A wandering mind can be your biggest deterrent in achieving the big 36. Commit to the topic at hand. Tell yourself that you are interested in the samurai sword. Your brain is easily manipulated. If you tell it to do something or think a certain way, it usually will. Remember, you only have to be interested in the topic for eight minutes. Also keep in mind that "indexing," as outlined in Chapter 13, can be a great way to focus yourself if a 1,000-word passage makes your mind swim.

Identify Main Idea and Tone

Once you have preheated your brain, zoom in a little further on the passage. Be careful not to zoom in too much; don't get preoccupied with the details and examples within the passage. As long as you gain an overall understanding of the arguments in the passage, there is no need to remember the details precisely. Getting bogged down by details causes problems for many students when reading nonfiction passages.

Identify the main idea of the entire passage as a whole and the role of each paragraph in expressing it. Identifying the main idea of a passage often stupefies people, but in reality it is fairly simple. Ask yourself the following questions: *What is the topic of the passage? What is the author saying about the topic?* It won't take you long to identify whether the topic is samurai swords or the life cycle of a butterfly. The next step is to decipher what the author is saying about samurai swords or the life cycle of a butterfly. The author may be trying to express the beautiful craftsmanship of the samurai sword. Or, she could be identifying it as one of the deadliest weapons in history. The purpose of the passage may be stated explicitly in either the introduction or the conclusion. In rare cases, you'll have to infer the main idea of the passage once you have read the passage completely.

Deciphering tone is similar to identifying the main idea. Instead of asking yourself what the author is saying about the topic, ask, *What is the author's attitude toward the topic?* Some reading questions may ask you to infer the author's tone. Is it cautionary? Celebratory? Pensive? Critical? Detached? The author may be warning you about a new contagious disease, or he could be celebrating a new astronomical discovery. Identifying the tone of the passage helps you eliminate answer options. If an answer choice doesn't match the tone of the passage, it's almost always wrong.

> **REMEMBER**
>
> Don't get caught up in the details of a passage. Read for the main idea.

Index the Passage!

The process of indexing is outlined in detail in Chapter 13. Learn and practice this process! Observing and briefly noting the purpose of each paragraph will help immensely when it comes to answering questions efficiently and accurately. Don't forget to learn and practice this invaluable technique!

STRATEGIES FOR APPROACHING NONFICTION QUESTIONS

Guess First, Then Find the Answer

Once you have read the passage using the previous six strategies, move on to the questions. Before reading answer options, come up with an answer on your own. If one of the answer options matches your guess, then that answer is probably correct. If there are two or three options that are similar to your initial response, then at least you have narrowed your options. If you are unable to even guess at the answer, the question will likely take you longer than others. Leave the question until you have finished answering the rest of the questions for that passage.

Know the Types of Questions: "Right There" and Inferential

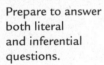

TIP

Prepare to answer both literal and inferential questions.

Use key words within the question stem to help you locate the correct answer. Some questions are "right there" or literal questions, questions that can be answered by looking in the text to find a specific detail. These answers are easy to find; go back to the text and locate them. The better your index, the easier it is to locate the section of text that addresses the topic in question. Some "right there" questions are so easy that you won't need to go back to the text. If you are unsure or hesitant about your answer, look it up. There will always be proof.

Other questions ask you to make an inference or "educated guess" about something not stated directly. ACT inference questions may give you a line from the text and ask you what the line "suggests" about the author's message, the author's attitude, or the topic in general. Key phrases like "it can be inferred that" and "it is most likely that" also indicate an inferential question.

The ACT also tests your knowledge of vocabulary by asking you what a word means based on its context. Vocabulary-in-context questions are also inference questions because you guess about a word's definition based on surrounding information.

PRACTICE PASSAGE: SOCIAL SCIENCE

The subsequent social science passage and ten questions that follow it are similar to what you will see on the ACT reading test. Read the passage using the strategies outlined in this chapter, and answer each of the questions independently before moving on to the answer explanations. The answer explanations include more specific strategies for responding to questions, so be sure to read them.

Find a watch or a clock. Try not to spend more than eight minutes reading the passage and answering the questions. Zoom out and see the big picture of the passage. Zoom in on the title, then index the passage itself. Find the topic and the main idea. Be careful not to zoom in too close as you read; getting bogged down in details slows you down. In the margins, summarize the main point or key ideas within each paragraph in a few words.

The following passage is taken from the United States Department of State's Bureau of Western Hemisphere Affairs, January 2008.

History of Chile

About 10,000 years ago, migrating Indians settled in fertile valleys and along the coast of what is now Chile. The Incas briefly extended their empire into what is now northern Chile, but the area's barrenness prevented exten-

Line
(5)
sive settlement. The first Europeans to arrive in Chile were Diego de Almagro and his band of Spanish conquistadors, who came from Peru seeking gold in 1535. The Spanish encountered hundreds of thousands of Indians from various cultures in the area that modern Chile now occupies. These cultures supported themselves principally through slash-and-burn agriculture and hunting. The conquest of Chile began in earnest in 1540 and was carried

(10)
out by Pedro de Valdivia, one of Francisco Pizarro's lieutenants, who founded the city of Santiago on February 12, 1541. Although the Spanish did not find the extensive gold and silver they sought, they recognized the agricultural potential of Chile's central valley, and Chile became part of the Viceroyalty of Peru.

(15)
The drive for independence from Spain was precipitated by usurpation of the Spanish throne by Napoleon's brother Joseph in 1808. A national junta in the name of Ferdinand—heir to the deposed king—was formed on September 18, 1810. The junta proclaimed Chile an autonomous republic within the Spanish monarchy. A movement for total independence soon won

(20)
a wide following. Spanish attempts to reimpose arbitrary rule during what was called the "Reconquista" led to a prolonged struggle.

Intermittent warfare continued until 1817, when an army led by Bernardo O'Higgins, Chile's most renowned patriot, and José de San Martín, hero of Argentine independence, crossed the Andes into Chile and defeated the

(25)
royalists. On February 12, 1818, Chile was proclaimed an independent republic under O'Higgins's leadership. The political revolt brought little social change, however, and 19th-century Chilean society preserved the essence of the stratified colonial social structure, which was greatly influenced by family politics and the Roman Catholic Church. A strong pre-

(30)
sidency eventually emerged, but wealthy landowners remained extremely powerful. Toward the end of the 19th century, the government in Santiago consolidated its position in the south by ruthlessly suppressing the Mapuche Indians. In 1881, it signed a treaty with Argentina confirming Chilean sovereignty over the Strait of Magellan. As a result of the War of the Pacific

(35) with Peru and Bolivia (1879–83), Chile expanded its territory northward by almost one-third and acquired valuable nitrate deposits, the exploitation of which led to an era of national affluence. Chile established a parliamentary democracy in the late 19th century, but degenerated into a system protecting the interests of the ruling oligarchy. By the 1920s, the emerging middle and

(40) working classes were powerful enough to elect a reformist president, whose program was frustrated by a conservative congress. In the 1920s, Marxist groups with strong popular support arose.

Continuing political and economic instability resulted with the rule of the quasidictatorial General Carlos Ibañez (1924–32). When constitutional

(45) rule was restored in 1932, a strong middle-class party, the Radicals, emerged. It became the key force in coalition governments for the next 20 years. During the period of Radical Party dominance (1932–52), the state increased its role in the economy.

The 1964 presidential election of Christian Democrat Eduardo Frei-

(50) Montalva by an absolute majority initiated a period of major reform. Under the slogan "Revolution in Liberty," the Frei administration embarked on far-reaching social and economic programs, particularly in education, housing, and agrarian reform, including rural unionization of agricultural workers. By 1967, however, Frei encountered increasing opposition from

(55) leftists, who charged that his reforms were inadequate, and from conservatives, who found them excessive. At the end of his term, Frei had accomplished many noteworthy objectives, but he had not fully achieved his party's ambitious goals. In 1970, Senator Salvador Allende, a Marxist and member of Chile's Socialist Party, who headed the "Popular Unity" (UP) coalition of

(60) socialists, communists, radicals, and dissident Christian Democrats, won a plurality of votes in a three-way contest and was named President by the Chilean Congress. His program included the nationalization of private industries and banks, massive land expropriation, and collectivization. Allende's program also included the nationalization of U.S. interests in

(65) Chile's major copper mines.

Elected with only 36% of the vote and by a plurality of only 36,000 votes, Allende never enjoyed majority support in the Chilean Congress or broad popular support. Domestic production declined; severe shortages of consumer goods, food, and manufactured products were widespread; and infla-

(70) tion reached 1,000% per annum. Mass demonstrations, recurring strikes, violence by both government supporters and opponents, and widespread rural unrest ensued in response to the general deterioration of the economy. By 1973, Chilean society had split into two hostile camps.

A military coup overthrew Allende on September 11, 1973. As the armed

(75) forces bombarded the presidential palace, Allende reportedly committed suicide. A military government, led by General Augusto Pinochet, took over control of the country. The first years of the regime in particular were marked by serious human rights violations. A new Constitution was approved by a plebiscite on September 11, 1980, and General Pinochet became President

(80) of the Republic for an 8-year term. In its later years, the regime gradually permitted greater freedom of assembly, speech, and association, to include trade union activity. In contrast to its authoritarian political rule, the military government pursued decidedly laissez-faire economic policies. During its 16 years in power, Chile moved away from economic statism toward a largely

(85) free market economy that fostered an increase in domestic and foreign private investment. In a plebiscite on October 5, 1988, General Pinochet was denied a second 8-year term as president. Chileans voted for elections to choose a new president and the majority of members of a two-chamber congress. On December 14, 1989, Christian Democrat Patricio Aylwin, the candidate of a

(90) coalition of 17 political parties called the Concertación, was elected president. Aylwin served from 1990 to 1994 and was succeeded by another Christian Democrat, Eduardo Frei Ruiz-Tagle (son of the previous President), leading the same coalition, for a 6-year term. Ricardo Lagos Escobar of the Socialist Party and the Party for Democracy led the Concertación to a narrower victory

(95) in the 2000 presidential elections. His term ended on March 11, 2006, when President Michelle Bachelet Jeria, of the Socialist Party, took office.

1. The author's use of the word *reportedly* in line 75 in reference to Allende's suicide suggests that:
   A. Allende's suicide was witnessed by the military.
   B. Allende's suicide was never confirmed.
   C. Allende's suicide was falsified.
   D. Allende's suicide never happened.

2. The passage states that the Spanish primarily sought which products when initially conquering Chile?

   I. gold
   II. land for agriculture
   III. silver

   F. I only
   G. I and II only
   H. I and III only
   J. I, II, and III

3. The passage suggests that the history of Chile has been:
   A. one-sided.
   B. peaceful.
   C. turbulent.
   D. democratic.

4. Which of the following reforms were included in Salvador Allende's program to improve Chile while he was the President of the Chilean Congress?

   I. nationalization of private industries and banks
   II. massive land expropriation
   III. nationalization of U.S. interests in Chile's major copper mines

   F. I and II only
   G. II and III only
   H. I and III only
   J. I, II, and III

5. According to the passage, during Allende's governance, which of the following did NOT occur?
   A. mass demonstrations
   B. inflation reaching 1,000% per annum
   C. majority support of his policies
   D. decline of domestic production

6. In the context of this passage, the word *junta* (lines 17 and 18) most nearly means:
   F. heroic leader.
   G. governmental council.
   H. conquistador.
   J. together.

7. According to the passage, Chile was declared an independent state in 1818. Why did the revolt that led to this independence result in little social change?

   I. family politics
   II. raids by the Mapuche Indians
   III. influence of the Roman Catholic Church

   A. I only
   B. II only
   C. II and III only
   D. I and III only

8. According to the passage, when Chile's border expanded northward the result was:
   F. the discovery of silver and a resulting era of affluence.
   G. sovereignty over the Strait of Magellan.
   H. the acquisition and exploitation of nitrate deposits.
   J. the acquisition of a fertile agricultural area.

9. According to the author, the government's military rule during the 1980s was not typical because it:
   A. was influenced by the Roman Catholic Church.
   B. expanded the territory of Chile northward.
   C. pursued laissez-faire economic policies.
   D. provided a welfare system for the rural poor.

10. According to the passage, which of the following can NOT be proven true of the government of Chile?

    F. The president can be denied a second term in office.

    G. Chile has had an elected president since the time of Diego de Almagro.

    H. Presidential candidates run for office within a multi-party system.

    J. The government has been overthrown by a military coup.

Strategy Review

Before reviewing the answers and explanations, compare your approach to the text with the following strategies for reading this passage.

1. **See the big picture.** Note that the passage is 7 paragraphs and 96 lines long. Allow yourself 4 minutes to get through the passage.

2. **Zoom in.** Read the title and realize that the passage will explore the history of Chile.

3. **Preheat.** Before reading, ask yourself, *What do I already know about Chile?* Even if you recently realized that Chile isn't just a soup to eat in the depths of winter, your brain will be ready to accept new information.

4. **Clear your mind.** Clearing your mind of outside distractions is critical. Forget about the D you just received on your biology lab. Forget that there is only one week until prom and you have yet to ask your girlfriend to go with you. Think only about Chile and what you can learn about it by reading this passage.

5. **Identify main idea and tone.** While reading, identify the main idea and tone of the passage. Within each era of Chile's history there have been disagreements between different parties, ambitious reform efforts that were not always met with support, and turbulent shifts of power between elected individuals and more authoritarian regimes. The tone of this passage is neutral toward any particular group or era; it is merely informative. The straightforward and informative tone matches the main idea of the passage. What is the author saying about the topic? He wants to describe the shifting and volatile nature of Chile's political history by discussing its leaders, from Chile's beginnings as a European country of interest to its more recent political leaders.

6. **Index the passage.** While identifying the main idea and tone of the passage, index the passage as well. In the margins, mark the content or purpose of each paragraph. For example:
   - Paragraph 1: Early settlers
   - Paragraph 2: Independence from Spain
   - Paragraph 3: Independent republic
   - Paragraph 4: Radical Party dominance
   - Paragraph 5: Frei and Allende reforms
   - Paragraph 6: Allende's downfall
   - Paragraph 7: Pinochet coup and recent leaders

TIP

Don't go overboard with underlining or highlighting. Stick to key names and words.

Your summaries for each paragraph don't have to match these examples. Underlining key names or key words, especially within historical passages with multiple historical figures, can also be effective. But don't overdo it. One problem with underlining key information is that you may get a little "high-light happy" and highlight more than necessary. However, because the question stems often include the names of the leaders, underlining the names within the passage may be helpful when searching for answers.

7. **Guess first, then find the answer**. After reading the question stem, try to answer the question before reading the answer options. If one of the answer options resembles the answer in your mind, you have narrowed down the answer options. Indexing the key ideas of each paragraph helps you locate answers quickly. Use key phrases and words within the question stem and the overall gist of the question to lead you to the correct locations within the index.

Answers and Explanations: Social Science

1. **(B)** Use your inference skills to answer this question. First, using your personal understanding of how the word *reportedly* is often used, you may have determined the correct answer immediately. Finding the location of the answer to this question is easy because a line reference is given to you in the question stem (line 75). Read the context surrounding the word *reportedly*: "As the armed forces bombarded the presidential palace, Allende reportedly committed suicide." Think about removing the word from the sentence. Without it, the phrase would read, "Allende committed suicide," which is much more factual. Therefore, the word is being used to indicate that Allende may not have committed suicide and that Pinochet's military may have "reported" that he did to hide the fact that they killed him. Options C and D claim that the suicide never happened, and option A claims that the suicide was witnessed and therefore verified. Because the word *reportedly* indicates that the suicide can be neither confirmed nor denied, these three options are incorrect.

2. **(H)** Questions with multiple variables require more time. Make an educated guess before reading the answer options; trust your memory of the passage's content to eliminate some options. This question asks about the first conquistadors in Chile; therefore, the answer will most likely be in paragraph 1. The phrase "primarily sought" is a key in the question stem, because it eliminates other products that they found after arriving in Chile. Paragraph 1 explains that in 1535 the Spanish conquistadors came from Peru "seeking gold" (lines 5 and 6). Upon reading this, you might rush to choose option A, which offers "gold" as the correct response. Be careful! Later in the paragraph, in lines 11 and 12, the author explains that gold and silver were sought by the Spanish conquistadors, which makes option III a correct response. It wasn't until after the Spanish arrived in Chile that they discovered the profitability of the land; therefore, option G does not work.

3. **(C)** There is no place to "find" any of the answer options explicitly stated within the text; instead, the question relies on your sense of the passage as a whole. First, attempt to eliminate answer options. Option A, "one-sided," logically doesn't make sense because of the many different groups vying for power within Chile. Option B seems unlikely because there are frequent references to violence during Chile's progression as a country. Options C and D make the most sense. Because of the multiple references within the passage to Chile's democratic process of voting, you may have been tempted to choose option D. However, option C is the best response because of the many ups and downs apparent in Chile's history and because not every era of Chile's history has been democratic.

4. **(J)** The key phrase within the question stem is "Allende's program." Refer to the index and note that the introduction of Allende's program is in paragraph 5. The ACT likes to test your ability to remember details located within a list. Line 71 introduces the details of Allende's program. Three items are included in the list: "nationalization of private industries and banks, massive land expropriation, and collectivization." Two of these items are on the list within the question stem, so you know that at least I and III are correct. When skimming quickly, your brain may stop at the end of that sentence. By continuing on to the next sentence you'll notice that the author adds another detail to the list, "the nationalization of U.S. interests in Chile's major copper mines." Options I, II, and III are each part of Allende's program; therefore, J is correct. Read the surrounding context to confirm the correct answer.

5. **(C)** Read the question stem carefully. Notice the word *NOT*! Then, by looking at your index, recognize that paragraphs 5 and 6 mention Allende. This question, again, tests your understanding of lists of details. Throughout paragraph 6, an inventory of negative details are given about the results of Allende's governance. One option for answering this question is to comb the details to identify which of the answer options did NOT happen during Allende's regime. Another approach is to look at the answer options again and eliminate some of them. Three of the four options are negative results of Allende's leadership: options A, B, and D. Option C stands out as you review the answer options. Logically, if, according to paragraph 6, the result of Allende's governance is primarily negative, Allende would probably not have gained "majority support of his policies" (option C). Early in the paragraph (line 67) the author introduces the description of Allende's governance by explaining that Allende *did not* enjoy majority support. Because the phrase "majority support" comes directly from the text, this option is distracting. Unless you remember the word *NOT* when reading the phrase "majority support," you might assume that this option is correct as well. Option C is the only response that works.

6. **(G)** Vocabulary-in-context questions are easily answered by replacing the word in question with the answer options and deciding which option works best. The word *junta* appears twice in the passage. Consider the original sentence in lines 16–18: "*A national* ___ *in the name of Ferdinand—heir to the deposed king— was formed on September 18, 1810.*"

   - A national *heroic leader* in the name of Ferdinand . . .
     This option works if you only consider the first half of the sentence. Include the rest of the sentence to make an informed decision: A national *heroic leader* in the name of Ferdinand . . . was formed . . . A national heroic leader can't "be formed" as the rest of the sentence suggests.
   - A national *governmental council* . . . was formed . . .
     This option makes the most sense so far and probably fits with your initial assessment of the word's definition. Check the other options just to be certain.
   - Option H: A national *conquistador* . . . was formed . . .
   - Option J: A national *together* . . . was formed . . .
     Again, you can't "form" a *conquistador* or a *together*, just as you can't "form" a *heroic leader* (option F).

   Another strategy is to analyze the function of the original word within the sentence or passage. The word *junta* is used as a noun. Ask yourself: *What actions did the junta perform or what actions did it receive?* First of all, it was "formed" by the government (line 17), and second of all, it made a "proclamation" (line 18). Which of the options can be formed and also make a proclamation? Option G, "a governmental council," is the only option that makes logical sense. Don't be fooled by your understanding of the word *junta* in Spanish, which sounds a little like the word for "together," *juntos*. Context is always more important, because more often than not you will be tested on a word that has multiple possible meanings.

7. **(D)** The most helpful part of the question stem is the date. The passage's chronological order makes it easy to locate 1818 within the passage (paragraph 3, line 25) and quickly read the surrounding area. The passage explains that the "political revolt brought little social change" because of the "stratified colonial social structure." Because "stratified colonial social structure" is not one of the options, keep reading. The "stratified colonial social structure" was "influenced by family politics and the Roman Catholic Church," both of which are options within the question. Answer choice D is the correct response. Option II is only included as a distraction. Your memory of the passage and your logical thinking might suggest that raids by Indians would certainly cause a society to become stagnant. Within the context of the passage, however, there is no "cause and effect" link between Indian raids and social change. Find the correct answer within the passage if you have any doubts about your initial response.

8. (**H**) If you haven't noticed by now, ACT answer options often contain phrases that can be found word for word in the text, as in option G, "sovereignty over the Strait of Magellan." Your ability to remember a phrase from the text is not enough to give you the correct answer. Make sure the phrase is associated with the question stem. You may be tempted to choose the first response that you remember seeing in the passage. Answer options always include distracting choices that can trick you. Another trick the ACT uses is making one word within the answer option incorrect, as in option F. When Chile's borders expanded northward, its people did not find *silver*, they found *nitrates*. Each incorrect answer option plays on the words used within the text. When you have found the area of the passage that talks about Chile expanding its territory northward, you will notice a few key words that are used in other answer options as distracters: *affluence* and *acquisition*. If you don't read carefully, one of them could trick you into choosing that response because it "sounds" like something that comes directly from the text. Lines 34–37 give you the correct information about Chile's northward expansion, making H the correct response.

9. (**C**) Your background knowledge may help you eliminate a couple of answer options immediately. The phrase "not typical" along with its description of "military rule" can guide your elimination process. Most governments ruled by the military tend to restrict the behavior of their citizens and discourage free thought and action. For this reason, options C, "pursued laissez-faire economic policies," and D, "provided a welfare system for the rural poor," would be more atypical of a militaristic government than the other options. Also, many governments controlled by a dominant religious group have spent time expanding the territory of the country they govern; therefore, option A, "was influenced by the Roman Catholic Church," and B, "expanded the territory of Chile northward," might actually be typical of a militaristic government. Whether your background knowledge helps you narrow down the options or not, you will still need to find the correct answer within the passage. The date included in the question helps locate the correct response. Skim the passage to find the 1980s, which are mentioned in paragraph 7. In order to answer this question correctly, you have to sift through quite a bit of text. The first half of the paragraph discusses Pinochet's militaristic government and its negative impact on Chile. The phrase "in *contrast* to its authoritarian political rule," located in line 82, identifies any other governmental actions mentioned as not typical of an authoritarian government. Even if you don't know that laissez-faire economic policy means that the government takes a "hands-off" approach, you will still be able to identify option C as the correct response.

10. (**G**) Complicated questions like this one force you to think about the passage as a whole. Sifting through the appropriate details takes time. Read the question stem carefully; don't let that tricky word *NOT* throw you off course. Eliminate

answer options that you know are true, and then work on the other options. Options F and J are confirmed true in paragraph 7. Line 74 indicates that a military coup took over the government, which eliminates option J, and lines 86–87 explain that Pinochet was denied a second term as president, eliminating option F. Option H can be proven true as well; throughout the passage, multiple political parties, including Socialists, Communists, and Christian Democrats, are mentioned. The validity of option G is more difficult to determine. The passage refers to multiple presidential elections. The key word in this option is *Diego de Almagro*. Refer to the section of text that discusses Almagro and work your way forward. After Almagro, the passage introduces Valdivia and O'Higgins. The passage does not claim that either figure was president and doesn't mention any elections surrounding their rise to power. Later in the same paragraph, you learn that a parliamentary democracy was established. From that information, you can infer that presidential elections only occurred after Valdivia and O'Higgins. There is not enough information to confirm that option G, "Chile has had an elected president since the time of Diego de Almagro," is true of the Chilean government.

PRACTICE PASSAGE: NATURAL SCIENCE

Natural science passages can be more difficult for many readers because they contain more scientific jargon or technical vocabulary than other passages. Use the context of the passage to figure out the gist of the message. Details may drag you down. Read only to identify the main ideas and the structure of the passage.

> ### STRATEGY REMINDERS
> - **See the big picture**. Notice the length of the passage and look at the number of paragraphs. Prepare mentally to read it in four minutes.
> - **Zoom in**. Identify the topic by focusing on the title and skimming the first paragraph to look for clues.
> - **Preheat**. What do you already know about this topic?
> - **Clear your mind**. Focus on the topic at hand and only on the topic.
> - **Identify main idea and tone while indexing the passage**. Summarize the focus of each paragraph in the margins. Identify the main idea of the passage by asking yourself, *What is the author saying about the topic?* Identify the tone of the passage by asking yourself, *What is the author's attitude toward the topic?*

The following passage is adapted from the United States Department of Agriculture Forest Service's report titled "Forest Issues and Disease Conditions in the United States" (August 2005).

Emerald Ash Borer

The emerald ash borer (EAB) (*Agrilus planipennis* Fairmaire) is a nonnative insect originally from Japan, Korea, Taiwan, northeast China, and adjacent parts of Russia. It was unknown on the North American continent until
Line its discovery in the Detroit, Michigan, area in July of 2002. Subsequent
(5) surveys showed that a large area of infestation was present, covering at least six counties surrounding Detroit. This "core" area was put under quarantine in the fall of 2002. Infestations were also discovered across the border in Windsor, Ontario, Canada. Following further surveys in 2003, the quarantine was expanded to 13 counties, and by fall 2004 the quarantine included
(10) 20 Michigan counties and Lucas County in northwest Ohio. A number of scattered isolated infestations outside of the quarantine area occur in the lower peninsula of Michigan and northeastern Indiana. It appears that these sites have been present for several years and probably represent introductions via infested ash firewood, logs, or nursery material.
(15) The EAB infests walnuts and elms in its native habitat. In North America, EAB is found (so far) only on ash (*Fraxinus* spp.), an abundant tree species in urban areas, rural woodlots, and riparian areas.

To contain further spread of EAB in Canada, government officials cut and destroyed all of the ash trees in a 30-km × 10-km zone extending from
(20) Lake St. Clair to Lake Erie. This "ash free" zone, in concert with an aggressive regulatory program to prevent the artificial movement of infested ash material out of the infested area, is intended to contain the existing infestation so that effective eradication activities can be implemented.

In Michigan and Ohio, EAB infestations are too extensive and numerous
(25) to be contained with the kind of "ash free" zones implemented by the Canadians. Instead management efforts have shifted to containment of EAB in the lower peninsula of Michigan and neighboring Lucas County in northwest Ohio by focusing survey, eradication, and ash reduction efforts in key "Gateway Areas." These gateways include northern Michigan south of the
(30) Mackinac Straits, St. Clair County just across the river from Canada, and along the borders with Ohio and Indiana.

Initially little was known about EAB biology and habits. Studies and evaluations have been underway since 2002 to investigate host range, biology, trap designs and possible attractants, and control options. Our understand-
(35) ing of EAB is improving but still limited. Control options are also limited; wood-boring insects are notoriously difficult to kill with insecticides once they bore under the bark or into the wood of trees.

The USDA Forest Service is an integral partner, along with the Animal and Plant Health Inspection Service (APHIS) and State authorities, in the
(40) EAB containment and eradication effort, providing scientific and technical

expertise, including survey, restoration, and public outreach and communi-
cations assistance. In 2004, the USDA Forest Service implemented EAB
surveys on Federal and State forest lands in Michigan and on public and
private forest lands in nearly 20 Eastern States. Special emphasis was placed
(45) on areas of known ash decline, around nurseries, and in areas where firewood
introductions were likely. EAB detection surveys will continue and be
expanded to other States in 2005. The USDA Forest Service also supports
and conducts critical technology development activities with university and
research cooperators to advance our understanding of EAB biology and
(50) dispersal habits, chemical control tactics, management strategies, survey
techniques, and monitoring, among others.

    Ash trees throughout southern Michigan had exhibited decline and
dieback symptoms for years. "Ash yellows," a condition caused by a myco-
plasmalike organism (MLO), was prevalent in the area and was one of the
(55) presumed causes. Ash yellows and another malady referred to as ash decline
were so prevalent that dying ash trees did not draw close scrutiny. EAB has
killed millions of ash trees so far and has the potential to decimate the more
than 800 million ash trees in Michigan forests. Ash species are common
across the Great Lakes region and the Northeastern United States. Ash is
(60) also a common roadside, shade, and yard tree. No ash species appear to be
resistant to EAB infestation and mortality. EAB appears capable of infesting
and killing much of the ash across North America.

    Scientists estimate that EAB had been in the United States for perhaps
5–10 years prior to its detection in 2002. EAB was previously unknown
(65) outside of Asia and was not on any exotic pest "watch list."

1. According to the passage, which trees does the EAB infest in its native habitat?
  A. walnut and elm
  B. oak and ash
  C. pine and cedar
  D. ash and walnut

2. According to the passage, the Canadian solution to EAB infestation of an
"ash free" zone is not viable in Michigan and Ohio because:
  F. management efforts shifted to the lower peninsula of Michigan.
  G. not enough research has been completed on EAB.
  H. EAB infestations are too extensive and numerous.
  J. U.S. government regulations have prohibited "ash free" zones.

3. Which of the following is NOT true of EAB eradication?
  A. The EAB is difficult to kill with insecticide once it bores under tree bark.
  B. No ash species appear to be resistant to EAB.
  C. Studies and evaluations of EAB within the United States have been underway
since 2000.
  D. "Ash free" zones have been declared in Canada.

4. Which infestation area triggered surveys of EAB?
   F. Detroit, Michigan
   G. Windsor, Ontario, Canada
   H. Lucas County, Ohio
   J. lower peninsula of Michigan

5. According to the passage, EAB has been found on ash trees located in which of the following areas?

   I. urban areas
   II. rural woodlots
   III. riparian areas

   A. I only
   B. II only
   C. II and III only
   D. I, II, and III

6. As it is used in the passage, the word *concert* (line 20) most nearly means:
   F. to perform.
   G. to plan or act together.
   H. to arrange by agreement.
   J. to organize by.

7. Which of the following are purposes of the Canadian "ash free" zone?

   I. prevention of artificial movement of infested ash material out of the infested area
   II. ash reduction efforts in key "Gateway Areas"
   III. destruction of all ash trees in a 30-km × 10-km zone

   A. I only
   B. I and II only
   C. II and III only
   D. I and III only

8. Which of the following tree decline and dieback symptoms hindered the discovery that EAB was killing ash trees in southern Michigan?
   F. ash yellows and ash decline
   G. ash yellows and ash deterioration
   H. ash decline and ash flaking
   J. yellow bark and ash decline

9. According to the passage, which of the following could transfer EAB to other areas?

    I. purchasing wood chips that were harvested from wood in Michigan and using them in Indiana

   II. placing extra ash firewood in your vehicle after camping in Michigan and driving to California

 III. standing near an ash tree in Michigan and then traveling to Florida

  A. I only
  B. II only
  C. I and II only
  D. I and III only

10. According to the passage, which is true of EAB prior to 2002?
  F. EAB was on a watch list.
  G. EAB was not in the United States.
  H. EAB was known outside of Asia.
  J. EAB was previously unknown outside of Asia.

Strategy Review

Preheating: Did you preheat your brain? While zooming in on the origins of the passage, the title, and the first paragraph, you should have noticed some key words and phrases: *U.S. Forest Service, disease conditions, emerald ash borer (EAB), infestations, 2002, Michigan,* and *Canada*. You should have thought, *What do I already know about bug infestations?* If you live in Michigan, you may be highly familiar with the EAB. If you live in Colorado or another state with infestations of pine beetles, you may understand the devastation caused by such pests. Even if you are unfamiliar with bothersome bugs, you might connect to an idea you already have about the Forest Service or about other diseases. Your ability to connect to the topic in some form greatly enhances your retention of the material.

    Finding the Main Idea and Tone; Indexing the Passage: The main idea and the tone of the passage may be clear within the first paragraph, or you may have to wait until you have read the entire passage to identify them. In the margins, summarize the contents of each paragraph. Your index may not use the same wording as the following one; however, you should have identified similar ideas for each paragraph.

Paragraph 1: Origins of EAB, Canada and U.S.

Paragraph 2: EAB infestation in native habitat and ash trees in U.S.

Paragraph 3: EAB control in Canada

Paragraph 4: EAB control in Michigan and Ohio

Paragraph 5: Current control options

TIP

Even if you're not familiar with the topic of a passage, try to make a connection with it on some level.

Paragraph 6: Government partnerships and research

Paragraph 7: Late discovery of EAB in Michigan

Paragraph 8: Reasons for no EAB warnings before 2002

Finding the Answer: Did you focus on key words and phrases from the question stems to guide your search? Those key phrases along with your memory of the passage and your notes in the margin should have helped you identify the location of answers within the passage.

Answers and Explanations: Natural Science

1. **(A)** The key phrase in this question is "native habitat." Your notes for paragraph 2 should have guided you directly to the answer, which is stated word-for-word in line 15: "The EAB infests walnuts and elms in its native habitat." Each of the other options "sounds" correct, so finding the answer is more productive than relying on your memory of the passage's details.

2. **(H)** The question asks you why an "ash free" zone won't work in Michigan and Ohio. Paragraph 4 discusses EAB control in these two states. The first sentence of the paragraph provides the answer: "infestations are too extensive and numerous to be contained with the kind of 'ash free' zones." The answer is "right there" in the passage. Option F is distracting because it contains a phrase used within the passage: "management efforts shifted to the lower peninsula of Michigan" (lines 26–37). The limited research available on EAB infestations (option G) and governmental regulations (option J) sound logical if you can't remember the exact detail. These distracting and even logical answer options are the reason you need to look up the correct response.

3. **(C)** Notice the key word in the questions stem—*NOT*. Use "EAB eradication" as the key phrase to find the location of the answer within the index. Think about the passage as a whole and find the areas that specifically address the eradication of the EAB. Because "NOT" questions take more time than others, consider leaving this one until you have finished all other questions for this passage. If your eight-minute passage allowance has ended by the time you get back to this question, make your best guess and move on to the next passage. Option A, "The EAB is difficult to kill with insecticide once it bores under the bark of a tree," is proven true in lines 36–37; option B, "no ash species appear to be resistant to EAB," in lines 60–61, and option D, "ash free zones have been declared in Canada," in paragraph 3. Option C is not true because studies have been underway since 2002, not 2000. Because the dates are so close together, option C may also appear true in your haste to answer the question.

4. (**F**) You may remember from the passage that surveys were conducted upon the initial findings of EAB infestation. The key word in the question stem is actually *triggered*. This word means "started" or "initiated." Locate the section of the passage that discusses the beginning of the EAB infestation. Your index should help you determine that paragraph 1 is the place to look. Lines 3–4 give you the correct answer to this question. Option G is the most distracting because, later in paragraph 1, the word *surveys* is used immediately after a reference to Windsor, Ontario, Canada (line 8). Attending to key words in the question stem helps you choose between two close answers. Options H and J may distract you because they are specifically mentioned within the passage.

5. (**D**) This question may take extra time. Actually, this one is fairly easy once you find the location of the information within the passage. According to the question stem, you are trying to figure out where ash trees are generally located. When referring to your notes, you can predict that the answer will probably be located in paragraph 2 because it mentions ash trees in the United States. Even if you don't have strong notes for each paragraph, you can logically assess that an important detail such as where ash trees are located is in the early part of the passage. Line 17 indicates that ash trees can be found in "urban areas, rural woodlots, and riparian areas." Each of these is an option within the question; therefore option D is correct.

6. (**G**) First, find the word in the passage. Thankfully, the line number (20) is given to you in the question stem. Read the sentence, and before reading any of the answer options, replace the original word with another word that could be used instead. The word *together* fits nicely in the sentence. Sometimes you have to replace the word along with surrounding words to make it make sense: "This ash free zone *together* with an aggressive regulatory program . . . " Go back to the answer options and find the one that most closely resembles the word you have chosen. Option G, "to plan or act together," works best. Option F plays on your initial instincts regarding the definition of the word *concert*. Outside the context of the article, the first definition you would have for *concert* is "a musical performance." Don't allow personal context to distract you. What do you do if you can't think of anything to replace the word in question? A second strategy is to replace the word with each answer choice and decide which option makes the most sense. Options H and J may sound reasonable initially, but if you replace the definitions with the word in the sentence, option G makes the most sense.

7. (**D**) Locate the section of the passage that refers to Canada's "ash free" zone. According to the index, paragraph 3 should contain this information. Also, you could answer this question using logic. You may remember that "ash free" zones require that all ash trees be removed. Option II indicates that ash trees are only being reduced; therefore, eliminate it as an answer. Now, you only have to

choose between answers A and D. In paragraph 3, both options I, "prevention of artificial movement of infested ash material out of the infested area;" and III, "destruction of all ash trees in a 30-km × 10-km zone," are identified as part of Canada's "ash free" zone project in lines 21–22 and line 19, respectively, making option D correct.

8. **(F)** The answer to this question is not explicitly stated within the passage; you must infer the correct answer. The following are the key words and phrases in the question stem: *discovery, tree decline and dieback symptoms*, and *hindered*. According to the index, paragraph 7 discusses the late discovery of EAB. The discovery of EAB can only be described as "late" if it was hindered by something. Refer to paragraph 7 for the answer. The first sentence in paragraph 7 contains a key phrase from the question stem—*decline and dieback symptoms*. This paragraph lists two symptoms that "disguised" the underlying problem of EAB: ash yellows and ash decline. The paragraph states that these two problems "were so prevalent that dying ash trees did not draw close scrutiny," which means that they masked or hindered the discovery of the EAB infestation. Each of the incorrect options, G, H, and J, play on the wording of the correct response. They may all sound reasonable, but they do not include the exact wording of the diseases indicated in the passage: ash yellows and ash decline.

9. **(C)** This question asks you to infer based on the passage as a whole. First, figure out how EAB is transferred. Your notes on each paragraph may not be very helpful because multiple paragraphs discuss the spread or control of EAB. Skim each paragraph for ideas about spreading EAB. Lines 12–14 indicate how areas outside of the quarantine area were most likely infested: ash firewood, logs, or nursery materials. The wood chips mentioned in option I are a "nursery material" that could possibly transport EAB. Transferring firewood, as in option II, could transport EAB. Nothing in the passage indicates that just standing near an ash tree transports these pests. If EAB could be transferred in this way, people would have to be quarantined as well. Options I and II make sense; therefore, answer C is correct.

10. **(J)** Finding the correct paragraph may be difficult based on the question stem. You could find every reference to 2002 and possibly locate the correct answer, but it may take too long. Look at the answer options to see if they give you a clue where to look. You may remember that the last line of the passage refers to a watch list. Go to the last paragraph and see if it leads you in the right direction. According to the paragraph, EAB was NOT on a watch list or known outside of Asia; therefore, options F and H are not correct. EAB was probably in the United States for 5–10 years prior to 2002, so option G is not correct. Option J, "EAB was previously unknown outside of Asia," is correct. The wording of these options may fool you, so read carefully.

EIGHT KEY STRATEGIES FOR READING NONFICTION

1. **It's all in the timing.** Spend no more than eight minutes on one passage, unless it is your last one.

2. **See the big picture.** Take in the passage as a whole before you begin reading. Observe how many paragraphs and lines you will be reading. Tell yourself that you only have four minutes to read the passage.

3. **Zoom in.** Look carefully at the citation and the title. Skim the first paragraph for key words to identify the topic.

4. **Preheat your brain.** What do you already know about the topic? Make a connection so that the new information you are going to read about has something to attach to inside your brain.

5. **Clear your mind.** Remove all mental clutter. Think only about your background knowledge of the topic. Forget about school, parents, friends, and any other mental distractions that cause you to lose focus as you read. Remain focused on the topic at hand, seeking to learn all you can about it.

6. **Identify the main idea and tone.** Remembering specific details the first time through the passage is not important; you have time to look them up later. Use the following two questions to identify the main idea and tone of the passage: 1) What is the author saying about the topic?, and 2) What is the author's attitude toward the topic? By identifying the main idea and tone of the passage, you will be better prepared to answer inferential questions about certain sections or about the passage as a whole.

7. **Index the passage.** Summarize the purpose and function of each paragraph. Take brief notes in the margins that give you an index you can refer to while answering the questions.

8. **Guess first, then find the answer.** As soon as you have read the question stem, take a stab at the answer. Doing so helps you eliminate incorrect answer options. Next, identify key words or line numbers within the question stem, and use the index you created to find the answer in the text.

SCIENCE

CHAPTER 16

Overview of the Science Test

- Structure of the science test
- Test directions
- Passage types
- Order of questions

This chapter will give you a quick refresher course about the ACT science test, introduce you to some general strategies for success on any standardized test, and then explain the format of the rest of this section of the book. Throughout this section you will see various tip boxes, which will give you specific, easily remembered advice about the best ways to approach the test. And be sure to pay special attention to "**Inside the ACT 36 Mind**." These are like getting a backstage pass into the workings of the ACT test writers. They will give you insight into how the test is structured, help you recognize answer choices that are included to distract you into making mistakes, and let you in on some of the tricks that test writers use so that not everyone will score a 36. By learning about how the test is created, you will be better prepared to reach your goals.

Now, take a look at the ACT science test.

SPECIFICS OF THE TEST

The science section has the same general format on every ACT test. Knowing this format and the instructions for completing the test beforehand will allow you to spend your time focusing on the passages themselves. The general instructions for the ACT science test look like this:

SCIENCE TEST

35 Minutes—40 Questions

Directions: There are seven science passages in this test, each of them followed by several questions. Based on the information presented in the passage, choose the correct answer and fill in the corresponding oval on the answer sheet. You may refer back to the passages as often as you need.

Calculators are **not** allowed on this section of the test.

TIP

Now that you have read the instructions, do not waste time reading them again on test day. They will not change.

Passage Types

There are seven passages on the science section of the ACT, each one numbered with Roman numerals, such as "Passage I," "Passage II," etc. The passages may be single pages or multiple pages, and sometimes you may have to flip back and forth between pages, but the test writers seem to try to avoid this. The seven passages are classified into three different types, each with a specific number of questions. They are:

1. **Data Representation**—5 questions. There are 3 of these on the test.

2. **Research Summaries**—6 questions. There are 3 of these on the test.

3. **Conflicting Viewpoints**—7 questions. There is 1 of these on the test.

The rest of the science chapters will dissect passages and give you detailed descriptions and strategies for mastering each of the types.

TIP

If you are running out of time on the ACT, quickly fill in any blank questions on the answer sheet—even if you have not read the question.

Scoring

Every question on the science test is worth 1 point. There is no penalty for guessing incorrectly, so you should attempt to answer every question. Every 1 to 2 correctly answered questions raises your score by one point, especially in the 30 and over range.

> ### INSIDE THE ACT 36 MIND
>
> You've probably heard the idea that when in doubt on a test, "Guess answer choice C." On the ACT (and almost every other standardized test you may take), this is not true, especially since almost half of the questions do not even have "C" as an option. Also, test makers and test companies have designed the tests to avoid bias. They make sure that, statistically, no answer choice is used more than any other. Also, don't worry if one answer seems to come up several times in a row. If you know, or are pretty sure, that your answer choices are correct, do not change them because there is a weird pattern on your answer sheet.

SCIENTIFIC REASONING IS TESTED

Probably the most important thing to remember about the science section of the ACT is that this is a test of scientific reasoning, not a test of scientific knowledge. Unlike the tests you take in school, you are not expected to come in with any prior knowledge about any of the topics presented in the passages. As an ambitious student, you have probably taken several science courses, including some advanced ones, so you are naturally going to be more familiar with the concepts. More important, you will have had more exposure to scientific methods and processes—this is what is being tested.

Because there is no specific content you're expected to know, all of the information you need to answer the questions is found in the passages. Make sure to focus

TIP

There are no facts to learn for the ACT science section. You are being tested on how science is done, so think like a scientist!

on this data, and don't spend time over-thinking topics you may have studied in class. Overanalyzing the content of any passage will only waste valuable time.

Timing and Order

With 40 questions to answer in only 35 minutes, you have about 52.5 seconds to answer each one. That means you must practice working as quickly and as accurately through the questions as you possibly can. Don't bother sitting with a stopwatch to time yourself, and don't focus on the clock so much during the test that you get distracted. With some general strategies and practice, you can eliminate some of the time pressure.

You will be able to answer some of the passages more quickly, and some will take more time. What many students have found to be a highly effective strategy is to do the passages out of order. That's right—do not go through the test starting at question 1 and finishing with question 40. Go through the test by doing certain passages first and others last.

As explained earlier, the seven passages are broken down into three types, each with a different number of questions. Because some of these require more intensive reading, while others can be scanned quickly, they should be done in the following order:

1. Data Representation (5 questions)—Do these three passages first.

2. Research Summaries (6 questions)—Do these three passages second.

3. Conflicting Viewpoints (7 questions)—Do this one passage third.

The passages are most easily identified by the number of questions following each, so remembering to do them in numerical order, "5, 6, 7," will help you save time in the long run.

As soon as you open your test booklet to the science section, you should quickly scan through each passage, check the number of questions, and number the passages "1st," "2nd," or "3rd" on the top of each page. Then start answering the questions.

INSIDE THE ACT 36 MIND

The test writers need a way to separate out students so that not everyone will score a 36. That's one of the reasons there is not really enough time to complete the test. They very often put the Conflicting Viewpoints passage in the first half of the test because most students will slow down to carefully read the passage, creating tremendous time pressure to finish the rest. Many people get so stuck that they never get to two or more passages at the end of the test. If you leave the Conflicting Viewpoints passage and its seven questions for the end, you will have more time to complete all the passages more accurately. Statistics show that even if you run out of time and don't get to this last passage, you can still score in the high 20s by answering the other passages correctly.

For some students, going out of order is the hardest advice to follow. You may have spent years working methodically through tests from start to finish. If so, jumping around the test is going to feel uncomfortable at first. Rest assured that with practice it will become easier and easier, and your scores should improve as well.

The other issue involving order on the ACT is that the science section always comes last. By the time you get to this part of the test, you have been sitting for almost an hour and a half reading questions and filling in circles on an answer sheet. Your hand hurts from writing, your brain hurts from thinking, and your rear end hurts from sitting. You simply want to finish the test. Don't let test fatigue get in the way. Before the science section, give yourself a pep talk that you're in the home stretch and can see the finish line. Remind yourself to keep going strong.

KNOWING YOURSELF AS A STUDENT

The type of student you are and your academic preferences and abilities have a great deal of influence on how you might approach the ACT science section. Recognizing your strengths and weaknesses and using them to your advantage is an important part of your success. For the purpose of the ACT, students tend to classify themselves into three general categories: science students, English students, and math students.

Science Students

Some students see themselves as **science students**. They have taken all the biology, chemistry, earth science, and physics courses that are offered. They do experiments in their basements and enter science fairs and competitions for fun. They do well in both math and English classes, but the science ones are what they enjoy the most. For these students, this section is the one they have been looking forward to throughout the entire test; however, they have to be careful not to read too much into the data sets or to try to understand every aspect of the experiments.

English Students

Students who see themselves as **English students** breeze through the English and reading parts of the ACT and tend to sweat their way through the math. They enjoy reading and writing and see vocabulary as their friend. They often dread the science section because it does not seem to play to their strengths. Making notations in the margins about data and main ideas helps them from being overwhelmed by the numbers. English students are the ones who will have the most difficulty leaving the Conflicting Viewpoints passage to the end, but it is really to their advantage.

TIP

Don't give a half-hearted effort on the science section just because you're tired. When you're physically there taking the test, be mentally there as well.

TIP

For Science Students
Do not over-think the passage content.

TIP

For English Students
Don't panic over the numbers. Write your own notes in the margins to help you stay focused.

Math Students

Math students like numbers in whatever form they appear. They love doing equations and solving problems in their heads. They can do things with calculators that seem to defy logic. They dread the English and reading parts of the ACT, but they like the Data Representation and Research Summaries passages of the science section because they contain charts and graphs. Math students are the ones who are most likely to get stuck in a Conflicting Viewpoints passage and miss the opportunity to answer easier questions later in the test.

Which type of student are you? Or do you not fit into any of the types? In reality, being one type or another should not interfere with your ability to do well on the science section. Make sure to use your strengths to your advantage. Work on your weaker areas by using strategies presented in this section, as well as throughout the book. Skills learned in one area are definitely transferable to another.

TIP

For Math Students Don't recalculate all of the data or get lost in the numerical details. Focus on the main ideas of the passages.

Passage Types and Strategies

- Data representation
- Research summaries
- Conflicting viewpoints
- Strategies for maximizing scores

There are three main types of passages on the science ACT: Data Representation, Research Summaries, and Conflicting Viewpoints. Understanding the basics of each of the three will help you better approach and answer the questions.

DATA REPRESENTATION

Data Representation passages are often referred to as "graphing" passages because the most common thing about them is their use of graphs. There are three of them on every ACT, and they are always followed by a set of five questions. The graphs, figures, and data tables that are used in these passages can be related to any scientific content. They include types of illustrations you will find in your science textbooks and in journal articles. The questions generally ask you to pick data points off of a graph, interpret data trends on charts or tables, and analyze information presented in figures or equations.

   You should do Data Representation passages first because the questions can be answered most quickly. They usually do not have much to read, except for a brief introduction, and many of the questions are factual.

TIP

Spend no more than 3 to 4 minutes on each Data Representation passage.

INSIDE THE ACT 36 MIND

The graphs, figures, and data tables throughout the ACT are designed to intimidate the test-taker. Many of them will be arranged in unfamiliar ways, have multiple sets of data plotted in different directions, or show very complex experimental set-ups. Don't be intimidated by their complexity. The more of these you see during your review and practice, the easier they will seem.

RESEARCH SUMMARIES

The second type of passage is called Research Summaries. These passages are sometimes referred to as "experimental" because they generally describe scientific experiments. There are also three of these on the test, but they are always followed by six questions and should be done second. Like Data Representation, these passages are designed to test your graph skills, your ability to interpret trends, and your overall science reasoning ability, but they also focus on proper experimental design, drawing conclusions, and knowledge of the scientific method. Whether you have never even heard of the subject or have actually performed the experiment in one of your own classes, remember: The correct answers to the questions can usually be found quickly using the information in the passage.

Many times, you can recognize these passages because of headings like "Experiment 1," "Experiment 2," and "Experiment 3." They too may seem very complex and maybe a little bit scary, but try to look at this as a challenge, not as an obstacle. Because these are more complex than Data Representation passages, doing these second will help you maximize your time.

The best way to review for these passages is to make sure you understand the steps of the scientific method and the parts of a controlled experiment. If you are able to identify a hypothesis, recognize a control group, and explain independent and dependent variables from any experimental design, then you are prepared to handle Research Summaries passages effectively.

TIP

Spend no more than 5 to 6 minutes on each Research Summaries passage.

CONFLICTING VIEWPOINTS

Conflicting Viewpoints passages contain two opposing scientific views about some theory or process. Phenomena that occur over a long time period, such as evolution, or on a scale that is difficult to measure, such as global warming, are common topics. There is only one of these on the test, and it is always followed by seven questions. You are not likely to find many graphs or figures in these, just several paragraphs of reading. Strategies that you have already learned for the reading section of the ACT, especially for the natural science passages, will come in handy here.

Because these passages are so reading-intensive, you should do them last. For students who are strongest in English, the advantage of this is that if they spend too much time on the other passages, their strong reading skills should help them make up the time and get more of these questions correct. For math students, leaving the Conflicting Viewpoints passage until the end will help prevent them from being bogged down earlier in the test, giving them more time to focus on this at the end.

TIP

Spend no more than 5 to 8 minutes on the Conflicting Viewpoints passage.

"SCIeNCE" STRATEGIES

Although every individual will take the ACT in his or her own unique way, there are some general techniques and strategies that you should follow to maximize your score. You may be doing some of these already, or you may not have any kind of system. Regardless, if your goal is to earn a high score, then learning and practicing a systematic approach to the passages will put you closer to achieving a 36.

To help you remember this approach, use the acronym "**SCIeNCE**." It may seem a little bit goofy, but it just might help you focus. It's certainly worth trying, and it just might boost your score.

> "**SCIeNCE**" stands for the following:
>
> **S—Scan the passage.**
> **C—Check the main idea.**
> **Ie—Ignore the extras.**
> **N—Note the reference in the question.**
> **C—Choose the best answer.**
> **E—Eliminate the incorrect answers.**

The first three, **SCIe**, are used before you even begin answering any of the questions. They will give you an overview and help you focus on what's important.

S—Scan the Passage

This is the first thing you will do once you start looking at a specific passage. Take a brief amount of time to look over the topic, notice what the graphs and tables are presenting, and see how the questions look. Once you've scanned the passage, you'll know where to find some random piece of information you need to answer one of the questions.

TIP

Scanning the passage should take about 10 to 15 seconds.

C—Check the Main Idea

Figuring out the main idea is very important for all of the science passage types. What will help you even more is underlining, circling, or marking these in some way. With Conflicting Viewpoints, for example, writing the scientist's argument in the margin is a very helpful practice. Drawing trend arrows for data tables and graphs will also help you understand the passage better. More important, these notations will actually be the answer to some of the questions or will serve as signposts telling you where to look for the correct answer.

TIP

Finding the main idea and marking it in the test booklet will help you analyze the questions better.

Ie—Ignore the Extras

Science passages are filled with extra information and jargon that you do not need to understand and that you don't need to answer the questions. There may be three graphs in one passage, but the questions only refer to two of them. Entire data tables and descriptions of experiments may never be used. Complex equations may be included, but they may not be used for an answer. Don't get tied up in them.

INSIDE THE ACT 36 MIND

Test writers include extra information to confuse and intimidate the average test-taker. Many students are so tired by the time they reach the science section, and so scared of the complex graphs, that they give up and don't focus enough to answer the questions.

The last three letters of the acronym, **NCE**, are strategies that you will use while you're answering the questions themselves.

N—Note the Reference in the Question

TIP

If the question refers to a specific experiment, graph, table, look there immediately to find the answer. Don't waste time re-reading other sections of the passage.

Some of the most common types of questions in the ACT science section start out, "According to Figure 1," or, "Based on the results of Experiment 3." These are like runway lights for a pilot. They tell you exactly where to go to find the answer. Sometimes, the references are less obvious, like, "A scientist who follows the theory of gradualism would most likely agree with . . . ," but for the student who has checked the main idea, this reference will point to the exact place where an answer can be found. In more complicated questions, there may not be a reference at all, or the reference may be found in the answer choices themselves.

C—Choose the Best Answer

This is what the science test is all about. Once you read the question stem, you should have an idea of what the correct answer may be, or at least know exactly where to go back and find it. You will find many hints and tips for doing this throughout this section of the book.

E—Eliminate the Incorrect Answers

For the average test-taker, this step often comes before choosing the correct answer, but high-achieving students often pick the best choice and eliminate the others simultaneously. Once you have an answer, make sure to quickly eliminate the others— physically crossing them out is an excellent strategy, especially if you get stuck and need to return to the question later. You will then have fewer items to consider. And don't overanalyze your answer choices, especially for questions that have simple numbers as answers. If you have found the correct one, mark it and move on. Don't waste valuable time.

When you select your answer on your answer sheet, make sure to mark clearly. Even more important, if you change an answer, erase the old one completely. Some people find it useful to make very light marks on their answer sheets and then take a minute at the end of the test to darken them the rest of the way.

Now that you've been introduced to the **SCIeNCE** strategies, it's time to really examine the passages themselves and to practice these strategies. In the next few chapters, we embark on a dissection of the passages, exposing all of their inner parts. Once we've done this, you'll get a chance to use what you've learned with some full-length passages and question sets.

Passage Dissection: Introductions

CHAPTER 18

- Scanning the passage
- Checking the main idea

- Ignoring the extras

All three types of ACT science passages include some reading. Usually, a paragraph or two is used as an introduction to the passage. Data Representation and Research Summaries passages generally start out with a description of the experiment from which the data was collected. Conflicting Viewpoints present two different points of view on a scientific theory or topic. Any of these can be about chemistry, biology, physics, earth science, or a related scientific concept.

Sometimes you may be familiar with the subject because you covered it during a course, sometimes you may have actually performed a similar experiment, but most of the time, the test writers pick some pretty obscure information that few high school students would know. This doesn't matter! The test is not an achievement test—how much you've learned—but it is a reasoning one—how well you can solve problems.

TIP

For the introductions, use some of the same strategies that you use on the English and reading sections of the ACT.

APPROACHING INTRODUCTIONS

For Data Representation and Research Summaries passages, the test writers also tend to include lots of specific detail in the introduction. There are often equations, calculations, units, and many numbers. These details are included to show that the experiment is valid, and for the average test-taker, they are intimidating. For the well-prepared student, they should not really be a problem.

How should you approach the introductions to the Data Representation and Research Summaries passages then? Use the **SCIe** of the **SCIeNCE** strategies to quickly **S**can the section, **C**heck the main idea, and **I**gnore the **e**xtras.

For practice with these strategies, approach each example like you would an actual ACT passage. Try to time yourself to see how long it takes to scan, identify the main idea by circling and/or underlining, and skip the extras. Then analyze how you did by filling out the charts after the examples. (Answers follow.)

Example 1

Adding heat to a material causes the molecules to increase their molecular motion. Certain substances have the ability to retain this heat longer than other substances.

In solids and liquids, this property is described as *specific heat capacity* and is defined as the heat required to raise some unit (usually 1.0 g) of the substance 1.0°C and is calculated using the following formula: $\Delta Q = m \times c \times \Delta T$, where $\Delta Q =$ the amount of heat applied (J or Kcal), $m =$ substance mass (g), $c =$ specific heat capacity (J/ g °C), and $\Delta T =$ change in temperature ($T_{final} - T_{initial}$). The specific heat capacities for various metals are presented in Table 1 (not actually shown). The time course for each of them to return to their previous temperature after being heated to 100°C is graphed in Figure 1 (not actually shown).

Strategy Practice Chart
Scan the passage.
  Time: _____
Check the main idea.
  Main Idea: _____
Ignore the **e**xtras.
  Extras: _____

How did you do? Here are the suggested answers for this strategy practice. If you came up with the same ones (or something close), great! If you're having difficulty, don't worry. Improvement may take a little time and is the reason that you practice.

Scan the passage.
  Time: 5–6 seconds. Remember, you should spend less than 4 minutes on the entire passage
Check the main idea.
  Main Idea: Specific heat capacity = how much heat a substance can retain. Did you circle or underline this?
Ignore the **e**xtras.
  Extras: The equation and its definitions. Don't let yourself be distracted. That's what the test makers want you to do

TIP

Pay attention to the amount of time you spend scanning the paragraph. On the actual ACT, you won't have the luxury of reading slowly.

Let's try another example on a different topic. Use the same strategies again as you read through the introduction.

Example 2

Most earthquakes occur along fault lines between tectonic plates of the Earth's lithosphere—large pieces of the earth's crust that are continually shifting and moving along, above, and below each other. Forces cause the deformation of the crust and overcome the frictional resistance holding the plates in place, causing displacement of the adjacent layers by as much as several meters. When the plates uplift along these weaker faults, such as the San Andreas Fault—a transform fault boundary between the North American plate and the Pacific plate in California—massive amounts of energy are released. Geologists measure this energy with the use of a seismograph, a machine that records the presence of two different types of waves—P (primary) and S (secondary). P waves are compressional waves, like sound waves. They travel between 6 and 13 km/s through both solids and liquids. S waves are transverse waves, traveling more horizontally, and move half as fast as P waves through solids only. S and P intervals can be used to calculate the epicenter of an earthquake. Figures 1 and 2 (not shown) show S and P intervals for two different earthquakes. Table 1 (not actually shown) displays calculated distances from six different monitoring stations.

Strategy Practice Chart
Scan the passage.
Time: _____
Check the main idea.
Main Idea: _____
Ignore the **e**xtras:
Extras: _____

How did this passage go? Were you able to understand how the introduction is written? See if you used the strategies in similar ways.

Scan the passage.
Time: 5–6 seconds—no more than 4 minutes for the entire passage.
Check the main idea.
Main Idea: Earthquakes are measured using S and P waves. Circling or underlining will help guide you back to this when you're answering the questions.
Ignore the **e**xtras.
Extras: Description of San Andreas Fault, definitions of S and P waves, and travel rates.

The important thing to remember from scanning the introductions of Data Representation and Research Summaries passages is that the information is there if and when you need it to answer the questions. Because you will scan the entire passage, tables, and questions all at once, you should quickly become aware of what you might need later, and more important, where to find it.

Conflicting Viewpoints passages should be approached in the same way, except this time you have to use the **SCIe** of the **SCIeNCE** strategies twice. Each paragraph/section presents a different view, so you need to pay attention to the topic and organize your thoughts very well.

Following is a Conflicting Viewpoints sample. Once again, **S**can the sections, **C**heck the main ideas, and **I**gnore the **e**xtras. Fill out the chart and then check to see how you did.

TIP

Don't forget to circle/underline the main idea or to write the viewpoint in the test booklet right next to the passage.

Example 3

Scientist 1

While studying galaxies in the early 20ᵗʰ century, scientists noticed that some of the stars at the outermost portion of many galaxies were not rotating according to accepted Newtonian laws of gravity, which state that the gravitational force between two bodies decays at a rate of the inverse square of the distance between them. Visible baryonic matter, all matter made up of atoms and their subatomic baryons consisting of three quarks, could not account for this discrepancy, but the presence of dark matter and dark energy can. Dark matter accounts for approximately 23% of the mass in the universe, as compared to the 4% for baryonic matter. The remaining 73% of the universe consists of dark energy and other radiation. By studying the redshift in light waves and determining the velocities of stars and other satellites in thousands of galaxies, scientists have collected evidence supporting the existence of the dark matter. These studies show that the concentrations of mass are many times larger than the visible galaxy itself and must be due to dark matter. Thus, this evidence restores Newton's gravitational law.

Scientist 2

In our solar system, the farther away a planet is from the sun, the slower its orbit. But in other galaxies, the observable change in the expected velocity of distant satellites is due to changes in acceleration, not gravity. Modified Newtonian Dynamics, or MOND, uses Newton's Second Law, $F = ma$ (F = force, m = mass, and a = acceleration); however, it includes a new acceleration constant that helps explain the situation in galaxies where the force of gravitational acceleration is very small. There is virtually no evidence to absolutely support the presence of dark matter. This mysterious substance has been used to help observational data conform to standard laws of physics, but it has not been unequivocally proven. Dark energy, which fills up what is seen as empty space in the universe, is uniform throughout and helps explain MOND behavior of an accelerating, expanding universe. To help understand the bending of light in relation to various forces, MOND has been modified as TeVeS—Tensor-Vector-Scalar. The tensor aspect describes the curvature of the gravitation fields, the vector shows that the strength of gravity differs from place to place, and the scalar expression shows that light is affected by these properties.

Strategy Practice Chart
Scientist 1:
Scan the passage.
　Time: _____
Check the main idea.
　Main Idea: _____
Ignore the **e**xtras.
　Extras: _____

Scientist 2:
Scan the passage.
   Time: _____
Check the main idea.
   Main Idea: _____
Ignore the **e**xtras.
   Extras: _____

As you can see, the Conflicting Viewpoints passages are really not much different than the introductions to the Data Representation and Research Summaries passages—they are usually just longer. The strategies are the same. Check to see if you approached them like a student aiming for a 36 would.

Scientist 1:
Scan the passage.
   Time: 25–30 seconds—no more than 7–8 minutes for the entire passage.
Check the main idea.
   Main Idea: Dark matter and energy fit into Newton's law to explain the unexpected orbiting behavior of stars/satellites in galaxies. Did you circle or underline this? Writing "dark matter/Newton" next to the passage itself will help guide you as you're answering questions.
Ignore the **e**xtras.
   Extras: Definition of Newton's law, baryonic matter, percentages of matter in the universe, etc. You'll know where to find these if you need them.

Scientist 2:
Scan the passage.
   Time: 25–30 seconds—no more than 7–8 minutes for the entire passage.
Check the main idea.
   Main Idea: Newton's laws and dark matter cannot explain the galaxies' behavior. MOND and TeVeS use acceleration to explain it. Hopefully you underlined/circled this or wrote "no dark matter/non-Newton" next to the paragraph.
Ignore the **e**xtras.
   Extras: Newton's law equation, explanation of parts of TeVeS, etc. Again, if you need this information to answer questions, you should be able to quickly find it.

You've now completed the first part of the passage dissection, the introduction. Remember, this part can be different lengths in the Data Representation and Research Summaries passages. Sometimes it has a lot of information you'll need to answer the questions. Other times, it may only be a single sentence. You should be savvy enough not to spend too much time on the introduction, but perceptive enough not to ignore it either.

INSIDE THE ACT 36 MIND

Remember, the test writers often include one question that relies on a piece of obscure information that is tucked away in the introduction. For Conflicting Viewpoints passages, the introduction is the entire passage, so reading these more thoroughly is the way to succeed—it is also the reason to do this type of passage last.

We're now ready to move on to dissecting the next part of the ACT science passages—the tables, graphs, and figures. It's like looking at the muscle layer of a frog or fetal pig, but without the mess.

Passage Dissection: Tables, Graphs, and Figures

CHAPTER 19

- Scanning the data
- Focusing on trends
- Understanding the main idea
- Drawing trend arrows

You will find a huge variety of tables, graphs, and figures in the Data Representation and Research Summaries passages. You will see data tables with both numbers and descriptions. Graphs may be oriented vertically or horizontally. Line graphs can be simple linear relationships, have scales on both sides, or even combine several very different data sets. Bar graphs are often stacked with several different data points shown on the same bar. Some graphs are more like figures than graphs themselves. You will need to be prepared for any of these. (See Figure 1 and other examples on page 250.)

TIP

Conflicting Viewpoints passages are almost always all reading, so you usually won't see tables, graphs, and figures in them.

Figures may show experimental apparatus, chemical structures, diagrams of ecosystems, or almost any science-related concept. Flip through any science textbook and you'll get an idea of the wide variety of images you may see. Most of them are fairly straightforward if you don't get distracted by the numbers and unfamiliar topics.

Since you may have never seen some of the types of tables, graphs, or figures, and may be unfamiliar with the topic, remind yourself that the information needed to answer the questions is there. Unlike many testers, well-prepared students will calmly use their strategies to their advantage.

TIP

Don't try to become an expert on what the data on graphs and tables represent. Just focus on interpreting the trends.

APPROACHING TABLES, GRAPHS, AND FIGURES

Approaching tables, graphs, and figures requires the same strategies you tried when looking at introductions. Again, use the **SCIe** of the **SCIeNCE** strategies to quickly **S**can the section, **C**heck the main idea, and **I**gnore the **e**xtras.

When **S**canning, note the data that are presented in each of the figures, graphs, or tables. Don't take too much time—note the main idea and come back to the specific data or number when you need it.

Checking the main idea reveals if there are any general numerical relationships between data sets, if there are trends in the data and graphs, and which directions and sides the scales are on. For graphs or tables with linear relationships, students often find it useful to quickly draw trend arrows, showing the direction of the data. This can be done with both tables and graphs.

Sample Graphs and Tables

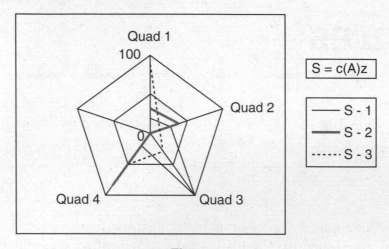

Figure 1

HPLC – Protein Sample # 7
C18 column 50% – 90% IPA/ACN over 50 minutes

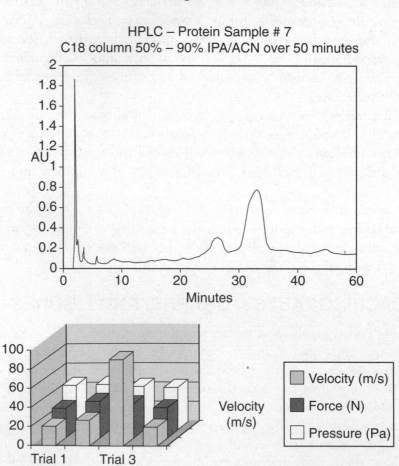

Temperature (°C)	Average Water Intake (ml)	Average Water Loss (ml)	Average PO_4 Release ($\mu g/cm^3$)	
35	8 ↑	12	3	
40	5	17	9	↔
50 ↓	3	28 ↓	4	

In the table above, Temperature and Water Loss are proportional—both sets of numbers increase—while Temperature and Water Intake are inverse—an increase in Temperature results in a decrease in Water Intake. PO_4 Release does not demonstrate a trend; the sideways arrow is one way of showing that.

Ignoring the **e**xtras is a major stumbling block for the less skilled test-taker. There is often a lot of extra information, and it is presented in ways that are sometimes unfamiliar. There are only five or six questions for each of these passages, so they obviously cannot require you to look at every piece of data. For example, in the table above, you may not need to know anything about PO_4 Release to answer any of the questions. Remember, you don't have to understand the concepts, you only have to be able to analyze the data well enough to answer the questions. Use the following examples to practice your strategies.

TIP

It doesn't really matter which way you draw trend arrows as long as you understand the relationships.

Example 1

A. altissima Extract Effects on Germination

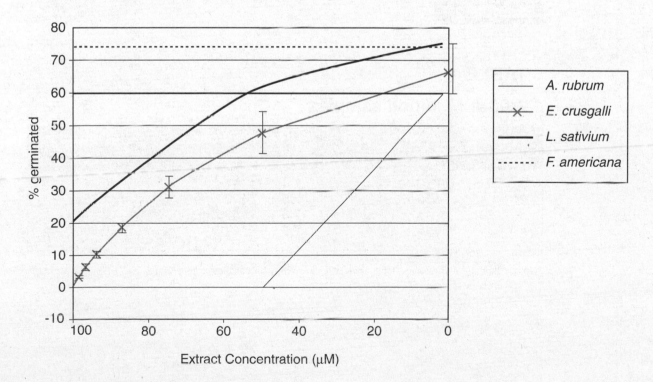

Strategy Practice Chart

Scan the graph.

Time: _____

Check the main idea (draw trend arrows/show relationship).

Main Idea: _____

Ignore the **e**xtras.

Extras: _____

Hopefully this was not too difficult and the strategies are becoming more familiar to you. Here is an idea of what you should have done with this graph.

Scan the graph.

Time: 4–5 seconds—just enough time to read the title, labels, and note any trends.

Check the main idea (draw trend arrows/show relationship).

Main Idea: Extract effects on germination—for most of the lines, higher concentrations = lower germination rates. Notice the scale on the x-axis of the graph goes from 100 to 0.

Ignore the **e**xtras.

Extras: Species names, specific units.

Here's another example on a different topic that uses a data table as a sample. Practice with your strategies to analyze this table.

Example 2

TABLE 1

7:00 A.M. blood samples

Patient	Volume (ml)	pH	Cholesterol* mg/dl	Bilirubin mg/dl
1	10	7.4	178	0.25
2	10	7.5	205	1.75
3	15	7.3	183	2.11
4	15	7.4	212	0.88

*Note: Cholesterol values are Total: Total/HDL ratios may be calculated from Test 2.

Strategy Practice Chart

Scan the table.

Time: _____

Check the main idea (draw trend arrows/show relationship).

Main Idea: _____

Ignore the **e**xtras.

Extras: _____

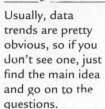

TIP

Usually, data trends are pretty obvious, so if you don't see one, just find the main idea and go on to the questions.

You may be shaking your head and wondering what you missed on this one. If you noticed, there really didn't seem to be any trends here. Hopefully, you didn't spend too much time looking for them. Frequently, there will be another table or graph with this kind of passage that will require you to compare the information with this table. From that you might be able to draw a trend.

Scan the table.

Time: 4–5 seconds—just enough time to read the title, labels, and note any trends.

Check the main idea (draw trend arrows/show relationship).

Main Idea: Patient blood samples for several different tests. There are no trends in this table.

INSIDE THE ACT 36 MIND

Sometimes, the ACT writers include tables, graphs, and figures that you do not need at all. They make the passage look much more complicated and are designed to waste the tester's time. Don't get caught in these traps.

Just remember, Data Representation and Research Summaries passages are designed to test your graph skills, your ability to interpret trends, and your overall science reasoning ability. Despite the sometimes confusing diagrams, you will need to understand the big picture, focus on only the relevant details, and work through these sections quickly. Doing these passages first will allow you to answer the most questions in the shortest amount of time.

We're now ready to complete our dissection of the passages with a look at the questions. This is the really juicy part because the questions are what need to be exposed to help you understand the workings of the science ACT.

Passage Dissection: Questions

CHAPTER 20

- Factual questions
- Inference questions
- Xtreme questions
- Question stems

O kay, now it's time to look at the "guts" of the science ACT—the questions. There are 40 questions in all, but there are really only three major question types. This chapter will examine these and give you some strategies to help you do well on them.

Because this is a reasoning test, the questions will be based on information that is in the passages and not on facts you've learned in science classes. The three types of questions that you are likely to see are: Factual, Inference, and what we'll call Xtreme.

QUESTION TYPES

Factual

Factual questions are based on facts or data that are clearly presented in either the introductions to the question or in tables, charts, and figures. These are the questions that most people get correct, and that you, as a student shooting for a 36, should rarely miss. The number of this type of question varies from passage to passage and from test to test, but there are generally two or three of these in a Data Representation or Research Summaries passage and one or two in a Conflicting Viewpoints passage. These questions can often be answered quickly and should not require much time.

Inference

Questions that require you to think a little bit more and find an answer that may not be a number in a data table or the main idea of the passage are inference questions. These require you to infer the answer based on some given information or draw a conclusion from an experiment. Inference questions often ask you to compare the results from two experiments or to figure out with which statement a scientist would disagree. Most of the questions in each passage are going to be inference because this is what tests your reasoning skills.

The answer choices are usually straightforward and do not include many tricks. They do require you, however, to consider each one before making the correct choice. If you've taken an honors or other advanced science class, these are the types of questions that your teachers ask you in class or when writing up lab reports. You have to take your time with inference questions, but they won't give you too many problems.

Xtreme

The "X Games" of questions, these are the ones the test writers design to separate out the very top students. Answering the Xtreme questions correctly will help you reach your goal of scoring a 36. These questions are often combinations of factual and inference questions. What makes them so difficult is that they often require you to pick out conflicting information from different experiments or graphs and then analyze them in a totally new way. One or two questions in Data Representation and Research Summaries passages are usually Xtreme. Two or three in a Conflicting Viewpoints passage is usually the norm. Xtreme questions will take the greatest amount of time to answer.

INSIDE THE ACT 36 MIND

Test writers often use their own little tricks to make the questions harder than they need to be. Many data tables have extra lines of information tucked into the bottom. Some introductions contain one sentence that at first seems to be extra information. Often there is a single sentence before one of the experiments that describes an additional variable not presented on the graphs. Depending on how the actual test is written and printed, this information may be a single line at the end of one experiment at the top of the right-hand column of text (see below*).

Why is this there? It's because we generally read from top left to bottom right in a diagonal fashion. If we are reading something fast, we are most likely to miss something that is in the bottom left or top right corner. It doesn't happen in every passage or on every test, but paying attention to hidden information will help you conquer these Xtreme questions.

Now that you know about the three types of questions, you probably wonder if there is a way to recognize them. Obviously they are not going to be labeled, and they are not going to be in order—passages often start with an easy factual question, but from then on they are pretty well mixed. Only by looking at the entire question will you be able to recognize the type.

To continue our dissection, we're now going to cut a little deeper and look at the structure of the questions themselves. We'll start with question stems and then look at the different kinds of answer choices.

TIP

Knowing each question type is not really that important. Being able to answer them correctly is what matters.

QUESTION STEMS

Question stems are what we normally think of as the question itself. In the ACT science section, there are several common question stems that are used over and over. The most basic ones usually start out with "Based on," or "According to," and then refer to one of the tables, graphs, figures, experiments, or scientists. Then they will ask you for some fact directly from the data or passage. The question stems for inference or Xtreme questions are just a variation of this, but they often include more information and are longer, even entire paragraphs.

Wording to Watch for

Here are the question stems that you'll likely see:

Based on . . . which of the following is most consistent . . .

Based on . . . one would conclude that . . .

According to . . . Scientist 1 would most likely argue that . . .

Based on the results . . . if (some condition) is changed, then . . .

According to Scientist 2's explanation, the reason that . . .

Which student would predict . . . based on (some change in the experiment) . . .

Which scientist would most likely agree with . . .

Assume that (some condition). On the basis of Table 2, one would conclude . . .

(A new piece of information) Based on this information and on . . . which of the following predictions is most likely true/false if . . .

If Experiment 2 had been repeated using . . . then which of the following figures best represents this new data?

A scientist hypothesized (some new information). Do the results of . . . support this hypothesis?

Which of the following statements best explains why (some part of the experiment)?

Suppose (some new fact). Which of the following statements about (this new fact) is most consistent with the information presented in the passage?

TIP

One of the surest ways of ensuring a high score is being so familiar with the test format that nothing is a surprise.

The more you familiarize yourself with the types of questions and the types of answer choices that they are often connected to, the better you will do on the test.

Now let's take a look at the kinds of answer choices you'll likely see.

ANSWER CHOICES

Like question stems, answer choices come in a variety of types. Some of them are simply numbers. Others are one or two factual words. There are usually some *if . . . then* statements. In Research Summaries and Data Representation passages, it is not uncommon to see new graphs or figures as part of the answer choices, and there is usually one question with almost an additional paragraph of reading involved in the answer choices—It should not be a surprise that these are often the Xtreme questions.

What to Look For

The following are the most common types of answer choices, but in any one test there can be a wide variety.

Simple Numbers

Numbers are almost always given in ascending or descending order. It is rare to find them presented randomly.
   A. 0.2
   B. 0.3
   C. 0.4
   D. 0.5

Combinations of Numbers

Again, there is usually an orderly pattern.
   F. a reading of 0.8 mg/ml at a pH of 3
   G. a reading of 0.7 mg/ml at a pH of 4
   H. a reading of 0.6 mg/ml at a pH of 5
   J. a reading of 0.5 mg/ml at a pH of 6

Ranges of numbers

Numbers ranges may be given by themselves or with other pieces of information.
   F. between 75 dB and 80 dB at 150 meters
   G. between 85 dB and 90 dB at 150 meters
   H. between 75 dB and 80 dB at 250 meters
   J. between 85 dB and 90 dB at 250 meters

Simple Words/Phrases

Most of the time, words and phrases will be in alphabetical order.
   A. cellular respiration
   B. fermentation
   C. glycolysis
   D. photosynthesis

Longer Phrases

Longer phrases can tell you whether a question is factual, inference, or Xtreme, depending on how they are related to the question and the passage. Many of the choices will be similar, so consider all of the options before choosing one.

    A. Scientist 1, because of the greater effects of electromagnetism
    B. Scientist 2, because of the greater effect of induced forces
    C. Scientist 1, because of the lesser effect of induced forces
    D. Scientist 2, because of the lesser effect of electromagnetism

Graphs or Figures

Probably the "scariest" kind of question for the average test-taker is one where the answer choices contain additional graphs or figures. What already looks like a complicated passage becomes even more challenging when new graphs are added. They require you to first understand the experiment and, often, then apply data from a table to answer the question.

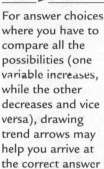

TIP

For answer choices where you have to compare all the possibilities (one variable increases, while the other decreases and vice versa), drawing trend arrows may help you arrive at the correct answer more quickly.

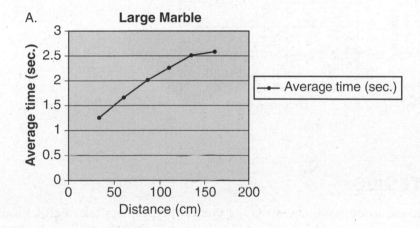

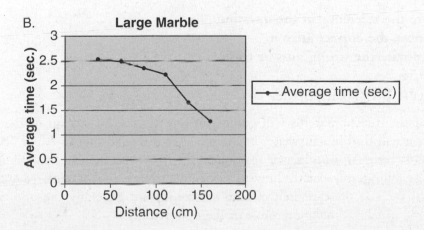

C.

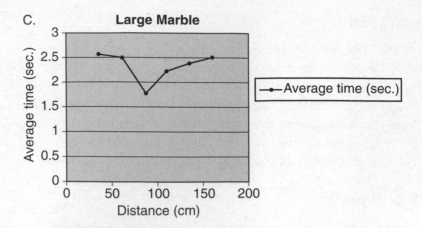

D.

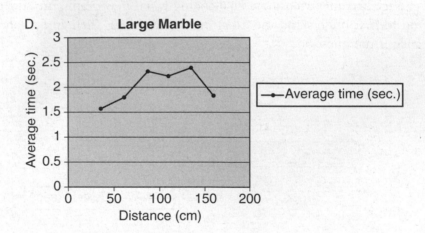

TIP

To answer questions with graphs or figures as answer choices, look back at your trend arrows on the data tables. You may have already "drawn" the data. Matching your notes up to the answer choices should get you through these questions in no time.

STRATEGIES

Now that you understand the variety of question types, let's take a closer look at the strategies for answering them. We've already used the **SCIe** parts of the **SCIeNCE** strategies, so now it's time to focus in on the **NCE** ones:

N—Note the reference in the question.
C—Choose the correct answer.
E—Eliminate the wrong answer choices.

N—Note the Reference

Many of the question stems will guide you directly to the section of the passage where you will find the answer. You will see "According to Figure 2," or "Based on Scientist 1," etc. As soon as you see these references—go there! They are like GPS directions telling you exactly how to navigate through the passage. Many factual questions include these references, and since they are generally the ones you can answer the quickest, make the most of the opportunity.

> ## INSIDE THE ACT 36 MIND
> While most of these questions are straightforward, the test writers will try to trick you on some of them. They will give a reference to one experiment or figure in the question stem and then give an entirely different reference in the answer choices. For example, you might see, "According to the results of Experiment 1 . . ." in the stem and then answers like, "Experiment 2 should be modified . . ." or, "Agrees most with the data presented in Table 2."

Some of the questions will not have obvious references. They may refer indirectly to the ideas of one of the scientists or the concepts of one of the experiments. A question may begin with a reference to punctuated equilibrium or to alluvial deposits. If you remember where in the passage you saw these topics, then you can quickly go back and find the answer. Students who have **S**canned the passage and **C**hecked the main idea will not have a problem.

What about questions without either a direct or indirect reference? Or ones that refer to both experiments? These will most likely be inference or Xtreme questions and where you will probably spend the most time. There are really no shortcuts to success for these questions. The best advice is to approach them methodically and quickly.

If you feel yourself getting stuck and using up too much time, circle or put a star by the question number, skip to the next question, and come back after you have completed the rest of the questions for that passage. Oftentimes, this technique will help you because some other piece of information in one of the other questions may trigger a response. Overall, how you handle these will depend more on the next two strategies—**C**hoose the Best Answer and **E**liminate the Incorrect Choices.

C—Choose the Best Answer, and E—Eliminate Incorrect Choices

Well, this is it—the final step in our dissection, where you get to see the guts of the ACT. Choosing the correct answer is what this test, and all of your hard work and preparation, is all about. Your goal is to choose all 40 of the correct answers and achieve your perfect score, a 36. Can you do it? By using your strategies and practicing with passages, you will get closer to the ultimate score.

Choosing the best answer and **E**liminating the incorrect choices are almost always done simultaneously by the advanced student. Other students will ponder over all four answers and then keep referring back to the passage to eliminate the wrong ones. While this might be effective on the tests you take in school, this does not work on the ACT—you simply do not have time!

As you read the question stem and answer choices and then refer back to the passage, you already should have an idea about what the correct answer will be. For factual questions, this usually involves picking out one of the numbers from a table or identifying the main idea of one of the scientists. Unlike in school, you are going to have to go back and refer to the passage because you will not know the topics and specific pieces of data. When you eliminate an answer choice, cross it out. Then make sure to carefully mark the correct answer on your answer sheet.

Choosing the best answer and **E**liminating the incorrect ones are more difficult in inference and Xtreme questions and will require more time. Take advantage of your references in the questions, as well as any trend arrows or notes you've made about the passage. If you have an idea about the correct answer even before you read the choices, then picking the right one will be much easier. When you have to analyze conflicting pieces of information, finding one part of an answer choice that is wrong means that the entire answer is wrong as well, and you don't have to spend more time going through it.

Example 1

Figures 1 and 2 show the germination rates over temperature increase and seedling mass under different salt concentrations for two different plant species.

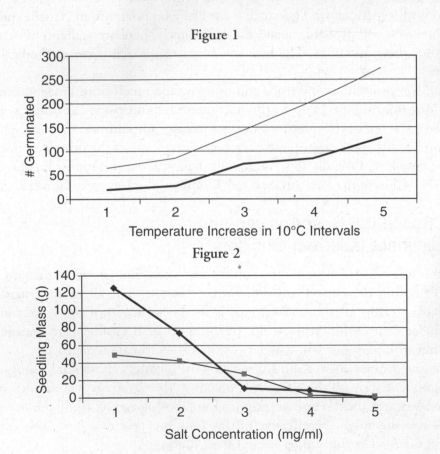

Figure 1

Figure 2

Based on the data in Figures 1 and 2, the researchers should make which of the following conclusions about the overall change in germination rates and seedling mass?

A. Increased temperature causes a decrease in the number germinated, and increased salt concentration causes an increase in mass.

B. Decreased salt concentration causes a decrease in mass, and decreased temperature causes a decrease in the number germinated.

C. Increased temperature and salt concentration have the same effects on the number germinated and seedling mass.

D. Increased temperature and salt concentration have opposite effects on the number germinated and seedling mass.

As you examine the answer choices, it is clear that both A and B are incorrect because the first part of each of the choices is false. Figure 1 shows that as temperature increases, the number germinated increases, so you don't even have to look at the second part of A because the answer is clearly wrong. Likewise, Figure 2 contradicts the first part of answer B, so don't bother with the rest; just eliminate it quickly and move on to the next choice. Answer C is also wrong, so the correct answer must be D.

Practice Sets

Okay, now let's put all of these skills together. Practice your strategies with the following sample sets of questions. Use the **SCIe** of the **SCIeNCE** strategies to quickly **S**can the section, **C**heck the main idea, and **I**gnore the **e**xtras as you read. Then focus on **N**oting the reference, **C**hoosing the best answer, and **E**liminating the incorrect choices. Analyze how you're doing by filling out the Strategy Practice Chart.

Practice Set 1

Temperature and precipitation data were collected over a three-month period for a specific region of the United States. Figure 1 shows the average daily low temperature as compared to the normal high and low temperatures. Figure 2 compares precipitation amounts and averages throughout the month.

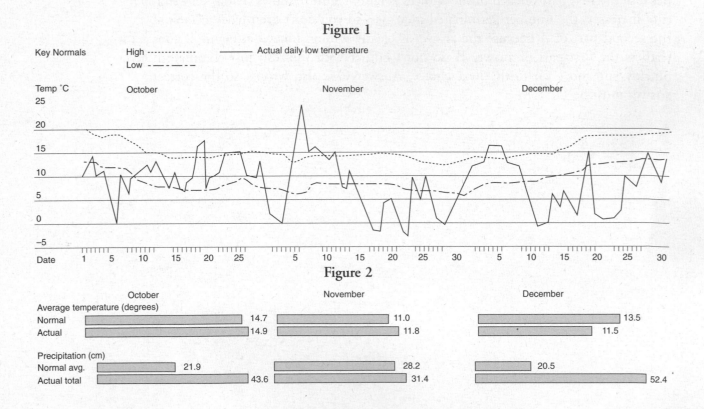

Figure 1

Figure 2

1. According to the data provided in Figure 1, the average low temperature on December 15 was approximately:
   A. 7.5°C.
   B. 10.0°C.
   C. 12.5°C.
   D. 15.0°C.

2. A student trying to analyze this entire three-month period would most accurately summarize it as:
   F. much warmer than average with much more precipitation.
   G. warmer than average with much less precipitation.
   H. average to slightly colder with much more precipitation.
   J. much colder than average with much less precipitation.

3. During which dates in Figure 1 was the actual daily low temperature most different from the normal high temperature for that same time period?
   A. October 5–7
   B. November 5–7
   C. November 28–30
   D. December 12–14

4. Suppose that, in January, scientists recorded actual average temperatures that were 10.1°C, instead of the normal average of 12.4°C. Normal precipitation is 23.7 cm. Normal high and low average temperatures follow the same pattern as December. Based on this information, which of the following is most consistent with the information presented in this passage?
   F. Precipitation will be lower than average because as temperatures get colder, precipitation amounts decrease.
   G. There should be higher amounts of precipitation because as temperatures get colder, precipitation amounts increase.
   H. There will be more days when the actual low temperature is above the average low temperature.
   J. Precipitation amounts may vary because there is not a direct relationship between temperature and precipitation.

Strategy Practice Chart

Note the reference in the question (if any).

Question 1: _____

Question 2: _____

Question 3: _____

Question 4: _____

Choose the best answer (explain your reasoning).

Question 1: _____

Question 2: _____

Question 3: _____

Question 4: _____

Eliminate the incorrect answers (explain your reasoning).

Question 1: _____

Question 2: _____

Question 3: _____

Question 4: _____

Do you think you used the **NCE** strategies well? Let's check your ideas. **N**ote the reference in the question.

Question 1:   Figure 1 only. Ignore Figure 2.

Question 2:   At first, seems to apply to both, but this can be answered using only Figure 2.

Question 3:   Only Figure 1.

Question 4:   No specific reference—the answers refer to information in both figures.

Choose the best answer.—Some of the answers were fairly obvious, especially for the factual questions. The inference and Xtreme questions were probably trickier, but close reading of the graphs should have resulted in success. **E**liminate the incorrect answers.—See the explanations below.

Did the strategies work for you? Did you have an idea of the correct answer even before looking at the choices? Did you eliminate answer choices that contained information that was clearly wrong? Here are the answers to the questions themselves.

Explanations and Tips

1. **(B)** A **Factual** Question—The average low temperature was 10.0°C.
   Wrong: **(A)** 7.5°C is the low for October 15. **(C)** 12.5°C would be reading the scale wrong. **(D)** 15.0°C is the average high temperature.
2. **(H)** An **Inference** Question—Figure 2 clearly shows that there is much more precipitation than average and that the overall temperature is slightly colder because of the lower temperature in December.
   Wrong: **(F)** Although both October and November have slightly warmer temperatures, December is significantly colder. **(G & J)** There is much more precipitation, so these choices are clearly incorrect.
3. **(A)** An **Xtreme** Question—There is the greatest difference—about 17.5°C—between the lowest temperature around October 6 and the normal high temperature.
   Wrong: **(B)** This time period is when the low temperature is the highest, but it is actually closest to the normal high. **(C & D)** These dates appear similar to (A), and (D) refers to one of the lowest temperatures on the graph, but the normal high temperature is much lower than in October.

TIP

Test writers usually include numbers for answer choices that can be found somewhere in the passage, such as in graphs and tables. They do not just make them up. Pay attention, and make sure that the number you pick is the actual answer to the question.

INSIDE THE ACT 36 MIND

Many times, with questions that have three answers that are similar and one that seems to be very different, the "misfit" answer choice is the correct one. Be careful, though. Test writers usually include at least two or three questions that work exactly the opposite, and they put in the obviously different answer just to trick you.

4. **(J)** An **Xtreme** Question—There is no correlation between the two variables. In October and November, there were warmer-than-average temperatures and increased precipitation. December had the coldest temperature but had increased precipitation as well.
   Wrong: **(F & G)** Some of the data contradicts each of these answers. **(H)** There should be fewer days when the actual low temperature is above the average low temperature, not more. Although this could be possible, it is not consistent with the data.

By, now, you should be getting the hang of the strategies and choosing the correct answers. If you are getting the answers wrong or got lucky with the right answer but used faulty reasoning, make sure to re-read the passage and find out where you are making your mistakes. Here's one more practice set to try.

Practice Set 2

Scientists use many methods to determine the identity and quantity of a substance in samples. Spectroscopy is a simple and powerful method for performing both qualitative and quantitative analyses. Light does not go completely through any liquid. Even in water some light is absorbed. The ratio of the amount of light not absorbed by a liquid (solvent) divided by the total amount of light the solvent was exposed to is called the transmittance and is represented by the following equation:

$$T = I/I_o$$

The amount of light that a solvent lets through is not nearly as important as the amount of light that something absorbs. The amount of light absorbed by something is called the absorbance, where

$$A = -\log \text{Transmittance} = I_o/I$$

The absorbance is given on a logarithmic scale, where an absorbance of 0 means no light is absorbed, an absorbance of 1 means 10% of light is absorbed, an absorbance of 2 means 1% of light is absorbed, an absorbance of 3 means 0.1% of light is absorbed and so on.

There is a general relationship between the amount of matter dissolved in a solvent and the amount of light that it absorbs. This relationship is called Beer's Law. Table 1 shows a Beer's Law standard curve for methylene blue—a substance used to compare absorbance values of other materials.

TABLE 1

Concentration	Absorbance
0	0.003
1	0.233
2	0.479
3	0.719
4	0.897
5	1.099

Experiment 1

When exposed to light, methylene blue turns from blue to colorless. Absorbance levels of various concentrations of methylene blue were measured, and then the samples were exposed to light for a standard amount of time. Final absorbance measurements were taken and are shown in Figure 1.

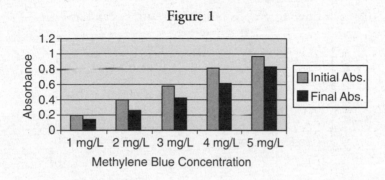

Figure 1

Experiment 2

Varying concentrations of a light-sensitive pigment are exposed to lights ranging in wavelength from 600 to 700 nm. Absorbance levels are measured at each point as shown in Figure 2.

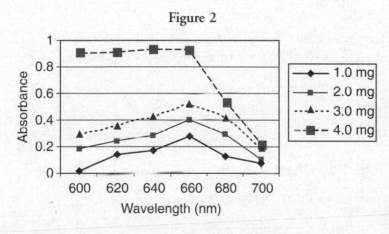

Figure 2

1. Based on Experiments 1 and 2, which concentration of the light-sensitive pigment at its highest absorbance is most similar in absorbance to the initial absorbance of methylene blue at the same concentration?
   A. 1.0 mg
   B. 2.0 mg
   C. 3.0 mg
   D. 4.0 mg

2. The relationship between transmittance and absorbance can best be described by which of the following?
   F. Higher absorbance equals higher transmittance.
   G. Lower absorbance equals lower transmittance.
   H. Higher absorbance equals lower transmittance.
   J. There is no relationship between absorbance and transmittance.

3. Which of the following graphs best represents Beer's Law?

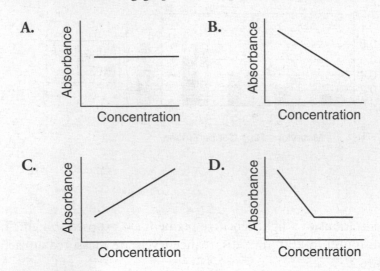

4. According to Figure 1, methylene blue at a concentration of 6.0 mg and exposed to light would have a final absorbance closest to:
   F. 1.2.
   G. 1.0.
   H. 0.8.
   J. 0.6.

Strategy Practice Chart

Note the reference in the question (if any).

Question 1: _____

Question 2: _____

Question 3: _____

Question 4: _____

Choose the best answer (explain your reasoning).

Question 1: _____

Question 2: _____

Question 3: _____

Question 4: _____

Eliminate the incorrect answers (explain your reasoning).

Question 1: _____

Question 2: _____

Question 3: _____

Question 4: _____

You should be finding the strategies easier to use every time you practice. Check the descriptions below and see if you're on the right track.

Note the reference in the question.

Question 1: Experiment 1 and 2.
Question 2: No specific reference, but the information is in the introduction.
Question 3: No specific reference, but the information is in the introduction.
Question 4: Figure 1 only.

Choose the best answer. As you go through more passages, picking the correct answer should get easier, and you should be getting more questions correct.

Eliminate the incorrect answers. See the explanations below.

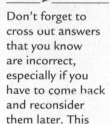

TIP

Don't forget to cross out answers that you know are incorrect, especially if you have to come back and reconsider them later. This will save you time.

Explanations and Tips

1. **(B)** An **Inference** Question—The absorbance is 0.4 for both the initial measurement of methylene blue and the light-sensitive pigment at a concentration of 2.0 mg.

    Wrong: (A) The light-sensitive pigment has a higher absorbance than methylene blue at 1.0 mg. (C & D) The light-sensitive pigment has a lower absorbance than methylene blue at 3.0 mg and higher at 4.0 mg concentrations.

2. **(H)** An **Inference** Question—Absorbance is the amount of light not passing through a substance, while transmittance is the amount of light passing through, so there is an inverse (opposite) relationship between the two. The introduction and equations state this.

    Wrong: (F & G) These answers are both wrong because absorbance and transmittance are opposites. (J) There is a relationship between absorbance and transmittance.

3. **(C)** An **Inference** Question—Based on Table 1, as concentration goes up from 0 to 5, absorbance increases from 0.003 to 1.099. Drawing trend arrows should have made this easy.

    Wrong: (A) Absorbance increases. It does not remain constant. (B) This graph shows absorbance decreasing. (D) Graph D shows absorbance decreasing and then leveling off, but Table 1 clearly shows an increase.

4. **(G)** An **Inference** Question—At each higher concentration of methylene blue, absorbance rises. Since at 5.0 mg it is above 0.8, then it should be closest to 1.0 at 6.0 mg.

TIP

When two answer choices mean the same thing but are stated in different ways, they are both wrong. This means you can eliminate them both and have a 50 percent chance of picking the correct answer.

TIP

When a question asks about graphs or tables with more than one data set, underline which one you're looking for in the question. That way, you're less likely to make simple mistakes.

Wrong: (F) 1.2 mg is too high, and the question asks about final absorbance. This would be correct for initial absorbance. (H & J) 0.8 and 0.6 are too low based on the trend of the data.

Congratulations! You've finished your dissection and have exposed the inner workings of the ACT science section. You should now be very familiar with the different sections of the passages—introductions; tables, graphs, and figures; and the questions. You have also learned and practiced the **SCIeNCE** strategies for each of them. Now you're ready to put everything you've learned into practice with actual passage examples.

Data Representation Passages

CHAPTER 21

- Three passages
- Five questions

- Answer these questions first

Now that you have dissected the science ACT, it's time to practice with an actual Data Representation passage. Don't forget that these passages usually contain multiple graphs, often with different scales on both vertical axes. They are very "number heavy," and contain a large amount of extra information that you do not really need to answer the questions correctly. They sometimes contain a sentence or two either at the beginning of the passage or sandwiched in the middle of several of the diagrams. There is often one question that relies on this information, and many less successful students often miss it.

When approaching the passage, use your **6 SCIeNCE** strategies:

S—Scan the passage
C—Check the main idea
Ie—Ignore the extras
N—Note the reference in the question
C—Choose the best answer
E—Eliminate the incorrect answers.

Before you check your answers, analyze how you used the strategies. Explanations of the problems and tips for answering the questions follow.

TIP

Remember, there are <u>3</u> Data Representation passages on each test, and they should be done first. You can always recognize them by the <u>5</u> questions that follow the passage.

SAMPLE PASSAGE

Researchers are working to develop non-natural protein mimics called peptoids. Peptoids differ from proteins in their backbone structure. Typical peptides consist of a central carbon atom, attached to an amino group (NH), a carboxylic acid group (C=O), a hydrogen atom (H), and a side chain called a replacement group (R) (Figure 1).

The structure of a peptoid is different because the replacement groups (R) are attached to the nitrogen atoms, rather than the carbon atoms (Figure 2).

Peptoids have an advantage over peptides in that they form stable, helical structures in solution, are highly resistant to degradation, and might be used to treat pneumonia or other lung infections, including those caused from inhaled biological warfare agents; however, some of them are toxic to cells.

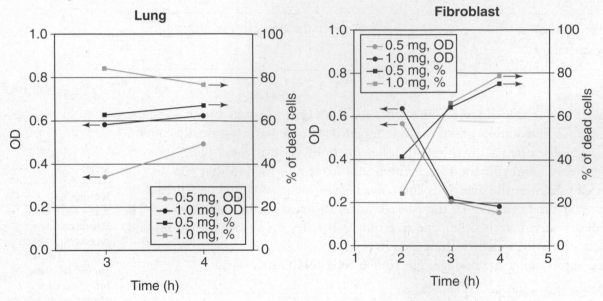

Figure 1: Peptide Structure

Figure 2: Peptoid Structure

Figure 3

Figure 3 shows the effects of two concentrations of peptoids (0.5 mg and 1.0 mg) on two cell types—lung and fibroblast. The optical density (OD) is a measure of the amount of light that is able to pass through the cell cultures and signifies the relative proportion of cells present in a culture. Lethal doses (LD) of a compound are considered to be when at least 50% of the cells have died due to exposure.

1. According to Figures 1 and 2, peptides and peptoids:
   A. contain entirely different atoms.
   B. only differ in the placement of some atoms.
   C. do not differ at all.
   D. behave in the exact same way.

2. At 3 hours, 1.0 mg of peptoid has killed approximately what percent of fibroblast cells?
   F. 20%
   G. 60%
   H. 70%
   J. 80%

3. According to Figure 3, over time, optical density (OD):
   A. increases for both types of cells.
   B. decreases for both types of cells.
   C. increases for fibroblast cells and decreases for lung cells.
   D. decreases for fibroblast cells and increases for lung cells.

4. A scientist trying to examine if there was any correlation between optical density and cell mortality at all peptoid concentrations could correctly draw the following conclusion:
   F. There is no consistent correlation between optical density and cell mortality.
   G. As optical density decreases, cell mortality increases at every peptoid concentration for all cell types.
   H. As optical density increases, cell mortality decreases in lung cells.
   J. Both optical density and cell mortality change throughout a 4-hour time period.

5. By what point in time was a lethal dose (LD) for both cell types first reached due to exposure of the peptoid?
   A. 1 hour
   B. 2 hours
   C. 3 hours
   D. 4 hours

SCIeNCE Strategies

Strategy Practice Chart
Scan the passage.

   Time: _____

Check the main idea (draw trend arrows/show relationship).

   Main Idea: _____

Ignore the **e**xtras. (What information did you skip?)

   Extras: _____

Note the reference in the question (if any).

   Question 1: _____

   Question 2: _____

   Question 3: _____

   Question 4: _____

   Question 5: _____

Choose the best answer (explain your reasoning).

Question 1: _____

Question 2: _____

Question 3: _____

Question 4: _____

Question 5: _____

Eliminate the incorrect answers (explain your reasoning).

Question 1: _____

Question 2: _____

Question 3: _____

Question 4: _____

Question 5: _____

Do you think you used the **SCIeNCE** strategies effectively? Savvy students practice approaching Data Representation passages almost like one of those complicated pictures where you have to find hidden objects—many things look similar, but it takes a keen eye to quickly spot what's correct.

TIP

Pay attention to graphs with multiple scales on opposite axes or sides. Also be aware that scales from one graph to the next are not always the same.

Scan the passage.—Taking 10–15 seconds to look over the passage should have told you that you were dealing with biochemistry concepts and laboratory experiments. Figures 1 and 2 deal with peptide and peptoid structure, while Figure 3 shows two sets of dual experiments.

Check the main idea.—In a Data Representation passage, you must make sure you understand the point of the passage, which is often found in the brief introduction to the passage. In this case, besides peptide and peptoid structure, the third paragraph explains the experiment; "the effects of two concentrations of peptoids (0.5 mg and 1.0 mg) on two cell types" should be circled or underlined. You should also have noted that the graphs have scales on both sides and can be read from either direction. In addition, the scales of the two graphs are not equal. The first graph shows a 1-hour time span, while the second one is 2+ hours.

If the data had been presented in a data table, rather than a graph, drawing a trend arrow to show the relationships would also be appropriate here.

Ignore the **e**xtras.—Data Representation passages are always filled with "extras." You'll need some of them for the tougher questions, but most of the time you can ignore the majority of the extra information. Do you really have to understand the differences in the structure between Figures 1 and 2? Is knowing the definitions of "optical density" and "lethal dose" going to help you? Probably not. The trick is to not get tied up in the details, but to know where they are if you actually need them.

Note the reference in the question.

Question 1: Figures 1 and 2 only. Ignore the graphs when you attempt this question.

Question 2: Only applies to the Fibroblast graph, so don't spend your time on the first one.

Question 3: Both Lung and Fibroblast graphs.

Question 4: No specific reference.

Question 5: Refers back to the introduction.

Choose the Best Answer.—See the answers and explanations below. Data Representation questions often have very obvious correct answers—as long as you've read the graph or data table correctly. Many of these are factual. Inference and Xtreme questions can be trickier, but remember, understanding table or graph trends will often make these pretty apparent as well. Review your trend arrows to see if they give you an easy answer to a question.

Eliminate the incorrect answers.—See the answers and explanations below.

How did it go? Were you able to use the strategies? You have probably used these techniques before and didn't realize it. That's why you're close to achieving your goal of a 36. Perfecting the strategies you already know and learning some new ones should get you even closer. Here are the answers to the questions themselves.

Answers and Explanations

1. **(B)** A **Factual** Question—Peptides and peptoids differ because the R group is attached to a different atom.

   Wrong: (A) Most of the atoms are the same. (C) The difference is what makes them two separate molecules. (D) The advantages of peptoids, because of their different structure, mean that they behave differently. Remember, the answers to factual questions often are clearly stated in the passage or quickly understood from a figure or graph.

2. **(H)** A **Factual** Question—Reading the Fibroblast graph and looking at the correct point shows that the answer is clearly between 60 and 80%.

   Wrong: (F) 20% is the amount for 2 hours. (G & J) The figures are clearly too low or too high on the Fibroblast graph.

3. **(D)** A **Factual** Question—Optical density increases for lung cells and decreases for fibroblast cells.

   Wrong: (A & B) These answers refer to patterns for other lines on the graphs. (C) This is the reverse of the lines on the graph.

TIP

The ACT is filled with questions where the correct answer is "right there" on the graph. Be careful that you don't misread the question and look at the wrong graph, the wrong place on the graph, or the wrong line.

TIP

Although factual questions tend to be easier, they require careful reading of the graphs. The answer choices may be designed to trick you. It is important in questions like these to make sure to eliminate the incorrect answers; on first glance, people sometimes choose an incorrect answer because they're working so quickly. Don't let the lack of time ruin your focus.

4. (**F**) An **Xtreme** Question—There is no correlation between the two variables. In Lung cells, as optical density increases, cell death increases at 0.5 mg and decreases at 1.0 mg.

   Wrong: (G) This is only true for fibroblast cells. (H) This is not true for 0.5 mg in lung cells. (J) The straight arrows on the end of the lines mean that the data stayed constant after that time. Lung cells only changed over a 1-hour time period.

TIP ✏️

Xtreme questions require you to look at multiple graphs and analyze them thoroughly. Once you read this type of question, you may want to work your way sequentially through the answer choices.

Xtreme questions are the questions that few students are expected to get correct most of the time. The ACT is designed to separate all the students who take the test into levels. So, if this was one of the first passages on the test, more students would get this correct. Later on, if this were passage 6 or 7, fewer students would get this one because they are tired, rushing, or out of time.

5. (**C**) An **Inference** Question—By 3 hours more than 50% of the cells had died for both cell types and at all concentrations.

   Wrong: (A & B) The lines are both below 50% for fibroblast cells, and there is not any data for lung cells at either of these times. (D) Although this answer is correct in that >50% of the cells have died, the answer does not agree with the question, which states, "by what point . . . first reached."

Now that you've had the chance to practice your strategies, you should be doing better on Data Representation passages and on the way to reaching your goals. In the next chapter we'll practice with a Research Summaries passage.

Research Summaries Passages

CHAPTER 22

- Three passages
- Six questions

- Tackle these second

Research Summaries passages usually consist of two or three experiments about the same concept.

Most of the time, these passages can be recognized by headings such as "Experiment 1," "Experiment 2," "Study 1," "Study 2," etc. However, they sometimes look more like Data Representation passages because they, too, will include graphs and data tables. In a few cases, they may even look like Conflicting Viewpoints passages because they will not have graphs and may have headings that look similar.

Don't forget to use your **6 SCIeNCE** strategies:

S—Scan the passage
C—Check the main idea
Ie—Ignore the extras
N—Note the reference in the question
C—Choose the best answer
E—Eliminate the incorrect answers

Once you've gone through the passage and answered the questions, analyze how your strategies worked as well. Explanations of the correct answers, wrong answers, and tips for answering the questions follow.

TIP

There are 3 Research Summaries passages on each test, and they should be done second. You can always recognize them by the 6 questions that follow each passage.

SAMPLE PASSAGE

When dropped, certain materials tend to bounce higher than others. As an object hits a surface, it becomes deformed to a certain degree and then returns to its original shape. In a sphere or ball, this property is referred to as elasticity. The more elastic a substance is, the more energy of this deformation is retained, the more it will be returned to its original shape, and then the higher and faster the sphere will bounce. The measure of this elasticity is the coefficient of restitution (e), and it can be calculated by several methods:

$$\sqrt{h_b/h_i} = e$$

h_b = bounce height
h_i = initial height

$$v_b/v_a = e$$

v_b = bounce/separation velocity
v_a = approach/impact velocity

Coefficients of restitution have values between 0 and 1.0.

A 2.0 m clear plastic tube was set up on top of a steel plate. A chamber at the top allowed for placement of spheres of varying diameters. An optical, electronic timing device recorded and calculated velocities, while a camera was used to measure the bounce heights. The inside of the tube could be converted into a vacuum chamber to discount the effects of air resistance, as shown in Figure 1.

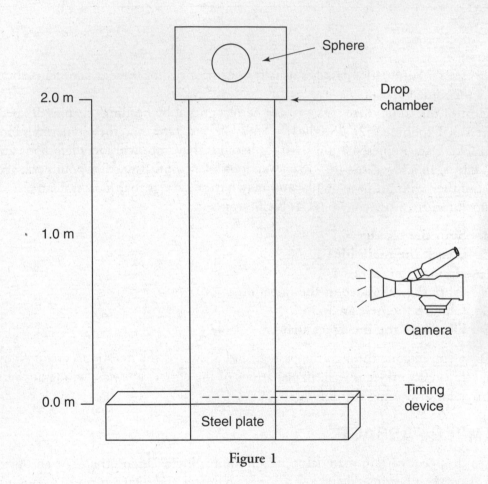

Figure 1

Experiment 1

Spheres of various substances with the same diameter were dropped from 2.0 meters in the vacuum tube. The bounce height (h_b) was measured and the resulting coefficient of restitution (e) was calculated. Each trial was repeated 10 times and averages were calculated. Results are presented in Table 1.

TABLE 1

Sphere	h_i (m)	h_b (m)	e
Clay	2.0	0.005	.05
Glass	2.0	1.13	.751
Ivory	2.0	1.49	.863
Plastic	2.0	0.78	.624
Rubber	2.0	1.83	.956
Steel	2.0	1.94	.984

Experiment 2

Using the same apparatus, various athletic balls were dropped from 2.0 meters. The approach/impact velocity (v_a) and bounce/separation velocity (v_b) were measured and the coefficient of restitution (e) was calculated. Each trial was repeated 10 times and averages were calculated. Results are presented in Table 2.

TABLE 2

Ball	v_a (m/s)	v_b (m/s)	e
Basketball	2.43	1.94	.798
Bowling Ball	2.58	0.570	.221
Glass Marble	1.49	1.11	.749
Golf Ball	1.78	1.28	.719
Soccer Ball	2.17	1.40	.645
Tennis Ball	2.04	1.83	.897

1. A sphere of unknown material was dropped in the apparatus and the bounce height (h_b) was measured to be 0.84 m. Based on the results of Experiment 1, the coefficient of restitution (e) is closest to:

   A. .547
   B. .613
   C. .648
   D. .871

2. Which of the following factors was NOT directly controlled by the student in Experiment 1?
   F. the bounce height (h_b)
   G. the initial height (h_i)
   H. the type of equipment
   J. the type of sphere

3. Which of the following types of balls has an elasticity coefficient most similar to ivory?
   A. basketball
   B. glass marble
   C. soccer ball
   D. tennis ball

4. Another student repeated Experiment 2 with a newly developed "Super Ball"—a very dense rubber ball that its inventors have made specifically for its incredible bouncing ability. Based on the results of Experiments 1 and 2, the most likely range of coefficients of elasticity for this ball would be:
   F. between 0.755–0.894
   G. between 0.951–0.997
   H. between 0.962–1.04
   J. between 1.23–1.55

5. Although the students running Experiment 1 and Experiment 2 used the same equipment and procedures, they collected different data and used different formulas to calculate the coefficient of restitution (e). Which of the following pairs of trials would best confirm that either of the two methods was accurate and consistent?
   A. Golf ball and glass marble because their e values were extremely close.
   B. Steel and basketball because their h_b and v_b were both 1.94.
   C. Ivory and glass marble because their h_b and v_a were both 1.49.
   D. Glass and glass marble because they were made out of the same material.

6. Based on the results from the two experiments, what is the most likely conclusion that can be drawn about the properties of materials and their elasticity?
   F. Balls used for sports are more elastic than spheres made of metal.
   G. Elasticity is always lower in large balls than in small balls.
   H. Spheres and balls that are softer have higher elasticity than those that are harder.
   J. Elasticity depends less on the size or softness of the sphere and more on its ability to return to its original shape.

Strategy Practice Chart

Scan the passage.

    <u>Time</u>: _____

Check the main idea (draw trend arrows/show relationship).

    <u>Main Idea</u>: _____

Ignore the **e**xtras. (what information did you skip?)

    <u>Extras</u>: _____

Note the reference in the question (if any).

    Question 1: _____

    Question 2: _____

    Question 3: _____

    Question 4: _____

    Question 5: _____

    Question 6: _____

Choose the best answer (explain your reasoning).

    Question 1: _____

    Question 2: _____

    Question 3: _____

    Question 4: _____

    Question 5: _____

    Question 6: _____

Eliminate the incorrect answers (explain your reasoning).

    Question 1: _____

    Question 2: _____

    Question 3: _____

    Question 4: _____

    Question 5: _____

    Question 6: _____

TIP

For Research Summaries passages, use the same types of strategies you learned for the reading and mathematics sections of the ACT because they rely on the same types of skills.

Were you able to use the **SCIeNCE** strategies for this passage? Research Summaries passages require you to understand an often complex experimental design and interpret diagrams, tables, and graphs quickly and accurately.

Scan the passage.—A quick (10–15 second) scan shows a brief introduction to the concept of elasticity, including several equations. A diagram of the experimental equipment is shown, and two different experiments are described with data presented in a table.

Check the main idea.—Research Summaries passages often contain one main idea and two or three sub-ideas. The concept of elasticity and a value known as a coefficient of elasticity are clearly main ideas. You would be wise to circle/underline these in the passage. For each experiment, you should do the same. Experiment 1 compares spheres and height, while Experiment 2 uses balls and velocity. Since the data is presented in a table, drawing trend arrows to show relationships would be helpful; however, these tables do not show any regular trends.

Ignore the **e**xtras.—Like Data Representation passages, Research Summaries are always filled with "extras." Once again, some of them are necessary, but most are not. Do you really need to compare the difference between numbers that use three decimal places? Most of the time the answers are far more obvious.

Note the reference in the question.

Question 1: Experiment 1.

Question 2: Experiment 1.

Question 3: The stem of Question 3 refers to Experiment 1, but the answer choices require you to look at Experiment 2.

Question 4: Experiments 1 and 2.

Question 5: Experiments 1 and 2.

Question 6: No direct reference at all.

INSIDE THE ACT 36 MIND

Every question is different and may ask you to focus on a different part of the passage. The best advice is to maximize your time by noting the reference and focusing only on that experiment to find the answer.

Choose the best answer.—See the answers and explanations below.

Research Summaries questions contain a variety of answer types. Some involve simply picking out a number from the data. Many others require you to interpret any trends and pick answers that would fit in between other choices. There is usually a combination of fact, inference, and Xtreme questions.

Eliminate the incorrect answers.—See the answers and explanations below.

Eliminating incorrect answers is a key step for the ambitious student. Research Summaries passages may contain three separate experiments and several graphs and data tables. With so much information to consider, you should always try to verify that the answer you picked as correct is the best one. Sometimes the questions contain correct answers—but they are for the wrong experiment. Don't get tricked by the test makers, especially in this section. That will prevent you from achieving your 36!

Hopefully, these strategies are becoming easier to use. With practice they will become second nature. What follows are the correct answers to the questions and explanations to help you understand the nature of the test.

Answers and Explanations

1. **(C)** A **Factual** Question—A bounce height (h_b) of 0.84 is closest to that of plastic (0.78, e = .624). Higher bounce heights result in higher e values, so the number has to be slightly higher than .624.
   Wrong: (A & B) Too low. (D) Too high.

2. **(F)** A **Factual** Question—The bounce height (h_b) is what the student is measuring and changes based on which type of sphere is dropped.
   Wrong: (G & H) The initial heights (h_i) and the type of equipment are the same for every trial of this experiment. (J) This is the experimental or independent variable in the experiment—what the student is actually testing.

> ### INSIDE THE ACT 36 MIND
>
> Every Research Summaries passage on the ACT includes questions based on experimental design and the scientific method. Remember, this is a test of scientific reasoning. Don't get distracted by the subject of the experiment. Focus on the proper set-up and, regardless of the topic, these questions should be easier.

3. **(D)** A **Factual** Question—A tennis ball has an e value of .897, while ivory has an e value of .863.
   Wrong: (A) (B) and (C) all have e values that are inconsistent with the question. (B) is wrong because the bounce height (h_b) for ivory is the same as the approach velocity (v_a) for the glass marble. The question asks for e values.
   Warning: Although this is a factual question, it requires <u>careful</u> reading of the data tables. As in Data Representation questions, the answer choices are designed to trick you. If you just look for numbers that are close and do not pay attention to the proper column or row on the tables, you are going to miss questions like these—exactly what the test makers want you to do.

4. **(G)** An **Inference** Question—Super Balls are made of rubber and should have similar coefficients of elasticity as other rubber balls.
   Wrong: (F) This range is too low based on the data. (H) The lower end of the range is fine, but the upper end is >1.0. (J) The entire range is too high.
   This question requires that you look at both of the experiments, but also that you refer back to the introduction. In the middle of the background information,

TIP

Be sure to look at the correct column on any table or graph and make sure the relationship between the numbers is clear.

TIP

Research Summaries questions are where understanding of experimental design and the scientific method really comes in handy. If you miss questions in these passages, review this topic using your class notes, textbooks, or online resources.

it states, "Coefficients of restitution have values between 0 and 1.0." Consequently, two of the answer choices can easily be eliminated. There are almost always questions like this in the Research Summaries sections, where the correct answer can only be determined by looking at both the description and the data.

ACT test writers seem to love questions like this. They not only test your ability to put together information from various sections of the passage, but they also make you really hunt for that information. Notice that the information you needed was placed right after the equations and right before a description of the equipment—two extra parts of the passage that you can usually ignore. You will also find this kind of information as a single sentence right above a graph or table, at the top of the right-hand column on the actual test, and crammed into additional rows at the bottom of tables or graphs. As you **S**can the passage note where these little bits of information are placed and be able to come back to them if needed.

5. **(D)** An **Inference** Question—The glass sphere and glass marble had very similar e values using both methods of data collection and calculation.

Wrong: (A) The e values were only determined using velocity. (B) There is no direct relationship between bounce height (h_b) and bounce velocity (v_b). (C) There is no direct relationship between bounce height (h_b) and approach velocity (v_a).

6. **(J)** An **Xtreme** Question—Realizing that harder materials sometimes have higher e values than softer ones and that smaller balls sometimes have lower e values than larger ones makes this the only correct answer choice.

Wrong: (F) Bowling balls are clearly less elastic than almost all of the spheres. (G) Small golf balls have a lower e value than larger balls, like basketballs. (H) Hard steel spheres have higher e values than softer ones like clay.

This is an **Xtreme** question because it asks you to draw a conclusion from the experiment. It also gives you answer choices with multiple options so that you have to refer back to both experiments and the data. In this case, the correct answer is the last one, but this is often not the case. Eliminating incorrect answer choices is a key step to getting these questions correct.

Did your strategy practice help? To perform even better, you should continue to work on understanding experiments, whether from passages, journal articles, labs, or textbooks.

The last chapter of this section features a Conflicting Viewpoints passage, so get ready to read!

Conflicting Viewpoints Passages

CHAPTER 23

- One passage
- Seven questions
- Tackle last

Below is an example of a Conflicting Viewpoints passage. This type of passage is often called a "theory" passage because it relies more heavily on unsupported evidence than on hard data like the Data Representation and Research Summaries passages.

These passages are usually identified by headings, such as "Scientist 1" and "Scientist 2," or topic titles, such as "Darwinism" and "Lamarckism." However, sometimes they will be headed "Experiment 1" and "Experiment 2," exactly like the Research Summaries passage headings. Be careful.

Remember, this is the passage designed to test your reading and science reasoning ability. It is also designed to waste time.

Use your **6 SCIeNCE** strategies:

S—Scan the passage
C—Circle the main idea
Ie—Ignore the extras
N—Note the reference in the question
C—Choose the best answer
E—Eliminate the incorrect answers

Explanations of the correct answers and the wrong answers and tips for answering the questions follow.

SAMPLE PASSAGE

Silver nanoparticles, which range in diameter from 4–20 nanometers (1 nanometer = 1 billionth of a meter), demonstrate unique properties, especially against various bacteria, viruses, and fungi. Silver has been used to treat infections for centuries, but with the advent of nanotechnology, the use of silver in nanoparticle form has opened new treatment avenues.

TIP

There is 1 Conflicting Viewpoints passage on each test, and it should be done <u>last</u>. You can always recognize this kind of passage by the 7 questions that follow.

TIP

Even if reading is your strongest subject, this section should be done at the end of the test because it requires you to go through the most material in the shortest amount of time.

Scientist 1

Silver nanoparticles have the potential to revolutionize the medical and consumer products industries. Various researchers have found that silver nanoparticles are effective killers of pathogenic bacteria such as *E.coli, B. subtilis,* and *S. aureus.* The antimicrobial mechanism of their action is not completely understood, but they may interact with the bacterial peptidoglycan layer, form pits in the cell wall, change membrane polarity, and/or form free radicals that damage the membrane. One thing that is known is that because the nanoparticles do not act via cell receptors, there is no immune response and thus no antibacterial resistance. Recent studies have also indicated that silver nanoparticles in the range of 1–10 nm attach to HIV proteins and inhibit the virus from binding to cells.

Because of these antimicrobial properties, silver nanoparticle technology has safely been incorporated into surgical instruments, hospital wound dressings, and a wide variety of consumer products, such as washing machines, food storage containers, bandages, and clothing. The possibilities for using the antimicrobial properties of this technology seem boundless.

Scientist 2

While silver nanoparticles may in fact have antimicrobial properties, the risks of their use potentially far outweigh the benefits. The Environmental Protection Agency has established regulations for companies that intend to sell products containing silver nanoparticles acting as bacteria killers. Before the products can be sold to consumers, these businesses will have to provide scientific evidence that there is no environmental risk posed by the nanoparticles. Further regulation has since defined the steps that companies would have to undergo before they could incorporate nanotechnology into their products and make claims regarding the antimicrobial properties. Consequently, various companies have dropped references to silver nanoparticles in their literature and packaging, but they have not changed the materials themselves.

Using silver medicinally, usually in the form of non-nanoparticle colloidal silver sold in health food stores as a dietary supplement, has some potential side effects. These include argyria, a permanent incorporation of silver into the skin resulting in a silver skin tone, neurologic problems, kidney damage, stomach distress, headaches, fatigue, skin irritation, and the potential interference with the body's absorption of some drugs. The effects of silver nanoparticles on the soil, air, wastewater, groundwater, and bacteria, algae, protozoa, fungi, plant, and animal life are not at all understood. Consequently, the technology is not without some huge implications, and its further use may result in the opening of a "Pandora's box" of problems.

1. According to the passage, silver nanoparticles may be effective against various bacteria because they:
   A. inhibit binding to cells.
   B. cause no immune response.
   C. interfere with the absorption of some drugs.
   D. form pits in the cell walls.

2. The information in the passage indicates that silver nanoparticles may be hazardous because:
   F. their effects are not completely known.
   G. of their antimicrobial effects.
   H. they can cause neurologic damage.
   J. they may result in permanent skin discoloration.

3. Scientist 2's views differ from Scientist 1's in that only Scientist 2 believes that silver nanoparticles:
   A. have potent antimicrobial properties.
   B. may pose an environmental threat.
   C. can be used safely and effectively in hospital equipment.
   D. are no longer being utilized in consumer products.

4. A company markets its use of silver nanoparticle technology. When the EPA steps in to regulate claims regarding the antibacterial properties of silver nanoparticles, the company may do which of the following and still follow the EPA guidelines?

     I. nothing and continue to sell its products as designed
    II. submit to rigorous testing of the properties and safety of the product
   III. change the packaging and leave the product unchanged

   F. I only
   G. II only
   H. II and III only
   J. I, II, and III

5. Suppose in vitro testing of silver nanoparticles finds that they reduce bacterial concentrations of *E. coli* and *C. botulinum* by 99.9% in petri dish cultures. However, food storage containers, which have silver nanoparticles incorporated into their chemical structure, have a negligible effect on these strains, as compared to similar containers that do not contain this material. Which of the following statements is most consistent with these results and with the information presented in the passage?
   A. Neither scientist would use this as conclusive proof of the antimicrobial properties of the particles.
   B. Scientist 1 would support the incorporation of the nanoparticles into the food storage containers.
   C. Scientist 2 would not support their use because of their apparent safety hazards.
   D. Both Scientist 1 and Scientist 2 would support their use in consumer products because of their strong antimicrobial properties.

6. Based on Scientist 1's explanation, using silver nanoparticles embedded into bandages to treat recurring bacterial infections would be more effective than current antibiotics because:
   F. the bacterial cell walls would be broken down.
   G. the risk of developing argyria would be decreased.
   H. the smaller size (1–10 nm) particles would inhibit growth the most.
   J. the bacteria would not go through natural selection and become resistant to the particles.

7. Which of the following developments would most greatly alleviate Scientist 2's concern about this new technology?
   A. Companies using silver nanoparticles clearly label their packaging.
   B. Testing shows that silver nanoparticles remain embedded in the products and do not have the potential to leak into the environment.
   C. The EPA drops the requirement that companies must prove there is no environmental risk.
   D. Studies on mice show few neurological side effects.

Strategy Practice Chart

Scan the passage.

    Time: _____

Check the main idea (draw trend arrows/show relationship).

    Main Idea: _____

Ignore the **e**xtras. (What information did you skip?)

    Extras: _____

Note the reference in the question (if any).

    Question 1: _____

    Question 2: _____

    Question 3: _____

    Question 4: _____

    Question 5: _____

    Question 6: _____

    Question 7: _____

Choose the best answer (explain your reasoning).

    Question 1: _____

    Question 2: _____

    Question 3: _____

    Question 4: _____

TIP

Don't forget to clearly circle, underline, or write the main idea in the margin for each scientist. This will help you answer the questions much more quickly.

Question 5:   _____

Question 6:   _____

Question 7:   _____

Eliminate the incorrect answers (explain your reasoning).

Question 1:   _____

Question 2:   _____

Question 3:   _____

Question 4:   _____

Question 5:   _____

Question 6:   _____

Question 7:   _____

Before we look at the answers, let's see how you used the **SCIeNCE** strategies.

Scan the passage. Taking 15–20 seconds to look over the passage (7 minutes total) should have told you that the passage was about biology, specifically silver nanoparticles. Scientists 1 and 2 both thought that the silver nanoparticles had benefits. Scientist 1 felt more positive about the technology. Scientist 2 was concerned about environmental effects.

Check the main idea. You should have circled/underlined "Silver nanoparticles . . . properties, especially against various bacteria, viruses, and fungi" from the introduction; "effective killers of pathogenic bacteria" and "safely been incorporated" from Scientist 1; and "the risks of their use potentially far outweigh the benefits" from Scientist 2. You should have also written something like "For silver np" next to Scientist 1 and "Against silver np" next to Scientist 2.

Ignore the **e**xtras. Do you really need to know about *E. coli* or particle sizes from 1–10 nm? Not necessarily. Although you are used to reading for information and for detail, this is not the time to do that. As you scan the passage, your brain will register the details. Then, if you need them later, you can always refer back to the passage.

Note the reference in the question.

Question 1:   No specific reference.

Question 2:   No specific reference.

Question 3:   Scientists 1 and 2.

Question 4:   No specific reference.

Question 5:   Scientists 1 and 2.

Question 6:   Scientist 1.

Question 7:   Scientist 2.

When you see these signals, make sure to zero in on those sections and those sections only. The test makers will try to distract you with information from the other scientist, but don't be fooled.

Choose the best answer. See the answers and explanations that follow.

Did you pick the best answer? As a good test-taker, your first instincts will often prove correct, but don't get too relaxed. Remember, sometimes the most obvious answer is correct, but for the Xtreme questions, it often is not. If you get stuck, eliminate the wrong answers and move on to a new question.

Eliminate the incorrect answers. See the answers and explanations that follow.

Eliminating incorrect answers in a Conflicting Viewpoints question is often more difficult than in Data Representation or Research Summaries passages because the answers are not obvious. They are rarely numerical, but knowing each scientist's main idea will speed up this process.

How did you do? With practice, these strategies will become second nature and will help you to achieve your goals. Now let's see how you did on the questions themselves.

Answers and Explanations

TIP

The factual questions should seem easier once you have identified each scientist's idea.

1. **(D)** A **Factual** Question—Scientist 1 lists the ways silver nanoparticles may kill bacteria, including forming pits.

    Wrong: (A) Refers to effect on HIV. (B) Describes a consequence, not a method of killing. (C) From Scientist 2's argument.

2. **(F)** A **Factual** Question—Scientist 2 is the only one to mention hazards, and the main idea is that the overall effects are "not at all understood."

    Wrong: (G) Is a positive effect of silver nanoparticles. (H & J) Refer to other side effects of silver, not necessarily silver nanoparticles.

    Be careful of answers like choice (G), which are clearly wrong. Misreading the question and not paying attention to the word *hazardous* would make this seem to be the most likely answer. Test writers rely on the fact that you are working quickly and skimming some of the material. Missteps like this can keep you from your 36.

3. **(B)** An **Inference** Question—Scientist 2 focuses on the environmental risks of this technology.

    Wrong: (A) Both scientists believe that the nanoparticles are effective against bacteria. (C) Medical use is referred to by Scientist 1 only. (D) Nanoparticles are no longer being advertised as used in consumer products, but the products themselves have not changed. This sounds correct, but requires you to read carefully.

INSIDE THE ACT 36 MIND

Pay close attention to which scientist's views are being discussed. Test writers purposely include multiple references to "Scientist 1" and "Scientist 2" in the question stems to try to confuse the average test-taker.

4. (H) An **Xtreme** Question—Options II and III may both be done by companies under the current EPA guidelines.

Wrong: **(F & J)** Both of these answers contain option I, which would not be permitted by the EPA. **(G)** While option II is correct, so is option III, which would eliminate this as the <u>best</u> answer.

These are Xtreme questions because they rely on you to not only infer what the correct answer is but also to reason the best combination of choices. If you can eliminate one of the options as wrong (in this case option I), then immediately eliminate all answer choices with that option in it (F & J). Then you have fewer choices to make.

INSIDE THE ACT 36 MIND

When you are given questions with multiple options, it is unlikely that the option that comes up the least is the correct one by itself. Conversely, the option that comes up the most is usually included in the correct answer. For example, in Question 4, option I is only included twice (answer choices F & J) and is listed by itself (choice F), while option II is part of three choices (G, H, & J) and is listed by itself (choice G). Option III is only included twice, but not by itself. Look for the option that comes up most often to be in the correct answer choice.

---

5. (A) An **Xtreme** Question—Although the nanoparticles are effective in a lab setting, they are not effective in consumer products, so neither scientist would use this as proof.

Wrong: **(B)** Scientist 1 believes this in general, but it is inconsistent with the results. **(C)** This is one of Scientist 2's concerns, but the results would not warrant putting the nanoparticles into the containers in the first place. **(D)** Although this answer is supported by the passage, it contradicts the facts presented in the question stem.

Many Science Reasoning questions on the ACT do not require reading the passage at all to find the correct answer. This is one of them. The tricky part about this question is that the closer you have read, the more likely you are to pick the wrong answer.

TIP

If an experiment does not work, then scientists are not going to draw positive conclusions about the results.

6. (J) An **Inference** Question—The key word here is *recurring*. The passage implies that bacteria are becoming resistant to various antibacterial chemicals, including antibiotics.

Wrong: **(F)** This may be one of the ways in which nanoparticles kill bacteria, but it does not explain why they would be more effective than antibiotics. **(G)** Argyria is referred to by Scientist 2 only. **(H)** Particles 1–10 nm in size have been shown to be effective against viruses, not bacteria.

Knowing some biology, although not required, definitely helps with this question. Understanding and recognizing the difference between viruses and bacteria, knowing how antibiotics work, and realizing how natural selection plays a role in antibacterial resistance give you an advantage over less advanced science students.

TIP

Although you don't have to be familiar with any of the passage topics to score a 36, the more science you do know, the better your chances are. Keep studying!

7. **(B)** An **Inference** Question—If silver nanoparticles remain in the materials and do not pose an environmental threat, then this would most alleviate Scientist 2's concern.

Wrong: (A) While this is an issue raised by Scientist 2, it is not the main idea of the argument. (C) Dropping the testing requirement would do nothing to alleviate the overall concerns. (D) Testing in mice would help; however, the neurological side effects are not a primary concern of this scientist.

Answering this question relies just as much on knowing common non-scientific vocabulary—in this case the word *alleviate*—as it does scientific principles.

After working through this practice passage, you should feel even more comfortable with Conflicting Viewpoints passages. Reading scientific articles and texts will expose you to more possible topics and help you out with this section, especially if this is the one that gives you the most problems. Keep practicing!

Tips for Boosting Your Science Score

CHAPTER 24

- Immerse yourself in science
- Review key terms
- Read more scientific publications
- Practice, practice, practice

Now that you've had a chance to study different kinds of passages, practice your strategies, and analyze your strengths and weaknesses, where do you go from here? You probably have already registered for the test and wonder what else you should be doing to better prepare yourself. Depending on your time frame, here are some reminders and suggestions to help you achieve your 36.

SUGGESTIONS FOR SUCCESS

Experience More Science

Students who have taken the most science classes in high school and have actively participated in their classes perform better on tests like the ACT. Scientific reasoning is a part of any good science curriculum, no matter what the subject. So go through your texts, notes, lab reports, journal articles, etc. and expose yourself to more topics from different sources. Here are some specific ideas for how to do this:

Read Graphs and Tables

Look at a graph or table without reading the caption and see if you can figure out the relationship with the data. Check the caption or description to see if you are correct.

Make Graphs and Tables

Take a complex data table and construct a graph from it. Do not use a calculator or computer to do it for you. Or, try constructing a data table from a graph.

Summarize Scientific Journal Articles

Find a journal article or even an abstract of an article. Write a phrase summarizing the main idea. Or, find scientific articles in the newspaper or online from a source such as Science Daily (*www.sciencedaily.com*), where hundreds of articles are

TIP

The more you practice making graphs by hand, the better your overall understanding of the concepts will be. Also, some other advanced science courses require this skill on their standardized exams, so you will be preparing for these tests as well.

posted every week, and write a one-sentence summary. Besides helping you to identify the main idea of a passage, reading these will expose you to a wider variety of topics.

Run Scientific Experiments

Take a lab activity that you've done or are doing in school and modify it. By changing a variable, collecting data, graphing results, and drawing conclusions, you will be using the same skills that the ACT requires in the passages. Your experiments do not have to be extensive or complicated at all. Ask your science teacher for some simple suggestions.

Use Scientific Vocabulary

Analysis of science textbooks has shown that there is often as much new vocabulary in a science course, especially biology, as there is in a first-year language course. Understanding the terminology is very important. What can you do? Here are a few suggestions:

Use Root Words

You have probably been given a list of Greek and Latin root words that are commonly used in science. Now would be a good time to look them over, as well as some of the terms that commonly use them.

Look Up Words

TIP

Don't spend time memorizing vocabulary for this test. The use of the terms might be different, and it would be rare to find the exact definitions used. Understand the **concepts**—don't memorize the words.

When you come across unfamiliar terms, either in an ACT passage, while reading a text or journal, or when reviewing experiments, look up the terms and make sure you understand them in context.

Keep a List

After finding and looking up unfamiliar terms, write them down in your own words on a list somewhere. The processes of putting them into your own words and writing them down will help you understand and remember them easier.

Review Published Vocabulary Lists

People have surveyed the ACT science section and put together lists of the most commonly used vocabulary terms. Use guides, such as *Barron's ACT*, or online sources to review these lists. Many of your teachers may also have quizzes that you could use to practice with these terms.

Practice, Practice, Practice

There is no substitute for being as familiar with the test as you can and for practicing the strategies. You probably own other guides that contain practice tests. Use the strategies that you learned from this guide to take the practice tests and then to analyze your performance.

Advice from High-Scoring Students

Now you're ready for the actual test. You have a sound knowledge base from your high school classes and from any outside studying you've done. You are familiar with the structure of the science section of the ACT and have become skilled at using **SCIeNCE** strategies. You have spent time practicing with passages so that there are few surprises. So, what else do you need to know? Can you reach your goal?

How about some advice from students just like you? These are people who've been in your shoes and have figured out a method to master the test. Here are four successful students' views of their "secret" to doing well on the ACT science section.

Approaching the Science Test

Do the passages in order of the number of questions—Data Representation (5 questions), Research Summaries (6 questions), and Conflicting Viewpoints (7 questions). Look over all the information in the passage (graphs, explanations, etc.) once—but thoroughly. Then go through the questions. The information should be fresh in your mind. If it isn't, then where you saw the information should be. Don't second-guess your answers, and most importantly, try to relax!
—Mark

Four Strategies That Work

1. *Make sure to do Conflicting Viewpoints passages last, especially if you are more of a math person than an English person—they can take too long and use up valuable time.*

2. *Graph trends are your friends, so make good use of them.*

3. *Don't be scared of unfamiliar vocabulary, or skip words that you think are too big. Most of the important terms are explained in the passages.*

4. *Background knowledge can be helpful. Use what you've learned in your science classes.*

—Rudy

TIP

Always try to practice passages under test-like conditions, especially when it comes to timing. Remember, you should spend only three to four minutes per Data Representation passage, five to six minutes for a Research Summaries passage, and no more than seven or eight minutes for a Conflicting Viewpoints passage.

Handling the Extras and Avoiding Panic

When you take the test and feel that you are rushing to complete all of the questions, you tend to overlook very basic information. Look for words that are important, take out most of the little details, and focus on words that are being repeated. Trust what you know, and do not second-guess yourself. Calm down, even if you mess up. There is almost always another chance to take the test again.
—Carly

What to Do if You Get Stuck

If one passage is taking up too much time, move to the next one and come back at the end. Sometimes seeing a brand new passage can clear your head a bit, so when you get back to the one you skipped, you're not as tired of the topic, and you'll be able to think through it better.
—Bianca

*   *   *   *   *

These students have all experienced success on the ACT science test. They come from different backgrounds, have different academic strengths, and even approach the tests differently. What they have in common is their ability to use test-taking strategies to achieve their goals. What worked for each of them was slightly different, just like what will work for you will not be exactly the same as what works for anyone else. Despite this fact, what all of these (and other) high-scoring ACT students agreed on was that trying basic strategies, such as **SCIeNCE**, and adapting them in ways that worked for each of them individually was the key to their good performance. Prepare well!

WRITING

Writing an Effective Essay

CHAPTER 25

- Consider the question
- Respond to counterclaims
- Use examples
- Take a position
- Defend your statements
- Write simply and clearly

Should you choose to complete the optional Writing section of the ACT, you will have just 30 minutes to plan and write a "position" essay in response to a prompt. Two graders will then score your essay, between 1 and 6, 6 being the best out of a possible six points. ACT combines those two scores to give you a writing score from 2 to 12. Finally, your essay score is combined with your score on the English section to give you an English/Writing score out of 36.

Rarely will you be asked to write an essay in thirty minutes—except on the ACT. The time allotted for this particular test dictates how you approach the process. Because you hardly ever have to craft an essay in such a brief time period, practicing this skill is essential.

Using the topics outlined in this chapter, set aside thirty minutes whenever you can to practice drafting an essay. Share your responses with your friends and analyze each other's work. Ask teachers to give you feedback. Do whatever it takes to get as much practice on and reaction to your essays as possible. Your peers and teachers will be able to tell you if the essay is comprehensible, logical, and persuasive. Besides writing your own essays, reading professional persuasive pieces helps you identify how solid arguments are developed and organized. Consider reading newspaper editorials and letters to the editor; mimicking the style of an effective writer can be good practice.

YOUR WRITING GOAL: SOLID, NOT PERFECT

An organized, purposeful, logical essay, free of distracting conventional errors, will achieve a high score. Thirty minutes is not enough time to spruce up your sentence fluency by combining sentences and adding transitions. It is also not enough time to review your word choice and beef up vocabulary. Although sentence fluency and word choice are factors, the ACT looks primarily for a solid writing sample that proves to potential colleges that you are strong enough to walk their hallways. Colleges want to see that you can handle the basics of writing: choosing a topic, staying focused on the topic, organizing your ideas, providing solid evidence and support for your ideas, maintaining a fluid style, and manipulating the conventional standards of written English.

> ### INSIDE THE ACT 36 MIND
>
> Because ACT essay graders spend only about one minute scoring each paper, your essay has to be solid, not perfect.

As in the other ACT sections, timing is everything. Memorize the following breakdown: 5–20–5. Spend 5 minutes choosing a topic and preparing your main points and examples. Take a position on the topic and develop an outline that puts forth your side and also refutes the other side. Once you have a solid outline, stick with it. With only 20 minutes to write the essay, don't stray from your plan of action. Use the last 5 minutes to edit the essay for conventional errors.

First Impressions Count

TIP

Ideas must be thoughtful, clear, and focused. And your writing must be legible.

The first thing anyone notices about a handwritten essay is its appearance: It's either tidy, a mess, or somewhere in between. The same is true for your ACT essay. You must write legibly. The chicken scratch that your English teacher can read only because he has had you in class for an entire year is not going to cut it. Even though, currently, your main mode of communication might be e-mail, blogging, online social networking, or text messaging, you will again have to reestablish handwriting basics. Remember, ACT essay graders spend approximately one minute reading your essay. If they have to spend the first thirty seconds deciphering whether you have written a "t" or a "d," they may not care to read much more. So take out your pencil and practice good penmanship.

THE TOPIC: A SOLID FOUNDATION

TIP

If you want your essay to be read and graded objectively, write neatly.

The foundation of any essay is its topic. All claims, details, and examples should help support that topic. Conveniently, the ACT writing test provides you with the necessary material for the topic. ACT prompts *always* ask you to take one side of a debatable issue. Prompts often have something to do with the teen experience! The following list contains sample topics written in the form of a question that may be posed to you:

TIP

Remember your essay must take a side—be it for or against.

- Should schools require uniforms?

- Should schools remove high school athletics in order to maintain a stronger academic environment?

- Should schools require students to complete community service hours or projects?

- Should high schools offer same-gender classrooms?

- Should the voting age be lowered to 16?

- Should teens be 18 before receiving their driver's license?

- Should all high school seniors be required to take an exit exam?

- Should grades be based on effort or actual achievement?

- Should every student be required to take an art class like drawing, sculpture, or painting or a performing arts class like theatre, music, or band?

The list could go on and on. Think about all of the debates surrounding teen life. Video games, graduation requirements, and even the value of after-prom costume parties could all become topics on the ACT writing test. All ACT prompts include context to define the topic more thoroughly. Consider the following two examples.

1. Some high schools want to require four years of physical fitness classes for all students. The obesity crisis is reaching epidemic proportions. Many health researchers suggest that inactivity is one of the greatest causes of the disease. Proponents of this idea feel that taking a physical fitness course each year of high school will help teach students good exercise habits as well as maintain healthier weights. Opponents feel that physical fitness should be the choice of the individual and that a required physical fitness course may take away the option for students to take more academic courses, which could further advance their academic success. Should students be required to take a physical fitness course each year of high school?

2. Some high schools are structured like colleges in that each student chooses a focus of study as a freshman or sophomore. Students may choose business, fine arts, medicine, journalism, or a host of other topics of study and then receive a specialized diploma reflecting that discipline. Some educators, parents, and students feel that having a focused area of study gives students an edge over students in a traditional high school setting because students aren't wasting their time studying information they will not use in future careers. Others suggest that freshmen and sophomores are too young to know which discipline they would like to pursue for the rest of their lives. Some people are also concerned that a narrow academic focus does not make for a well-rounded citizen. In your opinion, should schools offer specialized diplomas based on one focused area of study?

Regardless of the specifics of the question, all essay prompts will end with directions similar to the following:

In your essay, take a side on this question. You may write about either one of the two perspectives provided, or you may present a different point of view on the topic. Support your position with specific evidence and examples.

ACT WRITING CRITERIA

Throughout the rest of this chapter, you will see "writing criterion." Each represents an important element for writing a strong ACT essay.

Writing Criterion #1: *Take a side and stick with it*

Because the ACT gives you the topic, you just have to choose which side of the debate you want to support. Notice that the writing prompt doesn't say, "Choose which side you believe in deeply." Pick the more defendable side. If the only argument you can think of against taking a physical fitness class every year of high school is that you don't like to wear shorts, then you probably can't make a strong case for that position. Your defense of a topic must go beyond your personal fear of exposed legs. In fact, even though you might not want to take a physical fitness class each year of high school, you may be able to defend the idea because of how it may help the obesity crisis. Remember, you don't actually have to follow through and become an activist for the issue supported in the essay. No one is asking you to march into your principal's office with a proposal; you are just being asked to defend an idea on paper.

   As soon as you read the prompt, think of reasons to support both sides of the argument. Choose to defend whichever side has more support.

> ### INSIDE THE ACT 36 MIND
>
> For ACT writing test purposes, the only good argument is one you can defend quickly and easily. Once you have chosen a side, you have laid the foundation of your essay. Once you've begun, don't backpedal.

Writing Criterion #2: *Describe the context of the issue*

TIP

Use your own words to explain the issue. That shows the grader you comprehend the situation.

You will need to be able to explain why the issue is worthy of discussion. The ACT gives you a brief explanation of context, and your explanation of the context doesn't need to go far beyond that. However, if you choose only to restate the context exactly as the test has worded it, then your essay is functional but has a few cracks in its foundation. Explain the context of the issue in your own words. The ACT tests your ability to see the intricacies of an issue and why or how the issue originated. You might need to state the origins, complications, settings, or conflicts surrounding an issue. For example, why are people arguing over whether or not to structure high school like a four-year college? The ACT tests your ability to explain why this is even a debatable topic.

Writing Criterion #3: *Describe and discuss the multiple perspectives of the issue.*

OR

Writing Criterion #4: *Discuss the benefits, problems, and repercussions of the issue.*

OR

Writing Criterion #5: *Respond to arguments against your claims*

Notice the word *or* stuck between each of these criteria. You must do one of them in order to score a 6 on the writing test. The following guiding questions help you get to the center of the topic so that you can address at least one, if not more, of the writing criteria above.

Who, What, Why, and How

- **Who** does this issue affect?
  - **What** will it mean for the individuals involved?
  - **How** will it affect their daily lives?

- **What** are the pros or cons for the individuals, communities, or societies involved?

- **What** problems arise from the question? **How** will those problems manifest themselves? **What** are the benefits or the costs to each side?

- **What** would proponents of the other side of the topic say to refute my argument?

- **Why** is one point more substantial than the opposing viewpoint?

Spend the first two minutes of your five-minute preparation time choosing a side to defend and considering how the topic has become a debate in the first place. Explore the nuances of the question. Spend the next three minutes of the preparation time organizing your ideas. Each main argument in support of the side you have chosen becomes one of the supporting points of the essay. Each supporting point should also include a conflicting counterargument that you then disprove with reasoning and examples.

THE 5-MINUTE PREPARATION METHOD

1. Read the prompt carefully.
2. Identify the issue: Who, What, Why, and How?
3. Brainstorm support for each side.
4. Take a side (the side with the most support).
5. Establish two to three main arguments to support your side.
6. Identify counterclaims that attempt to refute your side.
7. Brainstorm examples and ideas that will support your side and disprove counterarguments.

The following graphic organizer illustrates how you might organize your thoughts. Use brief notes only. You may be able to use even briefer notes than shown on the chart below; often, a key word will trigger an entire thought.

- The top row identifies the topic.

- The next row identifies the context of the topic and its implications and complications.

- Two to three claims for **each side** are shown on the left and right sides of the chart.

- Once you have established the major claims for each side of the issue, pick the side with the more defensible argument. For the purposes of this chapter, assume that the "pro" side—students should be required to take a physical fitness class—is the more defensible.

- Once you have chosen a side, develop examples to support that side. While developing examples to support your side, consider examples that the other side might use. Then, figure out ways to refute them. When completing your own organizer, keep your notes brief.

Topic: Physical Fitness
Who? teens
What? obesity crisis, physical education, parent involvement
Why? inactivity, poor eating habits, lack of parent involvement
How (are problems manifested)? childhood diseases, rising health care costs

For: Class every year	*Against:* No class every year
Claim for:	**Claim against:**
• increases health for teens	• Parents should be in charge and students should have a choice
○ (example) teens are too inactive—television and video games	○ Refutation: they aren't getting the job done
• leads to healthier adult habits	○ Example: friends, parents as role models
○ (example) compare healthy and unhealthy adults	• Too many required courses already
• Relieves economic burden	• Colleges look at academics
○ (example) rising health care costs	○ Refutation: nothing is more important than good health
• Healthier bodies lead to healthier minds	• Athletes should be exempt
○ (example) compare two friends—healthy vs. not healthy	○ Refutation: many don't learn "life-long" exercise practices
○ (example) my personal health	

The following information defines the context, claims, and counterclaims more thoroughly so that you can see how the ideas within the template could be expanded.

Topic: Physical Fitness

Who, What, Why, and How? The issue springs from the obesity crisis in the United States. It is debatable because it infringes on the opportunity for students to take other academic classes and to make choices for their own learning. Another key tenet of the argument is that our society could suffer if the obesity issue is not solved: Health care costs are rising because of childhood illnesses related to obesity. Students need guidance on how to lead healthy lives. The question then arises whether or not high schools should be partially responsible for increasing the health of U.S. teens.

Claim for: Students need to be taught how to maintain a healthy weight through exercise in order to decrease the childhood obesity epidemic.

- **Examples for:** One of the causes of teen obesity is that teens spend too much time playing video or computer games, and watching television or movies. They do not know how to lead a healthy life.

- **Counterclaim:** Parents should be in charge of encouraging proper exercise and healthy habits, and students should have more choice in their courses of study. Colleges consider academic courses a higher priority on students' applications, and students should have course time available for academic class options.

- **Refutation of counterclaim:** Not all parents encourage students to maintain a healthy weight, and students with strong role models will not necessarily become strong role models for other students.

Claim for: Required physical education courses can lead to students having healthier habits as adults. It can also relieve some of the economic burden on families by lessening childhood obesity's impact on the rising cost of health care.

- **Personal example for:** Describe an adult you know that maintains healthy habits and one that doesn't and the way their habits affect their lives. You could also describe healthy role models in your life.

- **Counterclaim:** Many adults lead productive lives even while living with obesity. A student's personal success is determined by academic achievement and not by weight. There are already so many required courses that students don't often have the ability to choose academic courses or electives that interest them. Colleges look at the academic courses students are taking and will not pay attention to grades in physical fitness courses.

- **Refutation of counterclaim:** Physical health is more important than good grades or college; therefore, physical education supersedes academic courses. There is already plenty of time for academic courses, which dominate school curricula.

Claim for: Required physical education courses support academics because healthy bodies lead to healthier minds. Students' grades will improve if they are healthier.

- **Example for:** You could include a personal example of how participating in sports or physical activity made you feel better and have more energy to complete homework and participate in class.

- **Counterclaim:** Students who participate in athletics should not be required to take physical education classes. Sports provide enough exercise to reduce obesity, and they teach students how to lead a healthy lifestyle.

- **Refutation of counterclaim:** Not all sports are conducive to "life-long" health and activity. Students need to be taught a variety of activities that help maintain a healthy body. Sports like football and basketball may be too physically demanding as you age and can cause injuries.

ESSAY STRUCTURE

Writing Criterion #6: *The organization of the essay is identifiable and fluid. The introduction and conclusion are thoughtful and purposeful*

Think about the shape of the essay. A superb ACT essay will have a simplistic structure that is easy to see and understand. In other words, get to your point. An unfinished essay, as you might guess, won't score highly. One trap that higher level students fall into is overdoing the essay. You are accustomed to spending hours drafting, revising, and editing your work. You may have delusions that your thirty-minute essay has the potential to sound like something you took a week or more to complete. Don't fall into this trap. Keep the structure simple and clean with separate supports for each argument, designated in advance.

Organize your essay simply. In one paragraph, provide minimal background information and a thesis. Create a separate paragraph for each claim. Within each paragraph, refute counterclaims. Or, create a separate paragraph near the end of your essay to explore opposing claims and then refute them. Finally, conclude your essay by restating some key points and by tying it to the introductory hook. By keeping the structure simple, you should have time to finish and even revise at the end for obvious errors.

REMEMBER

Because you have a very limited amount of time, the structure of your essay should be clean and simple.

Elements of Structure

Introduction

- Restate the problem in your own words.

- Establish context: discuss the intricacies of the problem in your own words.

- Identify the side you are taking and briefly explain your reasoning.

Support Paragraphs

- Include a support paragraph for each claim that supports the side you affirm.

- Include details to "show" the reader the issues involved in the topic.

- Include examples to support your claim. Examples can be taken from your personal life—your experiences with your friends or family. They can also be taken from the news, literature, or history. Your goal is to show the reader the intricacies of the issue while justifying your side.

Refutation of Opposing Claims: Two Options

- The first option is to address opposing counterclaims within each support paragraph. Establish the claims made by the opposing side and refute them with reasons and examples that link to your original claim.

- The second option is to outline and refute opposing claims in a separate paragraph—at the end of the essay—prior to your conclusion.

Conclusion

- Reestablish the importance of the issue.

- Briefly restate your position using new wording.

- Review reasons why your side is the stronger of the two.

FLOW AND FOCUS

Writing Criterion #7: *Ideas are developed thoroughly and logically*

Writing Criterion #8: *Transitions demonstrate a clear progression of thought and are integrated fluidly*

Have you ever been in a large building where you can't figure out how to get from point A to point B? Maybe it happened when you first entered a new school. While confusion in an unknown place is inevitable, confusion in writing is caused by an inconsistent or choppy flow. Getting lost in an essay happens for two reasons:

- The organizational structure might be awkward. You may have crammed too many ideas in one paragraph, or you may have written a paragraph devoid of real purpose.

- Sentence fluency or flow within each paragraph and among ideas might be awkward. A key to stronger sentence fluency is to focus on transitions. The following list includes transitions that can be used within an essay.

Demonstrate cause and effect	Establish contrast	Add an idea or show sequence	Precede an example	Show a comparison	Establish a conclusion
as a result because consequently hence since so therefore thus	but however in contrast nonetheless on the contrary on the other hand still yet regardless	also besides furthermore in addition moreover next too finally	for example likewise for instance specifically	in the same way similarly also	in conclusion in short to conclude to sum up

Writing Criterion #9: *Incorporates a variety of sentences*

TIP

Hold your reader's attention by using a variety of sentence styles and lengths.

Sentence structure can also inhibit or enhance the flow of your essay. Too many short sentences makes an essay feel choppy and boring. Too many long, complex sentences makes an essay feel endless and confuses the reader. Consciously mix sentence lengths. Varied sentence structure is something a grader *can* notice in less than a minute. Making it obvious that you use different sentence styles and lengths will help you greatly.

Writing Criterion #10: *Ideas have been supported by specific details that show the reader the logic behind the author's claims*

Be sure to include examples and details that support your main arguments so readers will be clear about your position. Using appropriate details in your essay also helps defend against counterarguments.

SHOWING VS. TELLING

Identify the claim clearly within the first sentence of the support paragraph. For example: "Physical fitness classes should be required for each student because they teach students how to use exercise to maintain a healthy weight, which in turn teaches them to be healthier during their lifetimes." Maybe you, the writer, maintain a healthy weight by exercising daily. If so, by all means use your personal experiences to show the benefits of daily exercise. Maybe you or a friend of yours is obese and could use an exercise routine in order to lose weight. Personal examples like these are perfectly acceptable. Using examples from the media or from classes you have taken is also appropriate and encouraged. Effective examples "show" the reader the problem and "show" why your side is more beneficial overall.

Writing Criterion #11: *The essay demonstrates a strong understanding of the conventions of the English language*

Writing Criterion #12: *Word choice is specific and diverse*

Each essay has its own style and flair—that's what makes your essay unique. Sometimes, high-achieving students want to decorate their essays with a lot of fluff. Resist that tendency. Keep the style of your essay sophisticated and functional. Word choice must be specific and accurate. Demonstrate that you understand how words function—don't use an adverb when you should be using an adjective, and don't use a sophisticated word unless you are absolutely clear about its meaning. Chapter 4 addresses the ACT's expectations on word use. In short, cluttering your essay with extra decoration only detracts from your main message and shows that you are trying too hard to sound fancy. Dispense with the fanfare and focus on crafting a comprehensible essay.

CHECK YOUR CRAFTSMANSHIP: CLEAN UP YOUR MESSES

Writing Criterion #13: *Errors are minimal and rarely distract the reader*

TIP

Don't let sloppy grammar and spelling errors detract from an otherwise solid essay.

Are your commas thrown around sloppily, or do you know how to use them properly? Do you capitalize when you need to, or has text-messaging rendered you proper noun challenged? An essay that isn't proofread or fails to follow the standards of written English shows poor craftsmanship, and it takes only a second to sense it.

In the last few minutes of the time allotted, check your most common spelling problems. Do you always confuse *there, their,* and *they're*? Do you forget to add *ing* to the end of a word? Identify your personal tendencies and memorize how to correct them. Go back through the essay looking for your most common mistakes. In a grader's eyes, an essay that lacks attention to detail at the level of grammar, usage, capitalization, or spelling is at a disadvantage from the outset. Consistent and flagrant grammatical errors distract the reader, probably causing him to maintain a negative bias throughout the rest of the essay. No matter how wonderful your ideas, frequent errors make an essay challenging to read. Clean them up before submitting your final effort.

Sample Essays

Prompt: Some high schools are structured like colleges in that each student chooses a focus of study as a freshman or sophomore. Students may choose business, fine arts, medicine, communication, or a host of other topics of study and then receive a specialized diploma reflecting the discipline they have studied. Some educators, parents, and students feel that having a focused area of study gives students an edge over students in a traditional high school setting because students aren't wasting their time studying information they will not use in their future careers. Others suggest that freshmen and sophomores are too young to know which discipline they would like to pursue for the rest of their lives. Some people are also concerned that a narrow academic focus does not make for a well-rounded citizen. In your opinion, should schools offer specialized diplomas based on one focused area of study?

In your essay, take a position on this question. You may write about either one of the two perspectives provided, or present a different point of view on the topic. Support your position with specific evidence and examples.

Essay #1

Score: 6

When I graduate from college, I will be competing for jobs with graduates from countries like China, India, Britain, Sweden, and the United Arab Emirates. Every course I take in high school should be setting me up to compete with other international graduates. The current educational system offers a broad array of courses, requiring, or rather hoping, that students develop skills in each of the following areas: math, science, social studies, and English. If we are lucky, we get to take a smattering of classes in areas that interest us. Students waste time learning content they will never use. Not all students need to know the complexities of calculus or need to be able to write a memoir; granted, they all need basic reading, writing, speaking, and technological skills, but these foundational skills can be taught within the framework of an educational system that offers specialized diplomas. High schools should offer specialized diplomas that allow us to compete in a global economy.

If students are allowed to take classes that apply to their future goals, their engagement increases, inherently increasing student achievement. I am currently taking a calculus course because I want to become an engineer, and I know I will be using those skills in the future. Even more, I would appreciate taking a project-based math class that integrates the skills I will need as a future engineer. I am required to take English, and the only English elective that fit in my schedule is British Literature. I am currently reading Shakespeare and I have been assigned to write a sonnet. I do not understand when I will ever in my life need the ability to write a sonnet. If I were in an engineering-focused diploma program, I would be learning how to write proposals and convey my ideas through technical writing, rather than learning about iambic pentameter. I am bored in many of my classes and fail to see how the information applies to my future career choice.

Basic expectations about reading, writing, speaking, mathematics, technology, and civic mindedness should be inherent in any specialized degree. Specialized degrees don't lower their standards for these areas. A new high school just opened in my community that has business as its focus. The students learn the basic skills needed to become high-functioning citizens, yet they use the content of business as the backdrop for everything they learn. Some parents, educators, and students argue that students need to be exposed to all facets of knowledge in order to be successful and high-functioning citizens. I feel that functional citizens will be those who can get a job and be competitive in the international marketplace.

Opponents to specialized degrees say that teenagers are unable to make life-altering decisions as freshmen and sophomores. I agree that not all of my peers are able to make these decisions at this age; however, I think that some of us are, and should be given the opportunity to focus our education on a specific area of study. The key word is "opportunity." Some opponents may ask: what if a student wants to change his mind about his area of specialization? Because each degree teaches basic skills, it shouldn't be too difficult for a student to change his mind during the middle of high school. They may not be able to earn a specialized degree because they will be missing key content information, but they should still be allowed to switch to a different program or finish their degree in a "traditional" educational system. Or, the freshman year or both freshman and sophomore years could be the time when students are exposed to different areas of focus. The students then decide which diploma they would like to attain before leaving high school.

In an internationally competitive world, American students need to be as prepared as possible. Specialized degrees should be an option for all students. They will be more engaged if their strengths are encouraged and appreciated, and they may even be more willing to work on their weaknesses if they know that the assignments apply to a real life goal. I may never be good at writing a sonnet, but I am pretty sure the citizens of this country won't care when I build the strongest bridge in the world.

Comments on Essay #1

The student **takes a stand** by offering a "middle ground" proposal. Your solution does not have to fit into an all-or-none state of existence. The prompt states, "You may write about either one of the two points of view given, or you may present a different point of view on this question." The following question is at the core of the prompt: "should schools offer specialized diplomas based on one focused area of study?" The key word in the question is *offer*. It doesn't say *require* or suggest that specialized diplomas have to be mandatory. The prompt allows you to suggest an alternative to an all-or-none approach. Because of the persuasive nature of the ACT essay, many students write a one-sided essay without considering a more defendable alternative. For this essay, the student takes a side on the issue by saying, "High schools should offer specialized diplomas that allow us to compete in a global economy." The student reveals the **context of the issue** by introducing the competi-

> **NOTE**
>
> The items appearing in bold represent the writing criteria.

tive global economy, which exposes the need to revamp the current educational system to provide students with the edge they will need in the future.

The student **addresses the intricacies of the issue** by maintaining two main arguments in favor of specialized diplomas: 1) not all content is purposeful and meaningful for students' interests and future careers, and 2) education should focus on students' strengths and passions, which in turn increases student engagement and success. She has **addressed counterclaims** by taking a "middle ground" approach that allows her to easily refute the argument that not all students can choose a specialty area as freshmen. Since choosing to participate in a specialized degree is an option, not all students have to choose one. She then goes on to offer two alternatives for students who may want to switch programs in the middle of high school or who may need a little time to choose an area of focus. She elaborates on ideas by providing personal examples that explore the needless assignment in her British Literature class while also revealing her personal interests and examples of assignments and skills that she could learn in a specialized program.

Ideas within the essay are **easy to follow**. Each paragraph maintains a clear focus. The transitions are sophisticated and fluid. She identifies counterclaims when they would most logically appear in the mind of the reader. The **introduction and conclusion are purposeful**, even if they aren't flashy. The language of the essay demonstrates a solid understanding of the English language. The student uses a **variety of sentences** and **word choice that is specific and diverse. Conventional errors are minimal and rarely distract the reader**. In paragraph 4, the colon in the following sentence section is incorrect: "Some opponents may ask: what if a student. . ." A colon should not be used after a verb, and the word "what" should be capitalized because it begins a complete sentence after a colon. These errors are not obvious enough to distract the reader.

Essay #2

Score: 5

From the time wide-eyed children emerge from the womb all the way until, exhausted, they receive their high school diplomas and finally take their first steps into the enigma that is the "real world," they are literally bombarded with the mantras and clichés that have come to define our society: "be what you want to be," "the sky's the limit," and perhaps most tiredly, "dream it and you can achieve it." And while these may be true, they make it seem like a child with realistic expectations and a pragmatic life goal is nothing more than a slacker; a bum. In today's world, being "well-rounded" (perhaps more appropriately, being good at everything) is not only encouraged, but required. Kids load their college applications with clubs and extracurriculars to the point of nausea; and schools, in an effort to maintain balance in all programs, end up achieving nothing but mediocrity in most. Specialized pre-university education would be invaluable to children who know specifically what paths they would like to pursue, and certainly is a viable alternative for those who seek it.

That is why schools that offer specialized programs—whether they be in maths and sciences or arts and English—can and do succeed. In my hometown, a public specialized school (Denver School of the Arts, or DSA) is one of the most sought-after institutions of learning in the state. Thousands of children audition in order to gain entrance into the prestigious school, and all but the most qualified are turned away. Why is a public school, not a private institution with five-figure-a-year tuition, so highly sought-after? The answer is that those who seek admission understand the value of learning in the fields that they want to make a living in. Schools with specialized programs not only encourage competition; they encourage personal growth. While opponents of such magnet programs may contend that the outcome is a "less-rounded" human being, the fact of the matter is that that human is also one who is more passion-driven and internally charged, and certainly one who has stronger convictions about the world and their place in it.

While specialized schooling should be an option for those who desire it, there is a place for liberal education across all fields. In that respect, a focused area of study should be supported by required electives (if not extensive) in other arts. After all, it is the responsibility of the educator to expose the pupil to all facets of the world; and while a student may know where they fit in, they should know where others do too. Further critics of specialized schooling are correct in saying a child's plan may change, and it is because of that that a specialized education should be supported by pillars of a broad one, sparse, but enough to maintain their focus and give it perspective.

So while not all students know their life's trajectory, some do. And it is a responsibility of those that educate them to give them the option to follow that path: instead of teaching all children all things with equal balance, and mediocre results, why not give them the opportunity to let their real interests flourish? Maybe then they really can "achieve their dream," although perhaps not in terms so trite.

Comments on Essay #2

The student **comprehends the persuasive nature of the essay** by first identifying the foundation of the argument, student success. He then **takes a side** by offering reasons that support his conclusion that specialized degrees should be an option for all students. Just like the first sample essay, this student chooses to take a "middle ground" approach to the topic by suggesting that specialized diplomas should be optional, yet still offered to all students. The introductory remarks about the many clichés surrounding the topic of success help to **place the argument in context**. By identifying the reason this topic is important, the student has established a need for a decision to be made on one side or the other. He also demonstrates his understanding of context by addressing the term *well-rounded* and how this can really mean "mediocre" achievement in many areas of study.

In the introduction of the essay, he **identifies the intricacies of the issue** by showing a problem inherent in the current secondary educational system: Students are expected to be good at everything and students who are focused on *one* goal appear to be "nothing more than a slacker." The student continues by identifying the inherent flaws in a system that expects all students to excel in all areas: students are often over-involved in clubs and activities in an attempt to appear "well-rounded" for college, and often achieve "nothing but mediocrity" in many areas of study. The writer **acknowledges the counterclaims** by stating that students with specialized degrees may not be as well-rounded as students with a wider range of courses by suggesting that being well-rounded should not be the ultimate goal, and also that students receiving specialized degrees will be more "passion-driven and internally charged." The essay addresses another counterargument in paragraph three, when the writer notes that students attaining a specialized degree may change their minds about their life plans; therefore, a specialized degree "should be supported by pillars of a broad one . . . enough to maintain their focus and give it perspective."

The main issue of the essay is that the student has not **thoroughly developed his ideas**. The student continually indicates that a pre-university focus of study "would be invaluable to children" and that they would have "stronger convictions about the world and their place in it" while never truly explaining why this is true. The student gives an example of a school in his hometown that offers a specialized degree, but doesn't go on to explain why a specialized degree would give those students an advantage over others who have not received one. Also, when he explains how even a specialized education should be supported by "pillars of a broad one," there is ambiguity surrounding what he means by "pillars" and what it would look like to have a specialized education that "maintain[s] their focus and give[s] it perspective." There are not enough specifics to show the reader what this type of an education might look like. The student also claims that an education that provides a wide variety of classes produces mediocre results, and yet does not explain why this is true.

The essay **remains focused on the topic** for its entirety. Overall, **the organization is fluid. Transitions lead the reader through the essay** with no confusion except in the second paragraph. Instead of beginning the paragraph with the word *that*, a statement that identifies what the author means by *that* would be helpful before jumping into the main argument. The introduction is the strongest part of this essay. The ideas are relatable, thoughtful, and provocative. The clichés offered in the introduction hook the reader by focusing on the underlying reason for this debate to exist—student achievement. The **introduction clearly identifies the author's claim and sets the reader up well for the support that follows**.

The essay consists of **specific and diverse word choice** with a style that demonstrates an excellent **control of the English language. Conventional errors rarely distract the reader**; for example, in paragraph two, the author incorrectly uses the word *maths* instead of *mathematics*. He also incorrectly uses a semicolon in paragraph one: "more than a slacker; a bum." He should have used a colon instead; or, he could have rephrased the sentence altogether. The author also begins many sentences with the word *and*, which doesn't create as formal a tone as is needed for this essay. The author maintains **varied sentence structures** throughout the essay and demonstrates a solid understanding of the use of a comma.

Essay #3

Score: 4

Registering for freshman classes in high school is stressful. Kids worry about what will be the cool subjects, what their friends are taking, and who the best teachers are. Imagine if all those fourteen-year-olds had the added pressure of picking a specialty: deciding what to do with the rest of their lives. Schools should not require students to elect a specialty as a freshman or sophomore because most fourteen- or fifteen-year-olds are too immature to make such a critical decision. Additionally, the varied classes of a standard high school curriculum allow students to discover more about themselves and explore the different facets of society.

Incoming high school freshmen do not know themselves well enough to make a life-altering decision. The teen years are a time for people to discover themselves. If you are lucky, by fourteen you were self-assured, grounded, and knew exactly who you would be when you turned thirty. However, most of us aren't; we're more worried about what clothes to wear and who's locker we need to decorate next week. Freshmen are concerned with the immediate, not long-term, future and are rarely self-aware enough to know what they will become.

The typical, varied high school curriculum helps us learn more about ourselves so we are better equipped to make these decisions. Through taking art, cooking, and ecology classes, we learn what interests us and what we succeed at. Many people find that they excelled at middle school math, but are flustered when it comes to trig in high school. Similarly, kids might find that, while middle school U.S. history bored them, their high school civics class fascinates them. We need the varied curriculum to discover more about ourselves as we mature.

Proponents of specialized degrees may argue that students' interests and strengths aren't being developed enough in the traditional high school curriculum. I am taking an international business course that supports my future interests. It exposes me to the concepts so that I can make an informed decision about my college degree. We are also required to take courses that either enhance or develop our creativity. I have taken an introduction to theater class, and even though I do not plan to ever audition for a play, I feel that the experiences in this class helped me to become more outgoing and developed my interpersonal communication skills. I feel more confident when I have to speak in front of people. High schools should actually be encouraging students to reach beyond their comfort zones to explore other areas. You never know how another course may stretch you as an individual.

Finally, the wide array most high school students take exposes them to all parts of society. As a result, even if you decide to become a doctor, you will still know why lawyers are important. For society to function as a whole, we must all realize the importance of everyone else in the society. If we only studied one aspect of society from age fourteen on, it would be much harder to interact and cooperate with people in other sectors.

In conclusion, I believe that a varied high school curriculum is critical to the success of children in our ever-evolving society. I understand that others might claim that by specializing in high school, students are more prepared for college, but the children would loose the "big picture." Maybe we would be better doctors or lawyers, but we would not be as complete human beings.

Comments on Essay #3

The author **takes a side and sticks with it**; however, she does not understand the need to explore multiple facets of the issue. The student barely **establishes the context** within the conclusion of the essay when she explains that a student's preparedness for college is at the heart of the issue. She jumps into the topic by looking at one element of the issue: the immaturity of freshmen and sophomores when it comes to making a possibly life-changing decision, without exploring the inherent reasons a school system may consider a specialized diploma a viable educational experience. The essay **remains focused on the topic** and establishes three claims inherent in the discussion about specialized diplomas: 1) the inability of freshmen and sophomores to make a decision about their futures at such a young age, 2) the need for students to be exposed to a variety of educational content before they can choose a path that fits their passions and needs, and 3) the need for a varied curriculum in order to prepare students to function within society. The student **addresses counterclaims** by showing that there are already opportunities to pursue personal interests in the current model through her personal example of taking an international business course. She continues to support the argument that students who are required to take courses out of their "comfort zone" will often "stretch" themselves more than they would within a specialized degree by discussing the theater course she took.

The author **develops most ideas** by providing examples that reveal the current reality for many teenagers: They struggle to make decisions about what clothes to wear and which locker to decorate and rarely think about their future careers until much later in high school. She gives good examples to reveal why a student should be exposed to classes that offer diverse content when she explains how a student's attitude toward middle school math may change once he has taken trigonometry in high school. The author needs to further expand on her claim that taking a variety of classes in high school helps individuals "to interact and cooperate with people in other sectors."

The **organizational structure is easy to follow**. The **introduction and conclusion are purposeful**, even though they could be more developed. **Transitions are functional**, yet the fourth and fifth paragraphs begin with "finally" and "in conclusion," respectively. These transitions are too simplistic; the first half of the essay reflects more sophisticated transitions between ideas. Overall, the student demonstrates a **functional command of the style and conventions of English**. She varies her sentence structure and length. Her conventional errors do not impede the reader's understanding of the message; however, there are a few language and conventional issues within the essay. She should have avoided ending a sentence with the preposition *at* in the second sentence of paragraph two: "Through taking art, cooking, and ecology classes, we learn what interests us and what we succeed at."

Sentences should maintain a focused point of view, but some sentences within the essay shift between third- and second-person point of view. She also uses the contraction *who's* instead of the word *whose* in paragraph two.

FINAL PRACTICE

Use the following prompt to write your own essay. Refer back to the questions posed at the beginning of this chapter when looking for other topics to write about. Set aside thirty minutes; find a pencil and some paper. Spend five minutes preparing, twenty minutes writing, and five minutes reviewing and editing the essay. Share your results with a friend. Ask him or her to critique the essay using the writing criteria outlined in this chapter.

Practice Essay

Teachers vary in the amount of effort they acknowledge for the work a student does in class. Many students, parents, and teachers argue that students should be highly rewarded for their efforts, because much of what is learned in life is learned during the process of accomplishing a task. Others argue that it is not the effort that should determine students' grades, but students' final scores on a project, assignment, or test, because colleges and employers reward results and not effort. In your opinion, should grades be based on effort or actual achievement?

In your essay, take a side on this question. You may write about either one of the two perspectives provided, or you may present a different point of view on the topic. Support your position with specific evidence and examples.

KEY STRATEGIES FOR BUILDING AN EFFECTIVE ESSAY

1. Employ the 5–20–5 breakdown for the time allotted for the ACT writing test. Use the first five minutes to identify the essence of the topic, brainstorm claims for each side, choose a side, and then create a brief outline. Spend the next 20 minutes drafting a response. Then take the last 5 minutes cleaning up the clutter and correcting any grammar, usage, or spelling errors.

2. First impressions are important. Write legibly. Know which grammatical errors you frequently make and check for them.

3. Lay a solid foundation by choosing the more defendable angle on the topic and sticking to it. Identify the context of the issue. Explain why the topic is debatable and identify any complications and implications involved.

4. Respond to the counterclaims that might be made against your claims. A perfect writing score can only be achieved if you understand and address all sides of the topic.

5. Keep the structure simple by planning a different focus for each paragraph. Each claim within a paragraph should be defendable.

6. Maintain logical flow and sequence. Use transitions appropriately to help your reader move through the essay with ease. Consciously vary your sentence structure to give the essay a more sophisticated feel.

7. "Show" the reader why your side is more logical and reasonable. Use examples from your personal life and the world around you to support claims.

8. Keep your style functional and sophisticated, not fancy.

How to Use the CD-ROM

The software is not installed on your computer; it runs directly from the CD-ROM. Barron's CD-ROM includes an "autorun" feature that automatically launches the application when the CD is inserted into the CD-ROM drive. In the unlikely event that the autorun feature is disabled, follow the manual launching instructions below.

Windows®

1. Click on the Start button and choose "My Computer."
2. Double-click on the CD-ROM drive, which will be named **ACT_36.exe**.
3. Double-click **ACT_36.exe** to launch the program.

MAC®

1. Double-click the CD-ROM icon.
2. Double-click the **ACT_36** icon to start the program.

SYSTEM REQUIREMENTS

(Flash Player 10.2 is recommended)

Microsoft® Windows®	**MAC® OS X**
Processor: Intel Pentium 4 2.33GHz, Athlon 64 2800+ or faster processor (or equivalent).	Processor: Intel Core™ Duo 1.33GHz or faster processor.
Memory: 128MB of RAM.	Memory: 256MB of RAM.
Graphics Memory: 128MB.	Graphics Memory: 128MB.
Platforms:	Platforms:
Windows 7, Windows Vista®, Windows XP.	Mac OS X 10.5 and higher.
1024 × 768 screen resolution.	1024 × 768 screen resolution.